Investment Strategies - New Advances and Challenges

Edited by Gabriela Prelipcean and Mircea Boscoianu

Published in London, United Kingdom

Investment Strategies - New Advances and Challenges
http://dx.doi.org/10.5772/intechopen.105387
Edited by Gabriela Prelipcean and Mircea Boscoianu

Contributors
Abdulkarim Yusuf, Gabriela Prelipcean, Hu Xuemei, James Kolari, Jing-Long Huang, Luc Van Liedekerke, Min-Hsuan Fan, Mircea Boscoianu, Mu-Yen Chen, Olivier Sempiga, Seppo Pynnonen, Wei Liu

First published in London, United Kingdom, 2024 by IntechOpen
IntechOpen is the global imprint of INTECHOPEN LIMITED, registered in England and Wales, registration number: 11086078, 167-169 Great Portland Street, London, W1W 5PF, United Kingdom

British Library Cataloguing-in-Publication Data
A catalogue record for this book is available from the British Library

Additional hard and PDF copies can be obtained from orders@intechopen.com

Investment Strategies - New Advances and Challenges
Edited by Gabriela Prelipcean and Mircea Boscoianu
p. cm.

This title is part of the Business, Management and Economics Book Series, Volume 20
Topic: Economics
Series Editor: Taufiq Choudhry
Topic Editor: Jaime Ortiz

Print ISBN 978-1-83768-198-3
Online ISBN 978-1-83768-199-0
eBook (PDF) ISBN 978-1-83768-271-3
ISSN 2753-894X

For EU product safety concerns:
IN TECH d.o.o., Prolaz Marije Krucifikse Kozulić 3, 51000 Rijeka, Croatia,
info@intechopen.com or visit our website at intechopen.com.

IntechOpen Book Series

Business, Management and Economics

Volume 20

Aims and Scope of the Series

This series will provide a comprehensive overview of recent research trends in business and management, economics, and marketing. Topics will include asset liability management, financial consequences of the financial crisis and covid-19, financial accounting, mergers and acquisitions, management accounting, SMEs, financial markets, corporate finance and governance, managerial technology and innovation, resource management and sustainable development, social entrepreneurship, corporate responsibility, ethics and accountability, microeconomics, labour economics, macroeconomics, public economics, financial economics, econometrics, direct marketing, creative marketing, internet marketing, market planning and forecasting, brand management, market segmentation and targeting and other topics under business and management. This book series will focus on various aspects of business and management whose in-depth understanding is critical for business and company management to function effectively during this uncertain time of financial crisis, Covid-19 pandemic, and military activity in Europe.

Meet the Series Editor

Prof. Choudhry holds a BSc degree in Economics from the University of Iowa, as well as a Masters and Ph.D. in Applied Economics from Clemson University, USA. In January 2006, he became a Professor of Finance at the University of Southampton Business School. He was previously a Professor of Finance at the University of Bradford Management School. He has over 80 articles published in international finance and economics journals. His research interests and specialties include financial econometrics, financial economics, international economics and finance, housing markets, financial markets, among others.

Meet the Volume Editors

Gabriela Prelipcean is a professor and Ph.D. supervisor in economics at the Stefan cel Mare University of Suceava, Romania. She holds a Ph.D. at the Academy of Economic Studies of Bucharest, a postdoctoral NEC fellowships financed by the New Europe College (NEC), Bucharest, Romania, and a postdoctoral Fulbright scholarship in business at Elizabethtown College, Pennsylvania, USA. She teaches several courses and has wide experience as a researcher on the topics of investments, international economics, entrepreneurship, and the economics of extreme events. She is a member of the Academy of Management (AoM), Information Systems for Crisis Response and Management (ISCRAM), International Association for Research in Income and Wealth (IARIW), Global Consortium of Entrepreneurship Centers (GCEC), and European Regional Science Association (ERSA).

Mircea Boscoianu is a professor and Ph.D. coordinator in engineering and management at Transilvania University of Brasov, Romania. He holds a Ph.D. in aerospace engineering (Military Technical Academy, Bucharest) and in cybernetics and statistics (Academy of Economic Studies, Bucharest). He teaches several courses in Risk Management, Management in Aviation, and Strategic Management. He is the author and co-author of more than seven books and over 80 papers published in journals or presented at scientific events and is a director or member of various research projects. He is a member of international and national associations. He was president of the Saphire Program of the International Aeronautics Federation (2006–2008), vice-president of UVS Romania (2016-2018), and director of the Research Department of UVS Romania (2014–2016, 2018–present).

Contents

Preface

In the actual turbulent global context, which has a major impact on both the financial and capital Romanian markets, the entrepreneurial investment process has also been influenced. The need to finance is increasing alongside the negative impact of the restrictions and access barriers on the entrepreneurial processes. The entrepreneurial investments have become more complex and opaque, while the understanding of the movement of the markets and the reconfiguration of the opportunities and of the risks requires new research strategies and solutions.

The current multiple and contagious crises and turbulences in the markets are leading to a paradigm shift in investment strategies. Although the concerns related to the evaluation of strategic uncertainty are well known, in the context of competitiveness, the transformation of processes that take place in environments characterized by volatility, uncertainty, complexity, and ambiguity (VUCA) requires the permanent rethinking of specific strategies through the development of adaptive capabilities. This dynamic adjustment of strategies is particularly complex and starts from understanding the new dynamics of the environment and markets, the relationships between entrepreneurs and financiers, and how to integrate innovative solutions in this complex landscape.

The design of investment strategies must respond to the fulfillment of both long-term and short-term objectives and should be implemented efficiently and naturally in accordance with the company's internal resources and capabilities. The objective is to obtain a successful strategy characterized by effectiveness and robustness but also equipped with the adaptability to respond to different turbulences and crises.

Financial markets have evolved, and financing relationships naturally express themselves, providing efficient connections and diversification, and have proven to have good resilience in post-crisis situations. The conventional portfolio management has evolved, and through the integration of alternative investments (venture capital, private equity, real estate, commodities) and alternative strategies (arbitrage, but also other strategies specific to hedge funds) have allowed better risk management.

The current context of investment strategies is characterized by atypical behavior for a turbulent period in the wake of multiple crises after COVID-19, but also by an optimism arising from the development of new segments of interest, this context is difficult to analyze. It results in a reiteration of interest in simple theoretical models and their new applications (Section 1, with three chapters).

A special place is dedicated to specific strategies in emerging and frontier markets for which, although the literature has expanded recently, the research has not benefited from sufficient contributions to understand the mechanisms imposed by the new global context (Section 2, with three chapters).

Section 1. Investments Strategies – Theoretical Models and New Applications

Although in recent years theoretical models have often been criticized, especially in terms of the accuracy of the results from practical applications, there is an interest in deciphering the current problems resulting from the multiple turbulences that followed the Covid-19 crisis. Theoretical research is relaunched by the new problems identified.

Deepening the understanding of the effects of turbulence and crises on the reconfiguration of portfolio selection mechanisms—the way of evaluating all types of assets—the trading mechanisms in various market segments bring into discussion the harmonization of explanations related to the change of the risk spectrum, on the one hand, and the frictions in the markets with implications on the adjustment costs associated with effective participation in these markets, on the other hand [1, 2]. The issue of portfolio rotation, starting from the avoidance of risky assets in certain periods, is also related to participation costs and movements in the level of risk perception by investors.

In "The CAPM is Not Dead: It Works Better for Average Daily Returns", Prof. James W. Kolari et al. justify how the CAPM could contribute to understanding the new mechanisms in capital markets as a result of changing trading behavior across asset classes.

Portfolio selection captures the architectures of capital markets with a focus on equity, starting from the risk-neutral hypothesis. Thus, the utilities and therefore the weights of portfolio holdings start from the selections in relation to the equity premium. The CAPM model and subsequent versions or asset price models have been criticized in the literature due to the large number of simplifying assumptions that could alter the concrete results. For example, the impact of market frictions (trading and taxes associated costs, cognitive cost of planning) on the various selection preferences in equity portfolios implies a rethinking of the method of estimating risk aversion, disappointment aversion, and ambiguity aversion [3, 4].

This contribution [5] is focused on different cross-sectional tests of the CAPM. To mitigate problems with noise in the realized stock return series, it uses a smoothed data series of average daily returns per month. The tests using U.S. stock returns for equal-weighted portfolios demonstrate that beta is significantly priced for average daily returns but is not priced for realized monthly returns. The portfolio monthly returns do not linearly increase as beta risk increases, and the performances are situated in a fairly narrow range. By contrast, based on equal-weighted portfolios, average daily returns increase in a fairly steady linear manner as beta risk increases.

Finally, various opportunities to use CAPM for certain imposed conditions are presented. The identification of some areas of use is interesting and could open new directions of research for other types of evaluation models.

In "Stock and Futures Market Prediction Using Deep Learning Approach", Prof. Chen Mu-Yen et al. show the importance and necessity of predictions and proposes an elegant way of approaching price fluctuation predictions based on deep learning, an adequate instrument capable of solving nonlinear problems to capture the fluctuations of asset prices. Compared with machine learning (ML), deep learning (DL) autonomously regularizes the information features, reducing the complexity of the process. Recurrent neural networks (RNNs) are specifically suitable for dealing with time series analysis issues. The next step is a hybridization combining the RNN with adaptive boosting (AdaBoost), a new capability to predict the performances of different indices.

The application is based on deepening the understanding of the trend and volatility of the Taiwan 50 Index of TSEC starting from the Taiwan 50 ETF and the Taiwan Stock Exchange Index Futures (FITX). This contribution applies support vector regression (SVR), artificial neural networks (ANNs), the recurrent neural network (RNN), and the long- and short-term memory network (LSTM) to predict the trend of the Taiwan stock market. It is based on various financial and technical factors as inputs, as well as extracting variables from macroeconomic factors. The trained models are not only used to predict the fluctuation trend of the stock market but also are proposed as comparisons regarding their performances.

Based on the training by SVR, ANN, RNN, and LSTM, an interesting model is proposed capable of predicting the stock market fluctuation with adequate accuracy. Based on the stepwise regression for data dimensionality, the first experimental results showed that the foreign exchange and the technical indices are superior to the fundamental data, and the major institutional traders are inferior to the fundamental data. A comparison between SVR, ANN, RNN, and the LSTM models regarding the effectiveness and accuracy of market dynamics predictions demonstrated that SVR performs the worst and LSTM has the highest accuracy. Finally, this contribution analyzed the prediction performances for price fluctuation for the fundamental data, the foreign exchange, and the technical indices [6].

In "Aspects Regarding a Deep Understanding of the Prediction for Stock Market Movements", Prof. Hu Xuemei proposes an interesting discussion related to the possibility of predicting the stock return movement direction of financial markets. The idea is to mix the penalized logistic regression/group penalized logistic regression with technical indicators and also the group penalized trinomial logit dynamic models with technical indicators in order to predict up trends, sideways trends, and down trends. For the former, a coordinate descent algorithm is proposed to complete variable selection and to obtain a parameter estimator. A two-class confusion matrix is also introduced, using ROC and AUC to assess two-class prediction performance. For the latter, a rapidly convergent group coordinate descent algorithm is used, capable of simultaneously completing group selection and group estimation and providing the relatively optimal Bayes classifiers for class index information. A three-class confusion matrix using Kappa, PDI, ROC surface, and HUM is also introduced to assess three-class prediction performances [7].

Section 2. Specific Strategies in Emerging and Frontier Markets – Toward a New Agenda

Emerging markets (EM) have always offered opportunities for research, and in the current context, despite the mix of crises and turbulences, we are witnessing some convergence in relation to developed markets. New directions of interest are identified in the specialized literature through the analysis of the determining factors of EM performance and the integration of the new role of resilience. Besides current account balance, international reserves, and inflation [8], there are also specific market factors: understanding the role of the monetary pole in various phases of global financial cycles (which for EM actually represent exogenous shocks that test the resilience of these markets to major turbulences); understanding the reconfiguration of mechanisms for transmitting global risks to EM [9–11]; the problematic response to persistent inflation in some EMs [12]; and understanding the reconfiguration of flight to quality in periods of turbulence and crises.

In "Alternative Investment Vehicles Adapted for Entrepreneurial and Innovative Firms Financing in Emerging Markets", Gabriela Prelipcean and Mircea Boscoianu show the importance of AIVs (with a focus on crowdfunding, business angels, venture capital, and private equity) in emerging markets and the current solutions for adaptation to financing entrepreneurial and innovative firms. Even if in the specialized literature the focus is on developed markets and the approaches start from the harmonization of demand and supply, there are specific mechanisms that could determine a reorientation of AIVs in the case of EM as well. The idea of speeding up the introduction of AIVs in EM is related to the harmonization at the level of stakeholders but also to the need to integrate government intervention mechanisms in streamlining and making the access of entrepreneurial firms to capital more efficient, respectively the consolidation of the investment culture in general and that oriented on AIVs instruments in particular.

The research methodology for the portfolio's active management strategy starts from the understanding of the investors' motivation and from the possible alignment of the objectives with the offers that have been suggested by the fund managers together with the criteria used by investors to make asset valuations and the mechanisms for perceiving the investment opportunities.

The main contributions of this research are related to understanding the adjustment capabilities of the VCFs, the comparative analysis of the valuation models of the VCF portfolios adapted for emerging markets, the proposal for the integration of the dynamic capabilities and organizational resilience paradigms in a hybridized concept for a deep understanding of the evolutionary mechanisms and dynamics related to VCF, and the experimental investigations of portfolio investment decisions in EM from a triple natural perspective (investors–entrepreneurs–fund managers) [13].

In "Investment Indicators and Economic Growth in Nigeria: A Systematic Review", Dr. Abdulkarim Yusuf proposes an interesting review regarding the adaptation of the list of investment indicators in the sense of harmonization with economic growth. The adaptation of the research to the realities of Nigeria, an economy characterized by low investment flows, inadequate capital formation, and significant saving-investment gaps, requires the analysis of an extended set of behaviors that generate aggregate behavior functions: the behavior of households and the specification of consumption demand; the desire for money, assets, currency, job offer specification, savings, and investments; the behavior of companies and the specification of investment demand, financing assets, labor demand, monetary assets, and supply of goods; the behavior of the banking system and of commercial banks (specification of demand for liquidity depending on the interest rate); and the behavior of governmental institutions (specification of the governmental spending and the budget deficit depending on the fiscal policy) in a systemic approach. In this research, the domestic investment was disaggregated into private and public investment while foreign investment was disaggregated into foreign direct and portfolio investment.

The research demonstrates that credit to the private sector, domestic investment, economic liberalization, foreign portfolio investment (FPI), and interest rate have a significant positive impact on long-term growth, whereas foreign direct investment (FDI), capital expenditure, and inflation have a significant negative impact. In addition, the short-term analysis demonstrates that liberalization, private-sector credit, and portfolio investment are positively correlated with growth; on the other side, foreign direct investment, infrastructure spending, and inflation are profoundly negatively correlated. This results in the proposal for effective monetary and fiscal policy coordination to lower the cost of doing business, incentivize and open up opportunities for domestic and foreign investors, increase infrastructure spending to create jobs, reduce poverty, and sustain growth [14].

In "Investing in Sustainable Development Goals: Opportunities for Private and Public Institutions to Solve Wicked Problems That Characterize a VUCA World", Dr. Olivier Sempiga and Luc Van Liedekerke propose a unique way of identifying investment opportunities in sustainable development (SDG) in the current context.

Using a multivariate analysis of variance (MANOVA), the interest was to establish the relationship between SDG investing and a solution to wicked problems like global climate. The adoption of SRI represents an investment strategy that could improve economic, social, and environmental (ESG) performance. It represents a fine way of investing in SDG which could be a long-term solution to wicked problems. The search for the relationship between investing in SDGs and the solution of wicked problems is interesting because it contributes to the body of existing knowledge in order to inform policymakers in making strategic decisions. This research confirms the fact that wicked problems have been difficult to solve and are necessary for new ways to contribute to the philosophy of their understanding. In addition, this contribution will guide private and public institutions in examining their behaviors in tackling or contributing to challenges in the VUCA world and possibly how to navigate these new challenges [15].

Future work should be more focused on macro-level research in order to reexamine the extent to which SDG investments at different levels and in different sectors help tackle wicked problems. Future studies could also use other complementary quantitative methods.

Gabriela Prelipcean
Stefan cel Mare University of Suceava,
Suceava, Romania

Mircea Boscoianu
Transilvania University of Brasov,
Brasov, Romania

References

[1] Balloch CM, Richers J. Asset allocation and returns in the portfolios of the wealthy. LSE Financial Markets Group. 2023

[2] Gabaix K. In search of the origins of financial fluctuations: The inelastic markets hypothesis. Swiss Finance Institute Research Paper. 2022;20-91

[3] Barberis N, Huang M, Thaler RH. Individual preferences, monetary gambles, and stock market participation: A case for narrow framing. American Economic Review. 2006;**96**(4):1069-1090

[4] Bernheim RD, Rangel A. Beyond revealed preference: choice-theoretic foundations for behavioral welfare economics. Quarterly Journal of Economics. 2009;**124**(1):51-104

[5] Kolari JW. CAPM is not dead: It works better for average daily returns. In: Investment Strategies—New Advances and Challenges. IntechOpen. 2024

[6] Chen M-Y. Stock and futures market prediction using deep learning approach. In: Investment Strategies - New Advances and Challenges. IntechOpen. 2024

[7] Xuemei H. Stock return movement direction prediction. In: Investment Strategies—New Advances and Challenges. IntechOpen. 2024

[8] Aizenman J, Park D, Qureshi I, Uddin GS, Saadaoui J. The performance of emerging markets during the Fed's easing and tightening cycles: A cross-country resilience analysis. NBER Working Paper No. w32303. 2024. Available at: https://ssrn.com/abstract=4787394

[9] Furceri D, Loungani P, Zdzienicka A. The effects of monetary policy shocks on inequality. Journal of International Money and Finance. 2018;**85**:168-186

[10] Gomes FJ. Portfolio choice over the life cycle: A survey. Annual Review of Financial Economics. 2020;**12**(1):277-304

[11] Wu, JC, Xia FD. Measuring the macroeconomic impact of monetary policy at the zero lower bound. Journal of Money, Credit and Banking. 2016;**48**(2-3):253-291

[12] Neville H, Draaisma T, Funnell B, Harvey CR, Van Hemert O. The best strategies for inflationary times. Journal of Portfolio Management. 2021;**47**(8):8-37

[13] Prelipcean G, Boscoianu M. Alternative investment vehicles adapted for entrepreneurial and innovative firms financing in emerging markets. In: Investment Strategies—New Advances and Challenges. IntechOpen. 2024

[14] Abdulkarim Y. Investment indicators and economic growth in Nigeria: A systematic review. In: Investment Strategies—New Advances and Challenges. IntechOpen. 2024

[15] Sempiga O. Investing in Sustainable Development Goals: Opportunities for private and public institutions to solve wicked problems that characterize a VUCA world. In: Investment Strategies—New Advances and Challenges. IntechOpen. 2024

Section 1

Investments Strategies – Theoretical Models and New Applications

Chapter 1

The CAPM is Not Dead: It Works Better for Average Daily Returns

Wei Liu, James Kolari and Seppo Pynnonen

Abstract

In a series of papers, Fama and French showed that the CAPM failed to explain U. S. stock returns. Subsequently, they declared the CAPM dead. In its place, they proposed a number of different factors to better explain stock returns. Given that Sharpe received the Nobel Prize in Economics for the CAPM, their conclusion that it is dead is worth further investigation. This paper revisits cross-sectional tests of the Capital Asset Pricing Model (CAPM). To mitigate problems with noise in realized stock return series, we use a smoothed data series of average daily returns per month. Based on U.S. stock returns from 1965 to 2015, we find that, confirming Fama and French, beta is not priced for realized monthly returns. However, contrary to their findings, when we use average daily returns per month, we find that beta is significantly priced for average daily returns in equal-weighted stock portfolios. Further analyses reveal that popular factors proposed by Fama and French and others are more significantly priced for average daily returns also. Given that the CAPM is better supported by average daily returns per month than realized monthly returns, we conclude that it is not dead.

Keywords: asset pricing, average daily returns, beta risk, CAPM, cross-sectional regression

1. Introduction

One of the most controversial subjects in financial economics is the Capital Asset Pricing Model (CAPM) of Treynor [1, 2], Sharpe [3], Lintner [4], and Mossin [5]. Sharpe won a Nobel Prize in Economics in 1990 for his theoretical CAPM contributions to equilibrium asset pricing. The CAPM posits a linear relation between expected asset returns and beta (β) associated with the market portfolio. Unfortunately, based on extensive empirical tests in a series of research papers, Fama and French [6–10] concluded that, "In our view, the evidence that β does not suffice to explain expected return is compelling. The average return anomalies of the CAPM are serious enough to infer that the model is not a useful approximation." [9, p. 1957][1] Due to the CAPM's failure, a large number of multi-factors have been proposed by researchers to help

[1] Even early evidence raised suspicions about the CAPM. Seminal studies by Black et al. [11] and Fama and MacBeth [12] found a flatter relation between average returns and β than predicted by theory. See Levy [13] for an excellent survey of CAPM theory and empirical evidence.

explain cross-sectional stock returns (e.g., see Cochrane [14], Fama and French [10], Harvey et al. [15], Stambaugh and Yuan [16], Kolari et al. [17], and Kolari and Pynnonen [18]). According to Fama and French [9], these multi-factors add more to the explanation of average stock returns than CAPM beta.[2]

Why is it so difficult to find empirical evidence to support the CAPM? Elton [22] has argued that realized returns used in empirical asset pricing tests are poor estimates of expected returns. His main point is that occasional, large information surprises can dominate the estimate of mean returns even for long observation intervals such that unexpected returns do not tend to mean zero. This noise problem causes realized returns to be biased estimates of expected returns.[3] As anecdotal evidence, Elton observed that realized returns in the stock market have been less than the riskless rate for periods longer than 10 years (e.g., 1973 to 1984). Upon conducting simulation tests using individual U.S. stock returns, he found that information surprises could lead to the rejection of an asset pricing model.

Given the existence of information surprises, the present study seeks to not only use portfolios to mitigate information surprises but data smoothing to further remove noise from return series. To smooth data, we compute the average daily return in each month for stocks as an estimate of their expected daily return. Rather than a moving average that drops the last observation as it rolls forward in time, we compute independent average daily returns for each separate month. This simple mean daily return per month reduces the number of daily observations from an average of 252 trading days per year to 12 data points per year. Hence, the resultant smoothed series of average daily returns is much less sensitive to information surprises than daily returns.[4] By contrast, as observed by Elton, realized monthly returns compound daily returns and therefore multiply daily information surprises that leads to potentially biased estimates of expected monthly returns. Our main research question is: Do average daily returns work better than realized returns in cross-sectional tests of the CAPM?

Like Fama and French and many others, using realized monthly returns for U.S. common stocks from 1965 to 2015, no relation to market beta is evident based on Fama and MacBeth [12] cross-sectional tests. However, consistent with CAPM theory, our empirical results document a significant positive relation between mean daily returns and market beta. For equal-weighted portfolios, cross-sectional t-values associated with beta risk range from 1.66 to 2.61 across different test asset portfolios. As in

---

[2] It should be recognized that some evidence supports the conditional CAPM. For example, Ang and Chen [19], and Bali and Engle [20] have found that conditional time-varying measures of market beta (either stochastic or GARCH-based estimates) can predict cross-sectional variation in equity portfolio returns. Also, Kothari et al. [21] found evidence to support the static CAPM using annual returns from 1927 to 1990; however, further beta tests failed in the shorter period 1963 to 1990.

[3] Black [23] observed that past average returns used in testing asset pricing models provide highly inaccurate estimates of expected returns. Numerous studies have attempted to utilize analyst forecasts to proxy expected returns, including Ang and Peterson [24], Shefrin and Statman [25], Botosan and Plumlee [26], Brav et al. [27], and others. Another study by Campello et al. [28] used corporate bond yields to construct estimated expected stock return series for firms. More recently, Wu [29] employed analysts consensus stock price targets to estimate the expected returns of stocks. These studies have provided some evidence in support of the CAPM.

[4] See Madan [30] for discussion on estimating expected stock returns using daily data. They used approximately 10 years of daily returns to estimate mean returns for the entire sample period.

Bali et al. [31], for comparison purposes with realized monthly returns, we scale up daily returns to monthly percentage returns assuming 21 trading days in a month. In this respect, estimated market premia range from 0.44 percent to 0.86 percent per month for different test asset portfolios, which are economically meaningful. For Fama and French's [6, 7] widely-used size-BM (book-to-market) sorted test assets, the R-squared value indicates strong goodness-of-fit at 0.87. We conclude that CAPM is not dead as beta is better supported by average daily returns than realized monthly returns.

Further analyses augment the market factor with the size, value, and momentum factors. Due to multi-collinearity between these factors, we compute market-risk-adjusted excess returns as the dependent variable for test asset portfolios in cross-sectional regression tests. The results show that size and value are more significantly priced using average daily returns than realized returns. Also, pricing errors are driven to zero using average daily returns but not necessarily so for realized returns. When momentum is added to the three-factor model, it is significantly priced and supplants the size factor which becomes insignificant. We interpret these results to mean that zero-investment portfolios are needed to augment the CRSP market index to approximate the cross-section of average returns.

The next section discusses the problem of using realized monthly returns to proxy expected returns in testing CAPM beta. We propose average daily returns per month as an alternative choice for testing CAPM beta. Section 3 conducts empirical tests based on U.S. CRSP stock returns data. Further empirical tests of popular size, value, and momentum factors are provided. Section 4 concludes.

2. The problem of realized returns in testing the CAPM

The CAPM posits the following equilibrium relationship for the expected return on the ith asset:

$$E(R_i) - R_f = \beta_i \left[E(R_m) - R_f\right], \tag{1}$$

where R_f is the riskless rate of return, R_m is the market index rate of return, and β_i is the systematic market risk of the ith asset. Testing the above equation with real world data is nontrivial due to fact that investors' expected returns cannot be directly observed. Instead, as noted by Elton [22], researchers typically utilize realized returns to proxy expected returns in tests of the CAPM, which introduces a gap between empirical tests and CAPM theory. In an efficient market, all assets should move with the general market simultaneously, such that the length of the period to estimate expected returns is very small. Of course, for the smallest time scale, realized returns converge to expected returns. Unfortunately, the CAPM does not specify the length of the time period to compute expected return (see Kothari et al. [21], p. 190).

In practice, the following empirical form of the CAPM known as the *market model* by Markowitz [32] and Sharpe [33] is employed to estimate beta for common stocks:

$$R_{it} - R_{ft} = \alpha_i + \beta_i \left(R_{mt} - R_{ft}\right) + \varepsilon_{it}, \quad t = 1, \cdots T, \tag{2}$$

where $\hat{\alpha}$ is a mispricing term equal to zero in theory, ε_{it} is a random error term that represents idiosyncratic behavior of the ith stock's rate of return with $\varepsilon_{it} \sim N\left(0, \sigma^2_{i,Id}\right)$, and t is a time subscript. In cross-sectional asset pricing tests, it is common to use realized monthly returns for 60 months to estimate the market model. Subsequently, stocks are formed into (for example) 25 test asset portfolios based on their ranked $\hat{\beta}_i$ values and portfolio returns are computed for the next month (or next 12 months). In step one of cross-sectional Fama and MacBeth [12] tests, these monthly portfolio returns are used in a 60-month time-series regression to get $\hat{\beta}_p$ estimates for the 25 test assets. In step two, the 25 estimated portfolio betas are employed as independent variables in the following cross-sectional regression:

$$R_{pt+1} - R_{ft+1} = \alpha + \lambda\hat{\beta}_p + \varepsilon_{pt+1}, \quad t = 1, \cdots T, \tag{3}$$

where $R_{pt+1} - R_{ft+1}$ is the realized excess return of the pth test asset in the 61st month, and λ is the market price of risk associated with market beta. If the estimate $\hat{\lambda}$ is significantly different from zero, we infer that beta loadings associated with the market factor are priced in the cross-section of stocks. Also, the estimated intercept term $\hat{\alpha}$ should be statistically zero. A significant positive $\hat{\alpha}$ would imply mispricing in the sense that other factors are needed to fully price stocks.

As mentioned earlier, a potential problem in implementing the market model to test the CAPM is the common usage of realized rates of return rather than expected rates of return. In his AFA presidential address, Elton [22] defined realized returns as the sum of expected and unexpected returns, or

$$R_t = E(R_t) + I_t + \varepsilon_t, \tag{4}$$

where the unexpected return contains a systematic information component I_t plus a firm-specific component ε_t.[5] Due to information surprises, the unexpected return does not converge to zero over time. As such, realized returns do not equal expected returns. Information can have a large, permanent effect on unexpected returns and, in turn, realized returns. Elton argued that I_t follows a jump process that can influence factors in asset pricing models. In his words, "I believe that developing better measures of expected return and alternative ways to testing asset pricing theories that do not require realized returns have a much better payoff than any additional developent of statistical tests that continue to rely on realized returns as a proxy for expected returns."[6]

Elton's specification in Eq. (4) can be described as a random component model in which systematic component I_t consists of information surprises that potentially exist in stock returns. Instead of using realized monthly returns to estimate monthly expected returns, the alternative use of daily averages per month yields a model wherein I_t is the average surprise in month t and ε_t becomes a shrinked idiosyncratic random component with occasional daily noise effects averaging out. Replacing $E(R_t)$ in eq. (4) with the CAPM representation in Eq. (1), and denoting α_t as the daily average of I_t in month t, we can interpret the alpha term in Eq. (3) as the time-varying

---

[5] The existence of a noise component in realized returns is well recognized. See discussions in Brav et al. [27] and Wu [29] as well as citations therein, including Blume and Friend [34], Sharpe [35], Elton [22], Lewellen and Shanken [36], and Lundblad [37].

[6] See also Campbell [38] and Vuolteenaho [39] on decomposing unexpected returns into different systematic and firm-specific components. Vuolteenaho documented that unexpected returns primarily drive firm-specific realized returns.

mean of systematic information surprises. Consistent with Elton's model, we can redefine Eq. (3) as

$$\overline{R}_{pt+1} - R_{ft+1} = \alpha_{t+1} + \lambda\hat{\beta}_p + \overline{\varepsilon}_{pt+1}, \tag{5}$$

where the average daily return in month $t+1$ for the pth portfolio is

$$\overline{R}_{pt+1} = \frac{1}{M_{t+1}} \sum_{u=1}^{M_{t+1}} R_{pu}^{daily}, \tag{6}$$

with M_{t+1} = number of trading days in the month (e.g., $M_{t+1} = 21$ for most months), and $\overline{\varepsilon}_{pt+1}$ = average daily noise term in month $t+1$. The above specification with monthly averages of daily returns makes it possible to efficiently filter out the information surprise component I_t from the relation of stock returns and market risks in cross-sectional regression testing of the CAPM.

It is clear that average daily returns per month $\overline{R}_{pt}$ differ from realized monthly returns R_{pt} computed by cumulatively compounding daily returns for M_t days within each month, i.e., $\prod_{u=1}^{M_t}\left(1 + R_{iu}^{daily}\right) = \left(1 + R_{iu=1}^{daily}\right)\left(1 + R_{iu=2}^{daily}\right) \dots \left(1 + R_{iu=M_t}^{daily}\right)$. However, given that the CAPM is based on expected returns, the average daily return within 1 month is a potential proxy for the expected return that has not previously been considered in asset pricing tests. Consistent with Elton's [22] arguments, even though realized returns capture actual investor returns in each month, they are potentially biased estimates of expected returns as the additive daily effects of systematic I_t and occasional noise term ε_t become compounded into monthly returns. While average daily returns per month $\overline{R}_{pt}$ do not match realized monthly returns R_{pt}, the average daily return filters out most daily noise effects ε_t leaving occasional systematic component I_t essentially intact. This filtering makes it possible to single out its effect in modeling the expected return. Our specification [31] accomplishes this outcome by accounting for the I_t component via time-varying intercept term α_{t+1}, thereby reducing its biasing effect in our testing of the pricing relation predicted by the CAPM.

3. Cross-sectional tests using actual U.S. stock returns

The standard approach for testing the validity of asset pricing models is the two-step Fama and MacBeth [2] procedure. In this section, based oon U.S. stock returns, we conduct cross-sectional Fama-MacBeth regression tests by means of Eq. (3) in the previous section. First, we perform cross-sectional tests using a variety of beta-sorted test assets. Second, we repeat these tests using size and book-to-market (BM) sorted as well as industry portfolios downloaded from Kenneth French's website. Third, and last, we provide tests of popular multi-factors, including size, value, and momentum.

3.1 Beta-sorted test assets

Our data consist of all U.S. common stocks (share codes 10 and 11) in both CRSP and COMPUSTAT databases with at least 60 consecutive months of returns from January 1960 to December 2015. In any given month, we drop stocks in the bottom 10 percent market capitalization of this population to avoid liquidity issues associated with very small stocks. From these data we construct four sets of test assets comprised of 25 portfolio returns from January 1965 to December 2015:

1. Test assets I are value-weighted realized monthly returns for 25 test asset portfolios based on estimated betas using market model Eq. (2) for individual stocks and the CRSP market index. For all stocks with 60 monthly returns available from January 1960 to December 1964, 25 beta-sorted portfolios are formed and value-weighted one-month realized returns for these portfolios are computed in the subsequent month of January 1965. This procedure is repeated by rolling forward 1 month at a time until the end of the sample period to generate a time series of value-weighted realized monthly returns for each portfolio.

2. Test assets II are equal-weighted realized monthly monthly returns for 25 test asset portfolios based on estimated betas using market model Eq. (2) for individual stocks and the CRSP market index. The one-month-ahead rolling procedure used for test assets I is repeated.

3. Test assets III are value-weighted average daily returns per month for portfolios based on estimated betas using market model Eq. (2) by replacing R_{it} and R_{mt} with their daily average returns per month for individual stocks and the CRSP market index, respectively. The one-month-ahead rolling procedure used for test assets I is repeated.

4. Test assets IV are equal-weighted average daily returns per month for portfolios based on estimated betas using the market model [24] by replacing again R_{it} and R_{mt} with their daily average returns per month for individual stocks and the CRSP market index, respectively. The one-month-ahead rolling procedure used for test assets I is repeated.

Statistical properties of these test assets in the sample period are shown in **Table 1**. For value-weighted returns in test assets I and III, the mean CRSP index realized return and mean average daily return are the same at 0.89 percent per month. For comparative purposes with respect to monthly realized returns and later monthly risk premiums, we scale up average daily returns in each month as well as estimated daily risk premiums in cross-sectional tests by the number of trading days per month (i.e., $M = 21$) to obtain monthly return estimates.[7] Notice that the mean equal-weighted realized return in the sample period at 1.15 percent per month is approximately 30 percent greater than the mean value-weight realized return at 0.89 percent. Equal-weighted returns are clearly larger than value-weighted returns in our sample period. Turning to equal-weighted returns in test assets II and IV, the mean CRSP index

[7] Bali et al. [31] similarly scale up daily returns and risk premiums to monthly values assuming 21 trading days.

realized return is lower at 1.15 percent per month compared to 1.60 percent per month for average daily returns.[8]

Not only are (scaled) average daily returns consistently higher than realized returns (especially for equal-weighted returns), but the Sharpe ratios for test assets using equal-weighted returns are larger than those for value-weighted returns. As an example, the CRSP index has a Sharpe ratio of 0.21 for equal-weighted average daily returns compared to only 0.11 for both value-weighted realized and average daily returns. We interpret these results to mean that the equal-weighted market portfolio dominates the value-weighted portfolio and, therefore, is closer to the efficient frontier.[9] (Kothari et al. [21], p. 189) have commented that the question of whether the value-weighted stock index is preferred over an equal-weight stock index in CAPM beta tests is not settled. According to CAPM theory, they noted that the stock index most correlated with the true market portfolio is efficient.

The patterns of monthly returns in **Table 1** are particularly noteworthy. Average daily returns based on value-weighted portfolios increase from 0.79 percent per month for the low beta portfolio to 1.21 percent for the highest beta portfolio. However, portfolio returns do not linearly increase as beta risk increases for portfolios, and most portfolios have returns in a fairly narrow range (e.g., 0.90 and 1.10 percent). These patterns are evident in value- and equal-weighted realized monthly returns also. By contrast, based on equal-weighted portfolios, average daily returns increase in a fairly steady linear manner as beta risk increases for portfolios from 0.99 percent per month for the lowest beta portfolio to 1.60 percent for the highest beta portfolio. This descriptive pattern between equal-weighted, average daily returns and portfolio betas tends to support CAPM beta.

Monthly rolling cross-sectional Fama-MacBeth regressions are estimated for the test assets defined above. As described in Cochrane [41], we implement the following sequence of steps:

1. Estimate either market model Eq. (2) with realized monthly returns or with proposed daily average monthly returns to obtain a $\hat{\beta}_p$ estimate (factor loading) for each portfolio using monthly excess returns for the entire sample period January 1965 to December 2015.[10]

---

[8] The relatively high average daily return of 1.60 percent per month can be explained by the definition of realized returns. Assuming a stock's rate of return has average rate $\overline{R}$ and standard deviation σ_{AVG}, the realized rate of return in period T (i.e., 1 month) can be derived by means of a Taylor series expansion of the natural log function of each period's gross return $(1 + R_t)$ to obtain (after dropping higher order terms):

$$R_{1\to T} = \prod_{t=1}^{T}(1 + R_t) - 1 \approx \exp\left(\overline{R}T - \sigma_{AVG}^2 T/2\right) - 1, T = 1, \cdots, 21 \quad (6a)$$

where $\overline{R} = \frac{1}{T}\sum_{t=1}^{T} R_t$, and $\sigma_{AVG}^2 = \frac{1}{T-1}\sum_{t=1}^{T}\left(R_t - \overline{R}\right)^2$. Over time only one path of realized returns is observed by the investor. This path represents one draw from a distribution of many potential paths for realized returns. It is impossible for investors to know the true values of expected returns and volatilities. Investors may well perceive that $\overline{R}$ computed as the average of daily returns in a month provides a reasonable estimate of daily expected returns.

[9] Value-weighted portfolio returns introduce a size effect in the computation of returns that weights large stocks more heavily than small stocks. Since the equal-weighted CRSP index places more emphasis on smaller stocks and has a much larger Sharpe ratio than the value-weighted CRSP index, it appears that small stocks are needed to better approximate efficient portfolios.

[10] This approach is not feasible for individual stocks due to difficulties in gathering a sample of stocks with return series over the entire sample period.

Portf	Realized returns						Average daily returns					
	I. Value-weighted			II. Equal-weighted			III. Value-weighted			IV. Equal-weighted		
	μ	σ	$\frac{\mu-R_f}{\sigma}$	μ	σ	$\frac{\mu-R_f}{\sigma}$	μ	σ	$\frac{\mu-R_f}{\sigma}$	μ	σ	$\frac{\mu-R_f}{\sigma}$
1	0.69	4.15	0.07	0.81	3.10	0.13	0.79	4.09	0.09	0.99	3.13	0.19
2	0.83	3.77	0.11	0.90	2.98	0.16	0.92	3.56	0.15	0.96	2.95	0.19
3	0.88	3.69	0.13	1.00	3.11	0.19	0.85	3.57	0.12	1.06	3.09	0.21
4	0.95	3.70	0.15	1.04	3.39	0.19	0.99	3.71	0.16	1.21	3.37	0.24
5	0.80	3.90	0.10	1.06	3.68	0.18	0.91	3.91	0.13	1.21	3.70	0.22
6	0.96	3.92	0.14	1.13	3.85	0.19	0.94	3.90	0.14	1.25	3.88	0.22
7	0.91	4.06	0.13	1.16	4.08	0.18	1.03	4.27	0.15	1.29	4.06	0.22
8	0.97	4.39	0.13	1.11	4.28	0.16	1.05	4.34	0.15	1.26	4.23	0.20
9	0.95	4.39	0.13	1.14	4.48	0.16	0.93	4.35	0.12	1.31	4.51	0.20
10	0.90	4.47	0.11	1.18	4.69	0.17	1.09	4.38	0.16	1.30	4.64	0.19
11	1.01	4.58	0.13	1.22	4.86	0.17	0.94	4.64	0.12	1.32	4.80	0.19
12	0.88	4.74	0.10	1.11	5.01	0.14	1.01	4.72	0.13	1.36	4.96	0.19
13	0.87	4.87	0.10	1.21	5.14	0.16	0.85	5.01	0.09	1.30	5.13	0.17
14	0.80	5.04	0.08	1.28	5.37	0.16	0.96	4.96	0.11	1.42	5.38	0.19
15	1.02	5.12	0.12	1.26	5.57	0.15	0.98	5.29	0.11	1.43	5.49	0.19
16	0.94	5.38	0.10	1.13	5.75	0.13	1.03	5.33	0.12	1.38	5.64	0.17
17	0.94	5.70	0.09	1.23	6.03	0.14	0.87	5.68	0.08	1.34	5.94	0.16
18	0.83	5.93	0.07	1.21	6.36	0.13	1.12	5.78	0.12	1.39	6.20	0.16
19	0.95	5.86	0.09	1.11	6.55	0.11	1.04	6.18	0.10	1.43	6.41	0.16
20	0.94	6.38	0.08	1.21	6.95	0.12	1.03	6.36	0.10	1.42	6.67	0.15
21	0.79	6.68	0.06	1.16	7.22	0.10	0.88	6.59	0.07	1.50	7.18	0.15
22	0.93	7.23	0.07	1.14	7.81	0.09	0.89	7.10	0.07	1.50	7.63	0.14
23	0.81	7.69	0.05	1.13	8.36	0.09	1.16	7.92	0.10	1.45	8.15	0.13
24	0.99	8.36	0.07	0.95	9.23	0.06	0.99	8.41	0.07	1.56	8.92	0.13
25	0.94	9.42	0.06	1.00	10.71	0.06	1.21	9.54	0.08	1.72	10.46	0.13
CRSP	0.89	4.49	0.11	1.15	5.68	0.13	0.89	4.45	0.11	1.60	5.60	0.21

Based on CRSP data, test assets are created by estimating individual stock betas using the market model with U.S. common stocks' monthly excess returns for the 51-year sample period January 1965 to December 2015 and then forming the stocks into 25 beta-sorted portfolios, i.e., portfolio 1 [40] has the lowest (highest) beta. Both value- and equal-weighted, monthly excess returns are used for individual stocks and the CRSP market index, where excess returns are either realized or average daily excess returns. For comparison purposes to monthly realized returns, average daily returns are scaled up to monthly returns.

Table 1.
Statistical properties of test asset portfolios sorted on market beta.

2. Estimate cross-sectional OLS regressions using monthly excess returns in January 1965 as the dependent variable for all portfolios and $\hat{\beta}_p$ factor loadings from time-series regressions in step 1 as the independent variables for portfolios. The estimated coefficient denoted $\hat{\lambda}$ measures the beta risk factor price or risk premium.

3. Roll step 2 forward 1 month at a time to the end of the sample period December 1965.

4. Retain the monthly time series of 612 estimated factor prices of risk $\hat{\lambda}$ from January 1965 to December 2015. Use these series to compute the average value denoted $\hat{\bar{\lambda}}$ in percent per month.

5. Estimate t-statistics for the difference of mean values $\hat{\bar{\lambda}}$ from zero, which are corrected for errors-in-variables as in Shanken [42].

We evaluate the goodness-of-fit of the cross-sectional regressions using the adjusted R^2 statistic as suggested by Jagannathan and Wang [40] and Lettau and Ludvidgson [43]. This R-squared value can be computed via the pure cross-section approach in which a single cross-sectional regression is run:

1. As in the Fama-MacBeth approach, estimate either market model eq. (2) with realized monthly returns or proposed daily average monthly returns to obtain $\hat{\beta}_p$ factor loadings for each portfolio using monthly excess returns for the entire sample period January 1965 to December 2015.

2. Compute the time series average of 612 monthly excess returns for portfolios.

3. Estimate a single cross-sectional OLS regressions using the time series average monthly excess returns for all portfolios and the $\hat{\beta}_p$ factor loadings as the independent variables. The estimated coefficient denoted $\hat{\lambda}$ is the same as the time-series average value $\hat{\bar{\lambda}}$ in the Fama-MacBeth approach above.[11]

Fama-MacBeth test results using value-weighted monthly realized excess returns for both test asset portfolios and the CRSP market index are provided in Panel A of **Table 2**. We obtain $\hat{\bar{\lambda}} = 0.05$ percent per month with $t = 0.18$, which is far from significance. Also, $\hat{\alpha} = 0.45$ with $t = 2.43$, which indicates highly significant mispricing errors. Goodness-of-fit is very low with R-squared at only 0.04. These results are comparable to those of Fama and French [6–8] and many other studies that fail to accept the CAPM based on empirical tests. Similar findings are obtained with equal-weighted monthly realized excess returns in Panel B as well as value-weighted average daily excess returns in Panel C. The insignificance of beta with both value- and equal-weighted returns suggests that small and illiquid firms do not have an impact on the pricing evidence of market beta.

Using equal-weighted average daily excess returns for both test asset portfolios and the CRSP index in Panel D of **Table 2**, the market price of risk becomes marginally significant (at the 10 percent level) at $\hat{\bar{\lambda}} = 0.44$ percent per month with $t = 1.66$. Here the average estimated market premium is economically meaningful. Moreover,

---

[11] As Cochrane [41] observes, the Fama-MacBeth estimator for the standard error of $\hat{\lambda}$ adjusts for the cross-correlation of residuals and equals the pure cross-section OLS standard error of $\hat{\lambda}$ after correction for cross-sectional correlation. Hence, the two methods generate numerically equivalent cross-sectional results.

Panel A. Value-weighted realized returns				
$\hat{\bar{\alpha}}$	*t*-value	$\hat{\bar{\lambda}}$	*t*-value	R-squared
0.45	2.43	0.05	0.18	0.04
Panel B. Equal-weighted realized returns				
$\hat{\bar{\alpha}}$	*t*-value	$\hat{\bar{\lambda}}$	*t*-value	R-squared
0.65	4.45	0.07	0.25	0.05
Panel C. Value-weighted average daily returns				
$\hat{\bar{\alpha}}$	*t*-value	$\hat{\bar{\lambda}}$	*t*-value	R-squared
0.43	2.31	0.15	0.57	0.27
Panel D. Equal-weighted average daily returns				
$\hat{\bar{\alpha}}$	*t*-value	$\hat{\bar{\lambda}}$	*t*-value	R-squared
0.54	3.78	0.44	1.66	0.87

*Using 25 beta-sorted test assets described in **Table 1** with monthly excess returns for the 51-year sample period January 1965 to December 2015, we conduct cross-sectional Fama-MacBeth tests. In the first time-series regression step, the market model with monthly excess returns is used to estimate the market betas for the 25 test asset portfolios over the 51-year sample period. Here both equal-weighted and value-weighted returns are computed for test asset portfolios as well as the CRSP market index. Treasury bill rates are used to compute excess returns. Also, both realized excess returns and average daily excess returns are used. In the second cross-sectional step, the market price of risk denoted $\hat{\lambda}$ is estimated by regressing the excess returns for test assets in the first month of the sample period on their estimated full-sample betas. Subsequently, rolling forward 1 month at a time, this second step is repeated until the last month of the sample period to generate a time series of $\hat{\lambda}$ estimates, which are then averaged to obtain $\hat{\bar{\lambda}}$ for tests of their significant difference from zero. Using this monthly rolling approach, the portfolio beta for each test asset is the same in each monthly cross-sectional regression. For comparison purposes to results using monthly realized returns, risk premia based on average daily returns are scaled up to monthly premia. Standard errors are computed with Shanken [42] corrections to estimate t-values. R-squared values are based on the pure cross-section approach with a single cross-sectional OLS regression (see Jagannathan and Wang [40] and (Lettau and Ludviegson [43], footnote 17, p. 1254)).*

Table 2.
Cross-sectional Fama-MacBeth tests for the market factor using realized and average daily U.S. stock market returns for beta-sorted test asset portfolios.

the *R*-squared value indicates strong goodness-of-fit at 0.87.[12] Nonetheless, significant mispricing exists (i.e., $\hat{\bar{\alpha}} = 0.54$ with $t = 3.78$[13]), which suggests that other factors are needed to more fully price test assets. In forthcoming Subsection 3.3, we conduct further tests by augmenting the market factor with size, value, and momentum multi-factors in an attempt to mitigate mispricing errors.

Figure 1 plots average daily excess returns against estimated beta values for the 25 beta-sorted assets. The left-hand graph contains the results using value-weighted realized excess returns as in Panel A of **Table 2**. By casual inspection, there is little

[12] Levy [13] has observed that R-squared values in cross-sectional regressions with CAPM beta are typically low at around 0.04 with monthly data and 0.20 for annual data with individual stocks.

[13] It is interesting to note that, as the standard error of $\hat{\lambda}$ is 0.27, a similar size market price of risk estimate, i.e., $\hat{\bar{\lambda}} = 0.54$ (6.48 p.a) would result in only a borderline statistically significant *t*-value of $t = 2.00$, which suggests much lower power of the *t*-test of $\hat{\bar{\lambda}}$ compared to that of $\hat{\bar{\alpha}}$. Thus, the weak significance of $\hat{\bar{\lambda}}$ is attributable to the weak power of the standard *t*-test produced by the traditional Fama-MacBeth approach. The development of more powerful testing procedures is recommended that take into account highly correlated portfolios.

DOI: http://dx.doi.org/10.5772/intechopen.111932

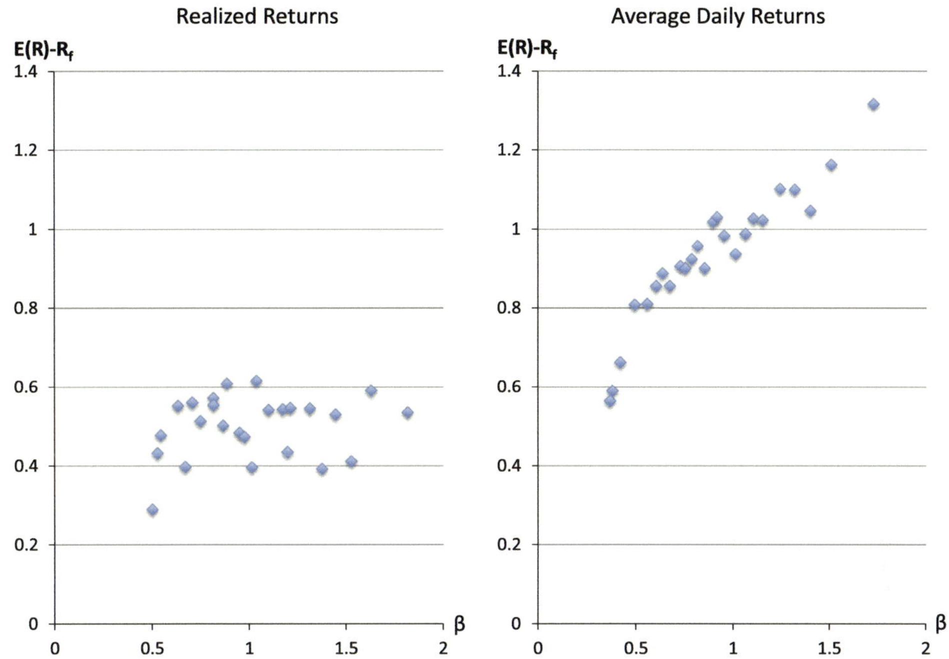

Figure 1.
The relation between average excess returns and market beta. The graph on the left shows the results for 25 beta-sorted test asset portfolios with the time-series average of market betas for each portfolio on the X-axis and the time-series average of value-weighted realized excess returns on the Y-axis. The graph on the right shows the results for the time-series mean of market betas for each portfolio on the X-axis and the time-series mean of equal-weighted average daily excess returns on the Y-axis (scaled to monthly returns). The graphs are based on results in Panels A and D of ***Table 2*** *using the pure cross-section approach for estimating R-squared values in the sample period January 1965 to December 2015.*

or no discernable relationship evident. By contrast, using equal-weighted average daily excess returns (scaled to monthly returns for comparison purposes) as in Panel D of **Table 2**, the right-hand graph illustrates a positive relation between average beta values and average daily excess returns. The linear relation shown there is almost a perfect depiction of CAPM theory. Also, it is consistent with earlier descriptive evidence in **Table 1** for equal-weighted average daily returns and portfolio betas.

3.2 Fama: French test assets and industry portfolios

Table 3 repeats the above cross-sectional tests of realized and average daily returns for widely-used test asset portfolios. From Kenneth French's website, we downloaded value- and equal-weighted returns for 25 portfolios sorted on quintiles of size and book-to-market (BM) as well as 30 industry portfolios. Average daily excess returns are computed from daily realized returns. Traditional test results in Panel A for value-weighted realized returns with 25 size-BM sorted portfolios reveal the following results: $\hat{\hat{\lambda}} = -0.33$ percent per month with $t = -0.77$. As in **Table 2**, the market factor is not significantly priced in the cross section of average stock returns. Again, mispricing errors are highly significant at the 1 percent level, and R-squared is relatively low at 0.06. The estimated market prices of risk for equal-weighted realized returns with 25 size-BM portfolios in Panel B are again insignificant but the coefficient signs switch from negative to positive. As before in **Table 2**, this evidence implies that small and illiquid firms do not affect market beta

Panel A. Value-weighted realized returns					
Portfolios	$\hat{\hat{\alpha}}$	*t*-value	$\hat{\hat{\lambda}}$	*t*-value	R-squared
25 Size-BM	1.06	2.76	−0.33	−0.77	0.06
30 Industry	0.66	2.84	−0.07	−0.23	0.01
25 Size-BM + 30 Industry	0.75	3.08	−0.10	−0.34	0.01
Panel B. Equal-weighted realized returns					
Portfolios	$\hat{\hat{\alpha}}$	*t*-value	$\hat{\hat{\lambda}}$	*t*-value	R-squared
25 Size-BM	0.71	2.49	0.06	0.17	0.00
30 Industry	0.72	3.31	0.05	0.17	0.00
25 Size-BM + 30 Industry	0.72	3.10	0.05	0.18	0.00
Panel C. Value-weighted average daily returns					
Portfolios	$\hat{\hat{\alpha}}$	*t*-value	$\hat{\hat{\lambda}}$	*t*-value	R-squared
25 Size-BM	1.23	2.44	−0.53	−1.32	0.17
30 Industry	0.69	3.05	−0.12	−0.41	0.03
25 Size-BM + 30 Industry	0.84	3.53	−0.21	−0.71	0.05
Panel D. Equal-weighted average daily returns					
Portfolios	$\hat{\hat{\alpha}}$	*t*-value	$\hat{\hat{\lambda}}$	*t*-value	R-squared
25 Size-BM	0.16	0.57	0.87	2.56	0.16
30 Industry	0.69	3.33	0.53	1.79	0.24
25 Size-BM + 30 Industry	0.34	1.54	0.79	2.61	0.21

From Kenneth French's website, we downloaded daily and monthly returns for Fama and French's [6–8] 25 size and book-to-market (BM) portfolios as well as 30 industry portfolios for the 51-year sample period January 1965 to December 2015. Value- and equal-weighted portfolio and CRSP market index returns as well as Treasury bill rates are downloaded. Implementing the Fama-MacBeth test procedure, in the first time-series regression step, the market model with monthly excess returns is used to estimate the market betas for the test asset portfolios over the 51-year sample period. Here both equal-weighted and value-weighted returns are used for test asset portfolios as well as the CRSP market index. Also, both realized returns and average daily returns per month are used. In the second cross-sectional step, the market price of risk denoted as $\hat{\lambda}$ is estimated by regressing the excess returns for test assets in the first month of the sample period on their estimated full-sample betas. Subsequently, rolling forward 1 month at a time, this second step is repeated until the last month of the sample period to generate a time series of $\hat{\lambda}$ estimates, which are then averaged to obtain $\hat{\hat{\lambda}}$ that is tested for significant difference from zero. Using this monthly rolling approach, the portfolio beta for each test asset is the same in each monthly cross-sectional regression. For comparison purposes to results using monthly realized returns, risk premia based on average daily returns are scaled up to monthly premia. Standard errors are computed with Shanken [42] corrections to estimate t-values. R-squared values are based on the pure cross-section approach with a single cross-sectional OLS regression (see Jagannathan and Wang [40] and (Lettau and Ludviegson [43], footnote 17, p. 1254)).

Table 3.
Cross-sectional Fama-MacBeth tests for the market factor using realized and average daily returns for size-BM sorted and industry test asset portfolios.

pricing. For value-weighted average daily returns in Panel C, the results are insignificant with negative coefficient signs similar to value-weighted realized returns in Panel A. The results for the 30 industry portfolios and combined 25 size-BM plus 30 industry portfoliios in Panels A to C are similar those for the 25 size-BM portfolios.

Using equal-weighted average daily excess returns in Panel D of **Table 3**, the estimated market prices of risk are statistically significant and economically substantial: $\hat{\hat{\lambda}} = 0.87$ percent per month with $t = 2.56$ for the 25 size-BM sorted portfolios,

$\hat{\hat{\lambda}} = 0.53$ percent per month with $t = 1.79$ for 30 industry portfolios, and $\hat{\hat{\lambda}} = 0.79$ percent per month with $t = 2.61$ for the combined 25 size-BM plus 30 industry portfolios. A recent study by Harvey et al. [15] argues that, due to the large number of proposed multi-factors, an asset pricing factor should be evaluated against a t-statistic threshold of 3.0 or more. Our t-values are somewhat less than this hurdle rate but market beta has the advantage of CAPM theoretical support. In this regard, Harvey et al. conclude that a lower threshold t-ratio may be justifiable for a factor with strong theoretical underpinnings.

In Panel D of **Table 3**, notice that the mispricing error terms $\hat{\hat{\alpha}} = 0.16$ and $\hat{\hat{\alpha}} = 0.34$ are relatively small and insignificant for the size-BM and size-BM plus industry portfolios, respectively. For these test assets, the magnitudes of the market factor prices of risk $\hat{\hat{\lambda}}$ are relatively high at about 0.80 percent or more per month and the associated t-values are significant at the 1 percent level. Hence, at higher estimated market factor prices of risk, mispricing error tends to disappear. In view of our earlier discussion of Elton's random component model, average information surprises embedded in $\hat{\hat{\alpha}}$ are diminished by significant market factor loadings. Finally, the estimated R-squared values in the range of 0.16 to 0.24 across test assets are relatively higher in Panel D using equal-weighted average daily returns than in other panels. These results are encouraging in terms of supporting the CAPM.

Some researchers (e.g., Lewellen et al. [44] and Daniel and Titman [45]) have recommended using industry portfolios as test assets (as well as combining them with Fama-French portfolios) due to their exogeneity with respect to model factors. However, empirical tests using industry portfolios have typically not supported the CAPM. Based on equal-weighted average daily returns in Panel D, the market price of risk is marginally significant (at the 10 percent level) for 30 industry portfolios with an economically meaningful risk premium of 0.53 percent per month. These results based on exogenous test assets support CAPM beta.

3.3 Cross-sectional tests of multi-factors

We next augment the market model with Fama and French's size and value factors plus the momentum factor. In unreported results, for both value-weighted and equal-weighted average daily returns, we find that the market factor is not significantly priced in cross-sectional tests models containing these factors. The primary reason for this insignificance appears to be multicollinearity between the market factor and the multi-factors. In our sample period the estimated correlations for value-weighted realized returns between the market factor and both size and value factors are 0.31 and $-$ 0.31, respectively. The size and value factors have an estimated correlation of -0.23. Correlations using average daily returns are similar or higher. For example, the market and size factors have a correlation coefficient of 0.56. Due to this collinearity issue, we tested the size and value factors as follows:

- Using the entire sample period, the market model is estimated by regressing test asset portfolios' monthly excess returns on CRSP market index excess returns.

- Risk-adjusted excess returns for (zero-cost investment) portfolios are computed for the entire sample period as

$$R_{pt}^{ex} = R_{pt} - R_{ft} - \hat{\beta}_p (R_{Mt} - R_{ft}). \tag{7}$$

- Risk-adjusted excess returns R_{pt}^{ex} are regressed on the *SMB* and *HML* factors to obtain $\hat{\beta}_{SMB}$ and $\hat{\beta}_{HML}$ as

$$R_{pt}^{ex} - R_{ft} = \alpha_p + \beta_{pSMB} SMB_t + \beta_{pHML} HML_t + \varepsilon_{pt}. \tag{8}$$

- Based on the second step in the Fama-MacBeth testing method, the market prices of risk $\hat{\lambda}_{SMB}$ and $\hat{\lambda}_{HML}$ are estimated.

Table 4 reports the results of this risk-adjusted excess return approach for testing the size and value factors. In Panel A using realized excess returns, size is marginally significant in the 30 industry portfolios, and the value factor is significant in the 25 size-BM portfolios and combined 25 size-BM and industry portfolios. In Panel B using average daily returns, both size and value factors are significant in the 25 size-BM portfolios and combined 25 size-BM and industry portfolios but not industry portfolios alone. Notice that $\hat{\alpha}$s equal zero for all three test asset portfolios. We infer from this evidence that the size and value factors are better supported via our risk-adjusted excess return procedure than the traditional three-factor model.

We repeated the above analyses for the four-factor Carhart [46] model with market, size, value, and momentum factors in **Table 5**. Most of the results for the size and value factors are similar to those in **Table 4**, with the exception that size is no longer priced in Panels A and B. It appears that, in this model, the momentum factor supplants size, as momentum is normally priced in Panel A to B.[14] Due to low estimated correlations in the sample period between size and momentum (i.e., -0.00 and $-$ 0.06 for realized and average daily excess returns, respectively), multicollinearity does not appear to be the reason for size dropping out.[15] Like the three-factor model, no mispricing error exists for tests using average daily returns, but mispricing occurs in the test assets using realized returns.

Overall, these results suggest that zero-investment portfolios are needed to augment the CRSP market index in order to better approximate the cross-section of average stock returns.

3.4 Robustness tests

We conducted a number of robustness checks. For example, we repeated cross-sectional tests in **Tables 2** and **3** of the CRSP market index using average daily returns in each quarter rather than each month. Smoothing over a longer period may further suppress information surprises. Also, further tests of average daily returns using a

---

[14] Recent work by Asness et al. [47] has shown that the size effect is masked to some extent by the quality of firms. Upon controlling for quality, they found that the returns to size are more stable and significant than otherwise. Also, momentum did not explain the returns to size-quality portfolios. Interactions between multi-factors were recommended for further study by the authors.

[15] The estimated correlations between momentum and the excess market returns are -0.13 and $-$ 0.27 for realized and average daily returns, respectively.

Panel A. Value-weighted realized returns							
Portfolios	$\hat{\alpha}$	*t*-value	$\hat{\lambda}_{SMB}$	*t*-value	$\hat{\lambda}_{HML}$	*t*-value	R-squared
25 Size-BM	−0.00	−0.00	0.06	1.42	0.51	4.05	0.67
30 Industry	0.15	4.07	−0.39	−1.88	−0.14	−0.21	0.25
25 Size-BM + 30 Industry	0.07	2.26	−0.02	−0.17	0.28	2.16	0.17
Panel B. Equal-weighted average daily returns							
Portfolios	$\hat{\alpha}$	*t*-value	$\hat{\lambda}_{SMB}$	*t*-value	$\hat{\lambda}_{HML}$	*t*-value	R-squared
25 Size-BM	−0.03	−1.00	0.35	2.18	0.71	5.20	0.67
30 Industry	0.03	0.99	−0.23	−0.78	−0.12	−0.62	0.03
25 Size-BM + 30 Industry	−0.02	−0.97	0.35	2.09	0.49	3.41	0.38

From Kenneth French's website, we downloaded daily and monthly returns for Fama and French's [6–8] 25 size and book-to-market (BM) portfolios as well as 30 industry portfolios for the 51-year sample period January 1965 to December 2015. Value- and equal-weighted portfolio and CRSP market index returns are downloaded in addition to the Fama-French size ((SMB) and value (HML) factors and one-month Treasury bill rates. Implementing the Fama-MacBeth test procedure, in the first time-series regression step, the market model with monthly excess returns is used to estimate the market betas $\hat{\beta}_p$ for the test asset portfolios over the 51-year sample period. Here both value- and equal-weighted returns are used for test asset portfolios as well as the CRSP market index. Also, both realized returns and average daily returns per month are used. Excess monthly returns for each portfolio are computed as follows: $R^{ex}_{pt} - R_{ft} = R_{pt} - R_{ft} - \hat{\beta}_p R_{mt} - R_{ft}$, where R_{mt} and R_{ft} are the CRSP index return and Treasury bill rate, respectively. Subsequently, these excess returns are regressed on the SMB and HML factors to estimate the multi-factors' loadings for the full sample period. In the second cross-sectional step, the market price of risk denoted as $\hat{\lambda}$ for each multi-factor is estimated by regressing the excess returns for test assets in the first month of the sample period $R^{ex}_{pt=1}$ on their estimated full sample multi-factor betas. Rolling forward 1 month at a time, this second step is repeated until the last month of the sample period to generate a time series of $\hat{\lambda}$ estimates for each multi-factor, which are then averaged to obtain $\hat{\bar{\lambda}}$ that is tested for significant difference from zero. Using this monthly rolling approach, the estimated portfolio SML and HML betas for each test asset are the same in each monthly cross-sectional regression. For comparison purposes to results using monthly realized returns, risk premia based on average daily returns are scaled up to monthly premia. Standard errors are computed with Shanken [42] corrections to estimate t-values. R-squared values are based on the pure cross-section approach with a single cross-sectional OLS regression (see Jagannathan and Wang [40] and (Lettau and Ludviegson [43], footnote 17, p. 1254)).

Table 4.
Cross-sectional Fama-MacBeth tests for the size and value factors using realized and average daily market beta risk-adjusted returns for size-BM sorted and industry test asset portfolios.

longer period provide some validation of our monthly results. Based on equal-weighted returns, **Table 6** shows that market beta is again significantly priced for 25 beta-sorted portfolios (viz., *t*-value = 1.91), 25 size-BM portfolios (viz., *t*-value = 2.88), 25 size-BM plus 30 industry portfolios (viz., *t*-value = 2.47), and 25 size-BM plus 30 industry plus 25 beta-sorted portfolios (viz., *t*-value = 2.37). For industry portfolios, market beta is not significantly priced (viz., *t*-value = 1.40), which contrasts with the nominal significance of market beta in Panel D of **Table 3** (viz., *t*-value = 1.79) As before, mispricing error is insignificant for the size-BM and size-BM plus 30 industry portfolios (i.e., average information surprises are eliminated). In general, these results using average daily returns per quarter corroborate our findings using average daily returns per month.

In unreported tests, we found that market beta was not significantly priced using median (rather than mean) returns per month. Also, we repeated the realized return tests in Panels A and B of **Tables 2** and **3** using daily (rather than monthly) realized

Panel A. Value-weighted realized returns									
Portfolios	$\hat{\alpha}$	t-val	$\hat{\lambda}_{SMB}$	t-val	$\hat{\lambda}_{HML}$	t-val	λ_{MOM}	t-val	R-squared
25 Size-BM	0.06	2.37	−0.08	−0.54	0.64	4.97	3.25	4.85	0.77
30 Industry	0.15	3.92	−0.36	−1.61	−0.01	−0.07	0.27	0.44	0.27
25 Size-BM + 30 Industry	0.10	2.84	−0.05	−0.34	0.36	2.65	0.97	2.08	0.31
Panel B. Equal-weighted average daily returns									
Portfolios	$\hat{\alpha}$	t-val	$\hat{\lambda}_{SMB}$	t-val	$\hat{\lambda}_{HML}$	t-val	λ_{MOM}	t-val	R-squared
25 Size-BM	0.02	0.74	−0.11	−0.53	1.03	6.52	3.08	3.94	0.71
30 Industry	0.04	1.32	−0.39	−1.17	0.07	0.32	1.53	2.11	0.27
25 Size-BM + 30 Industry	−0.01	−0.25	0.08	0.39	0.67	3.99	1.74	2.52	0.47

From Kenneth French's website, we downloaded daily and monthly returns for Fama and French's [6–8] 25 size and book-to-market (BM) portfolios as well as 30 industry portfolios for the 51-year sample period January 1965 to December 2015. Value- and equal-weighted portfolio and CRSP market index returns are downloaded in addition to the Fama-French size ((SMB) and value (HML) factors, momentum factor, and Treasury bill rates. Implementing the Fama-MacBeth test procedure, in the first time-series regression step, the market model with monthly excess returns is used to estimate the market betas $\hat{\beta}_p$ for the test asset portfolios over the 51-year sample period. Here both equal- and value-weighted excess returns are used for test asset portfolios as well as the CRSP market index. Also, both realized excess returns and average daily excess returns per month are used. Excess monthly market returns for each portfolio are computed as follows: $R^{ex}_{pt} - R_{ft} = R_{pt} - R_{ft} - \hat{\beta}_p(R_{mt} - R_{ft})$, where R_{mt} and R_{ft} are the CRSP index return and Treasury bill rate, respectively. Subsequently, these excess returns are regressed on the SMB, HML, and MOM factors to estimate the multi-factors' loadings for the full sample period. In the second cross-sectional step, the market price of risk denoted as $\hat{\lambda}$ for each factor is estimated by regressing the excess returns for test assets in the first month of the sample period, or $R^{ex}_{pt=1} - R_{ft=1}$, on their estimated full sample factor betas. Rolling forward 1 month at a time, this second step is repeated until the last month of the sample period to generate a time series of $\hat{\lambda}$ estimates for each factor, which are then averaged to obtain $\hat{\hat{\lambda}}$ that is tested for significant difference from zero. Using this monthly rolling approach, the estimated portfolio SML, HML, and MOM betas for each test asset are the same in each monthly cross-sectional regression. For comparison purposes to results using monthly realized returns, risk premia based on average daily returns are scaled up to monthly premia. Standard errors are computed with Shanken [42] corrections to estimate t-values. R-squared values are based on the pure cross-section approach with a single cross-sectional OLS regression (see Jagannathan and Wang [40] and (Lettau and Ludviegson [43], footnote 17, p. 1254)).

Table 5.
Cross-sectional Fama-MacBeth tests for the size, value, and momentum factors using realized and average daily market beta risk-adjusted returns for size-BM sorted and industry test asset portfolios.

returns to estimate market betas. However, market beta again was not significantly priced in these cross-sectional tests.

4. Conclusion

Based on empirical evidence using U.S. stock returns, Fama and French [6–10] concluded that Sharpe's [3] famous CAPM is dead. Since the Sharpe received the Nobel Prize in Economics for the CAPM, this conclusion is worth further investigation. Elton [22] has argued that empirical tests of the CAPM are flawed due the gap between theory based on expected returns and real world tests using realized returns. The main problem is daily informational surprises that can bias monthly compounded daily realized returns as proxies for expected returns. To address this problem, this paper sought to mitigate information surprises in realized returns by smoothing data series using the average of daily returns per month.

Equal-weighted average daily returns per quarter					
Portfolios	$\hat{\bar{\alpha}}$	***t*-value**	$\hat{\bar{\lambda}}$	***t*-value**	**R-squared**
25 Beta	1.28	2.75	1.77	1.91	0.94
25 Size-BM	0.09	0.12	3.12	2.88	0.25
30 Industry	2.24	3.34	1.43	1.40	0.22
25 Size-BM + 30 Industry	0.93	1.40	2.51	2.47	0.26
25 Size-BM + 30 Industry+25 Beta	1.09	2.09	2.23	2.37	0.34

*This table repeats equal-weighted return tests in Panel D of **Tables 3** and **4** using average daily returns in each quarter rather than each month. The 25 beta-sorted portfolios are described in the text and **Table 1**. From Kenneth French's website, we downloaded equal-weighted daily returns for Fama and French's [6–8] 25 size and book-to-market (BM) portfolios (i.e., 25 Size-BM) as well as 30 industry portfolios (i.e., 30 Industry) for the 51-year sample period January 1965 to December 2015. Equal-weighted CRSP market index returns as well as Treasury bill rates are downloaded. Average daily excess returns per quarter are computed for all data series. Beta-sorted test asset portfolios are created by estimating CRSP stocks' betas as described in Subsection 3.1 (i.e., test assets IV using average daily returns per quarter rather than per month). Implementing the Fama-MacBeth test procedure, in the first time-series regression step, the market model with average daily excess returns in each quarter is used to estimate the market betas for the test asset portfolios over the 51-year sample period. In the second cross-sectional step, the market price of risk denoted as $\hat{\lambda}$ is estimated by regressing the excess returns for test assets in the first quarter of the sample period on their estimated full-sample betas. Subsequently, rolling forward one quarter at a time, this second step is repeated until the last quarter of the sample period to generate a time series of $\hat{\lambda}$ estimates, which are then averaged to obtain $\hat{\bar{\lambda}}$ that is tested for significant difference from zero. Using this quarterly rolling approach, the portfolio beta for each test asset is the same in each quarterly cross-sectional regression. For comparison purposes to results using realized returns, risk premia based on average daily returns are scaled up to quarterly premia. Standard errors are computed with Shanken [42] corrections to estimate t-values. R-squared values are based on the pure cross-section approach with a single cross-sectional OLS regression (see Jagannathan and Wang [40] and (Lettau and Ludviegson [43], footnote 17, p. 1254)).*

Table 6.
Further cross-sectional Fama-MacBeth tests for the market factor using average daily returns for beta-sorted, size-BM sorted, and industry test asset portfolios on a quarterly basis.

Based on U.S. common stock returns from the CRSP database for the sample period 1965 to 2015, we conducted cross-sectional tests of the CAPM. A variety of test assets were employed, including beta-sorted, size-BM (book-to-market) sorted, and industry portfolios. Both value- and equal-weighted portfolio returns were computed for realized returns and average daily returns per month. Consistent with many previous studies, in the case of realized returns, the market price of beta risk was insignificant, pricing errors were highly significant, and R-squared values were relatively low. These lackluster findings have motivated researchers to conclude that the CAPM is dead. However, when we repeated the cross-sectional tests using average daily returns per month, the market price of beta risk became statistically significant. In these tests, cross-sectional t-values for beta risk ranged from 1.66 to 2.61 across different test asset portfolios. For beta-sorted test assets, the estimated R-squared value was relatively high at 0.87. And, even though most researchers cannot price the market factor using industry portfolios, we found some evidence that β is significantly priced in these exogenous portfolios. Lastly, for size-BM (book-to-market) sorted portfolios, mispricing error was insignificant, which suggested that average information surprises are diminished using average daily returns.

Subsequently, utilizing size-BM and industry portfolios as test assets, we tested multi-factor models by augmenting the market model with size, value, and momentum factors. For the three-factor model, the size and value factors were more significantly priced in different test assets using average daily excess returns than realized excess returns. Mispricing errors existed in both return cases. To take into account multicollinearity arising from the correlation between the market factor and multi-factors, we repeated the three-factor analyses by regressing risk-adjusted excess returns (after taking into account the market factor) on the size and value factors. Cross-sectional results for the size and value factors were similar to those for the non-orthogonalized three-factor model but now mispricing errors became insignificant (i.e., information surprises were diminished). Also, including the momentum factor in the latter risk-adjusted analyses revealed that it tends to supplant size as a priced factor in this model. We infer that multi-factors are important in helping to better explain the cross-section of expected returns.

Based on these findings, we conclude that CAPM is not dead as beta appears to be better supported by average daily returns per month than realized monthly returns. Using average daily returns, in Merton's [48] words, "... the capital market operates 'as if' the assumptions of the CAPM were satisfied." (Merton [37], p. 867) Further research is recommended on average daily returns, including other return smoothing approaches, different sample periods, asset classes, and countries.

JEL classification

C10, C20, G12

Author details

Wei Liu[1], James Kolari[1*] and Seppo Pynnonen[2]

1 Adam C. Sinn '00 Department of Finance, Mays Business School, Texas A&M University, College Station, USA

2 Department of Mathematics and Statistics, University of Vaasa, Vaasa, Finland

*Address all correspondence to: j-kolari@tamu.edu

References

[1] Treynor JL. Market value, time, and risk. Unpublished manuscript. 1961

[2] Treynor JL. Toward a theory of market value of risky assets. 1962. Unpublished manuscript

[3] Sharpe WF. Capital asset prices: A theory of market equilibrium under conditions of risk. Journal of Finance. 1964;**19**:425-442

[4] Lintner J. The valuation of risk assets and the selection of risky investments in stock portfolios and capital budgets. Review of Economics and Statistics. 1965;**47**:13-37

[5] Mossin J. Equilibrium in a capital asset market. Econometrica. 1966;**34**: 768-783

[6] Fama EF, French KR. The cross-section of expected stock returns. Journal of Finance. 1992;**47**:427-465

[7] Fama EF, French KR. The cross-section of expected returns. Journal of Financial Economics. 1993;**33**:3-56

[8] Fama EF, French KR. Size and book-to-market factors in earnings and returns. Journal of Finance. 1995;**50**:131-156

[9] Fama EF, French KR. The CAPM is wanted, dead or alive. Journal of Finance. 1996;**51**:1947-1958

[10] Fama EF, French KR. The capital asset pricing model: Theory and evidence. Journal of Economic Perspectives. 2004;**18**:25-46

[11] Black F, Jensen MC, Scholes M. The capital asset pricing model: Some empirical tests. In: Jensen MC, editor. Studies in the Theory of Capital Markets. New York, NY: Praeger; 1972

[12] Fama EF, MacBeth JD. Risk, return, and equilibrium: Empirical tests. Journal of Political Economy. 1973;**81**:607-636

[13] Levy H. The CAPM is alive and well: A review and synthesis. European Financial Management. 2010;**16**:43-71

[14] Cochrane JH. Presidential address: Discount rates. Journal of Finance. 2011; **56**:1047-1108

[15] Harvey CR, Liu Y, Zhu H. ... and the cross-section of expected returns. Review of Financial Studies. 2015;**29**:5-68

[16] Stambaugh RF, Yuan Y. Mispricing factors. Review of Financial Studies. 2017;**30**:1270-1315

[17] Kolari JW, Liu W, Huang JZ. A New Model of Capital Asset Prices: Theory and Evidence. Cham, Switzerland: Palgrave Macmillan; 2021

[18] Kolari JW, Pynnonen S. Investment Valuation and Asset Pricing: Models and Method. Cham, Switzerland: Palgrave Macmillan; 2023

[19] Ang A, Chen J. CAPM over the long run: 1926-2001. Journal of Empirical Finance. 2007;**14**:1-40

[20] Bali TG, Engle RF. The intertemporal capital asset pricing model with dynamic conditional correlations. Journal of Monetary Economics. 2010;**5**: 377-390

[21] Kothari SP, Shanken J, Sloan RG. Another look at the cross-section of expected stock returns. Journal of Finance. 1995;**50**:185-224

[22] Elton EJ. Expected return, realized return, and asset pricing tests. Journal of Finance. 1999;**54**:1199-1220

[23] Black F. Estimating expected returns. Financial Analysts Journal. 1993; **49**:36-38

[24] Ang JA, Peterson DR. Return, risk, and yield: Evidence from ex ante cata. Journal of Finance. 1985;**40**:537-548

[25] Shefrin H, Statman M. The style of investor expectations. In: Coggin T, Fabozzi F, editors. The Handbook of Equity Style Management. 3rd ed. Hoboken NJ: John Wiley & Sons, Inc.; 2003

[26] Botosan CA, Plumlee MA. Assessing alternative proxies for the expected risk premium. Accounting Review. 2005;**80**: 21-54

[27] Brav A, Lehavy R, Michaely R. Using expectations to test asset pricing models. Financial Management. 2005;**34**:5-37

[28] Campello M, Chen L, Zhang L. Expected returns, yield spreads, and asset pricing tests. Review of Financial Studies. 2008;**21**:1297-1338

[29] Wu L. Estimating risk-return relations with analysts price targets. Journal of Banking and Finance. 2018;**93**: 183-197

[30] Madan DB. Efficient estimation of expected stock price returns. Finance Research Letters. 2017;**23**:31-38

[31] Bali TG, Engle RF, Tang Y. Dynamic conditional beta is alive and well in the cross-seciton of daily stock returns. Management Science. 2017;**63**:3760-3779

[32] Markowitz HM. Portfolio Selection: Efficient Diversification of Investments. New York, NY: John Wiley & Sons; 1959

[33] Sharpe WF. A simplified model for portfolio analysis. Management Science. 1963;**9**:277-293

[34] Blume ME, Friend I. A new look at the capital asset pricing model. Journal of Finance. 1973;**28**:19-33

[35] Sharpe WF. New evidence on the Capital Asset Pricing Model: Discussion. Journal of Finance. 1978;**33**:917-920

[36] Lewellen J, Shanken J. Learning, asset prices, and market efficiency. Journal of Finance. 2002;**57**: 1113-1146

[37] Lundblad C. The risk return tradeoff in the long run: 1836–2003. Journal of Financial Economics. 2007;**85**: 123-150

[38] Campbell J. A variance decomposition for stock returns. The Economic Journal. 1991;**101**:157-179

[39] Vuolteenaho T. What drives firm-level stock returns? Journal of Finance. 2002;**57**:233-264

[40] Jagannathan R, Wang Z. The conditional CAPM and the cross-section of asset returns. Journal of Finance. 1996;**51**:3-53

[41] Cochrane JH. Asset Pricing. Revised ed. Princeton, NJ: Princeton University Press; 2005

[42] Shanken J. On the estimation of beta-pricing models. Review of Financial Studies. 1992;**5**:1-33

[43] Lettau M, Ludvigson S. Resurrecting the (C)CAPM: A cross-sectional test when risk premia are time-varying. Journal of Political Economy. 2001;**109**: 1238-1287

[44] Lewellen J, Nagel S, Shanken JA. A skeptical appraisal of asset pricing tests. Journal of Financial Economics. 2010;**96**: 175-194

[45] Daniel K, Titman S. Testing factor-model explanations of market anomalies. Critical Finance Review. 2012;**1**:103-139

[46] Carhart MM. On persistence in mutual fund performance. Journal of Finance. 1997;**52**:57-82

[47] Asness C, Frazzini A, Israel R, Moskowitz T, Pedersen LH. Size matters, if you control your junk, Chicago Booth Working Paper No. 15–21. Chicago, IL; University of Chicago, Booth School of Business; 2015

[48] Merton RC. An intertemporal capital asset pricing model. Econometrica. 1973; **41**:867-887

Chapter 2

Stock and Futures Market Prediction Using Deep Learning Approach

Min-Hsuan Fan, Jing-Long Huang and Mu-Yen Chen

Abstract

In recent years, numerous studies have been devoted to predict the price fluctuations of financial markets. Taiwan 50 Exchange Traded Funds (ETF) is one of the important indicators to measure the volatility of the component stocks of the Taiwan 50 Index. With the development of the financial market, the trading volume of Taiwan Stock Index Futures is also increasing. The three markets play the important roles of economic development in the Taiwan. This study predicts the trend of Taiwan 50 ETF and Taiwan index futures applying machine learning and deep learning approaches which have excellent data exploration capabilities. This study applies the support vector regression (SVR), artificial neural networks (ANN), recurrent neural network (RNN), and long short-term memory network (LSTM) to predict the trend of the Taiwan stock market. This study uses various financial and technical factors as inputs, and extract variables from the factors affecting Taiwan's economy to build models, and compares the benefits between models to explore future market.

Keywords: deep learning, machine learning, stock market, foreign exchange market, technical indices

1. Introduction

Stock market prediction has been commonly regarded as a challenging topic. Various econometric or statistical models were widely used in the prior studies [1, 2]. Although the prediction of stock market returns is a non-linear problem, many studies have proved that the non-linear models are not necessarily superior to the linear models [3–5]. Moreover, the linear technical indices are proved to help investors make investment strategies to improve investment performance. Zhu et al. used the variable moving average (VMA) on the basis of the moving average (MA) to successfully predict the stock price trends of Shanghai Stock Exchange Composite Index (SSEC) and the Shenzhen Stock Exchange Component Index (SZSE) [6].

Recent studies used the machine learning methods to solve the non-linear problems to capture the fluctuation of stock price. Chen and Hao proposed the hybridized framework of the feature weighted support vector machine (FWSVM) and the feature weighted K-nearest neighbor (FWKNN) to effectively predict the stock market indices of the SSEC and the SZSE [7]. They found that that these models can achieve a better prediction capability to both the SSEC and the SZSE in the short, medium and long term. Paiva et al. embedded support vector machine into an investment decision to predict the São Paulo Stock Exchange Index (Ibovespa) [8]. However, machine learning would require taking a lot of time in feature extraction, regularizing the extracted features, and then interpreting the roles through the expert knowledge.

Compared with the machine learning, deep learning autonomously regularizes the information features to reduce many steps in the machine learning process, and thus greatly saving labor costs and time. Recurrent neural network (RNN) which is on approach of deep learning approach is specifically suitable for dealing with the time series issues. Chen et al. proposed a hybrid model combining the RNN and the adaptive boosting (AdaBoost) to predict the stock indices, where the experiment results showed that the model has good prediction performance [9].

Taiwan 50 Exchange Traded Funds (ETF) was founded by the Yuanta Funds in 2003, consisting of 50 largest stocks by market value of the Taiwan Stock Exchange Corporation (TSEC). The Taiwan Stock Exchange Index Futures (FITX) was first launched by the Taiwan Futures Exchange (TAIFEX) in 1998, targeting on the weighted stock index issued by the TSEC, and changing in accordance with the fluctuation of the weighted stock index. The FITX has always been the largest trading commodity in Taiwan's future market. This study applies the support vector regression (SVR), the artificial neural networks (ANN), the RNN and the long short-term memory network (LSTM) to predict the trend of the Taiwan stock market. The trained models are not only used to predict the fluctuation trend of the stock market, but also compared to decide which one has the best performance. In this study, the Taiwan 50 ETF and the FITX are taken as the study samples. This study calculates the technical indices based on the stock data provided by the Taiwan Economic Journal (TEJ).

The remainders of this study are organized as follows. The literatures are reviewed in the Section 2. In Section 3, this study develops data collection and research models. Section 4 describes the experiment results and performance evaluation. The Section 5 concludes this work.

2. Literature review

2.1 Stock market and foreign exchange market

The three major institutional traders in Taiwan stock market refer to the foreign investors, the investment trusts and the dealers. Foreign investors specifically refer to the investors of the foreign stock markets except Taiwan, the investment trusts stand for the securities investment companies, and the dealers shall be the securities companies certified by the government to use their own company capital to trade on the TSEC. Wang analyzed the impact of institutional investors' sentiment on the stock market trading, and used four volatility models to analyze the stocks on the American Stock Exchange (AMEX) [10]. They found that the institutional investors take lower investment risks when they are pessimistic; on the contrary, they are take higher risks when they are optimistic about the stock market.

The foreign exchange market is a financial market distributed among countries to trade currencies. Except for the holidays and major festivals, the foreign exchange markets continuously operate and trade various currencies throughout the day. The foreign exchange rates fluctuate complexly as the foreign exchange market would be affected by various external factors, making it not easy to predict the currency exchange rates. Yong et al. proposed the Gaussian mixture model initialized neuro fuzzy (GMMINF) model to predict the exchange rates of the Australian dollar, the euro and the British pound against the US dollar, and obtain good prediction results at the closing price [11]. Henryíquez and Kristjanpoller suggested a hybrid model of an independent component analysis in combination with the neural network to predict the exchange rates of the euro, the British pound, the Japanese dollar, the Swiss franc and the Canadian dollar against the US dollar, where the results showed that the accuracy of the proposed hybrid model is higher than other econometric models [12].

2.2 Technical indices

Grodinsky proposed fundamental analysis and technical analysis to analyze the stock market price. Investors can use the fundamental analysis to evaluate the firm value or predict the fluctuation of the financial market through the economic theories and the financial statements analysis [13]. The fundamental indicators include earnings per share (EPS), price-to-earnings ratio (PER), price-book ratio (PBR), earnings before interest and tax (EBIT) and return on equity (ROE). Bunea et al. used the linear regression model to observe the financial statements of 1253 firms in Romania, where the results showed that the asset turnover and the PER have the greatest impact on the stock return [14]. Lončarski and Vidovič used the principal component analysis (PCA) to analyze the financial statements of the companies in the S & P 500 index, where the profitability, the growth prospects and the risk can be effectively reflected through the analysis of the financial statements [15].

The technical analysis was originated from the Dow Theory of Robert [16], where the theory proposed that the stock prices will fluctuate with the stock market. Elliott subsequently suggested the Elliott Wave Theory, explaining that the end time of the trend can be predicted [17]. Afterwards, Granville mentioned the moving average, providing the basis for most of the technical indices [18]. Common technical indices are also the moving average convergence diversity (MACD), the relative strength index (RSI) and the stochastic oscillator (KD).

Lin used 14 technical indices calculated to predict the fluctuation of the stock market, and regression analysis was used to analyze their relationship [19]. He found that the technical analysis can significantly improve the predictability of the stock price from the investment portfolio. Jiang et al. used the technical indices and macroeconomic characteristics as the inputs, and used the decision tree algorithms and deep learning to predict the S & P 500, the Dow 300 and the Nasdaq 100 indices, where the results showed that these models have achieved good performance [20]. Picasso et al. used 10 technical indices from the Nasdaq 100 index and the financial news related to the Nasdaq 100 index from the Intrinio API, where the emotional features were extracted from the texts, and were further combined with the technical indices as the training variable inputs to the Random Forest, SVM, feed forward neural network models [21]. The results showed that the proposed method can effectively classify the uptrend and downtrend in the stock portfolio.

2.3 Support vector regression

Machine learning is an innovative method combining statistics and computer science, by which allows the machine to learn from the past data and experience, find out the rules and make its learning as smart as the human beings. Nowadays, it has become popular in various application fields, such as visual images, natural language processing, search engine, voice handwriting recognition, data exploration and securities market analysis and prediction. In terms of securities market analysis and prediction, Patel et al. compared four models trained by the artificial neural network, the SVM, the Random Forest and the Bayesian in combination with the technical indices, where the results showed that the Random Forest has higher accuracy than the other models [22]. Lee et al. proposed the financial network index of investment strategy, using the logical regression, the SVM and the Random Forest, which justified that the proposed scheme can effectively predict the fluctuation of the stock market, specifically with the best performance in the short-term investment [23].

The support vector machine (SVM) was derived by Vapnik and Chervonenkis [24]. It is a supervised learning algorithm combined with classification and regression. In this study, the support vector regression (SVR), an extension of the SVM, is used. SVR has the capable of processing continuous data, and is suitable for deal with the time series data of stocks. Lahmiri used the SVR to analyze the stock data of a listed personal computer company, and the results showed that the accuracy of the model trained by the SVR is higher than other fundamental analysis models [25]. Mishra and Padhy selected 92 stocks in the Indian stock market, and used SVR to predict the stock market prices, where the results showed that the predicted prices are close to the actual prices, and the investment transactions of the selected stocks have high returns [26].

2.4 Artificial neural network and deep learning

Artificial neural network (ANN) is one kind of the machine learning, and simulates the human brain to make judgment. Rezaee et al. integrated the Fuzzy C-Means, the data envelopment analysis and the ANN to analyze the listed company data of the Tehran Stock Exchange (TSE) in Iran, where the results showed this method can help investors make decisions fast [27]. Wang et al. combined price volatility network with ANN to predict the copper price in the New York Mercantile Exchange (NYMEX), where the results showed that the proposed hybrid technology is more accurate than the traditional neural network in terms of the price prediction [10].

Deep learning extends from ANN, the continuously increases its hidden layers in addition to the input layer, the hidden layer and the output layer constituting the traditional ANN. LeCun et al. [28] proposed convolutional neural network (CNN) to process pictures, while Williams and Zipser [29] proposed RNN to deal with texts. Gunduz et al. [30] used the CNN to predict the stock price of the Borsa Istanbul Stock Exchange (BIST) in Turkey, where the results showed that it can successfully capture the hourly fluctuation of the stocks. Xu et al. used the RNN to classify the features of China Securities Index 300 (CSI 300) [31]. Chen et.al proposed a hybrid model combined with the RNN and the adaptive boosting to predict the CSI 300 Index, where the results showed that the hybrid model is superior to ANN and SVR [9].

The long short-term memory (LSTM) is an artificial recurrent neural network (RNN) architecture. The first RNN was proposed by Williams and Zipser [29]. When the first sequence of the RNN is performing the output operation, an additional set of vector information is also being output concurrently as the input to the subsequent sequence point. Therefore, the second sequence point have the previous sequence point and its own set of vector information. These two sets of vector information are subject to certain calculation before being output, which means that in addition to the latest information, the RNN model would simultaneously receive the previous information to achieve the effect of memory. Nevertheless, the RNN has one drawback—although this model has the effect of memory, it cannot keep long-term memory but only short-term memory. To resolve the aforesaid problem, Hochreiter and Schmiduber proposed an artificial neural network named LSTM [32]. The biggest difference between the LSTM and the RNN lies that the LSTM has many cell states, which can receive the long-term memories of the past. Fischer and Krauss used the LSTM, an ANN for sequence learning, to predict the S & P 500 index, where the results showed that the accuracy of the model was higher than that of the machine learning [33]. Cao et al. proposed a hybrid model combined with the empirical mode decomposition (EMD) and the LSTM to predict the stock prices using four stock market indices in the United States, where the results showed that the proposed model performs better than the fundamental analysis model [34].

3. Research methodology

According to prior literature, this study chooses the technical indices, the institutional investor and the foreign exchange market of Taiwan 50 ETF and the Taiwan Stock Exchange Index Futures (FITX), and then reduce these data dimensionalities to create the input variables. After training by the SVR, ANN, RNN and LSTM respectively, this study obtains the best model to predict the stock price fluctuation, and further verify the accuracy of each model to judge which model has high accuracy for the stock prediction.

3.1 Research framework

This study classifies each of Taiwan 50 ETF and the FITX into its own control group and experimental group. The control group is the fundamental data, while the experimental group includes the foreign exchange, the major institutional traders and the technical index. This study investigates the correlation of the research object against its own individual inputs, select the best model by analyzing the training results, use the best model to predict the price fluctuation of the research objects, and then evaluate the performance of the model. The details for the experimental design are illustrated in the following **Figures 1** and 2.

3.2 Datasets collection

This study use the data of Taiwan 50 ETF, the FITX, the foreign exchange rate, the technical indices and the three major institutional traders. The research period is from 2015 to 2018.

All data related to the Taiwan 50 ETF and the FITX come from TEJ database. According to Cao et al. [34], Xu et al. [31] as well as Mishra and Padhy [26], we use the opening price, the highest price, the lowest price and the closing price for the Taiwan 50 ETF and the FITX.

For the exchange rates of the foreign exchange market, this study uses the six foreign currencies are converted to the TWD in terms of the cash exchange rate and the spot exchange rate respectively, thereby a total of 12 variables. According to Yong et al. [11] and Baffour et al. [35], the exchange rates of the euro, the British pound and the US dollar were selected as the variables. The renminbi (CNY), the Japanese yuan (JPY) and the Hong Kong dollar (HKD) circulating in the regions near Taiwan are also included.

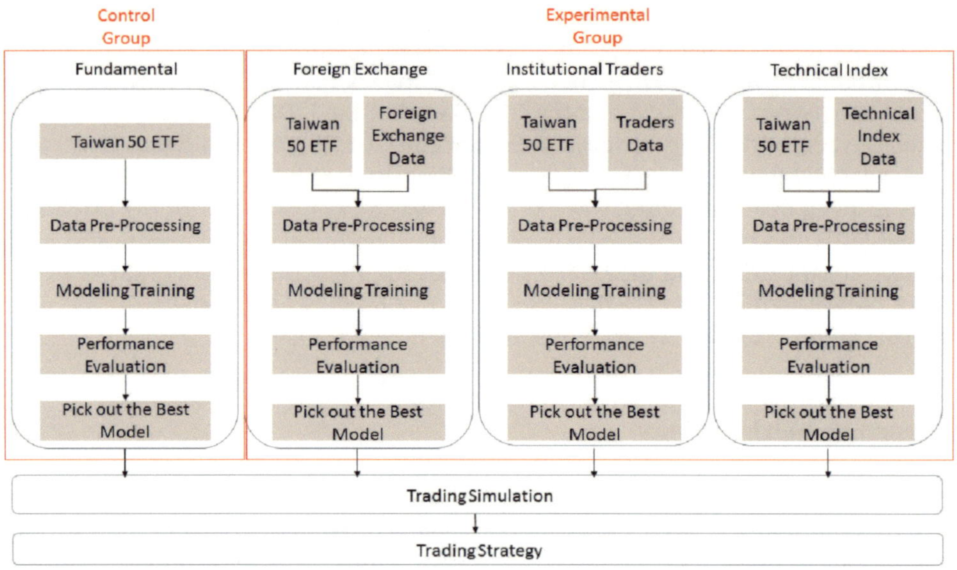

Figure 1.
The experimental design for Taiwan 50 ETF.

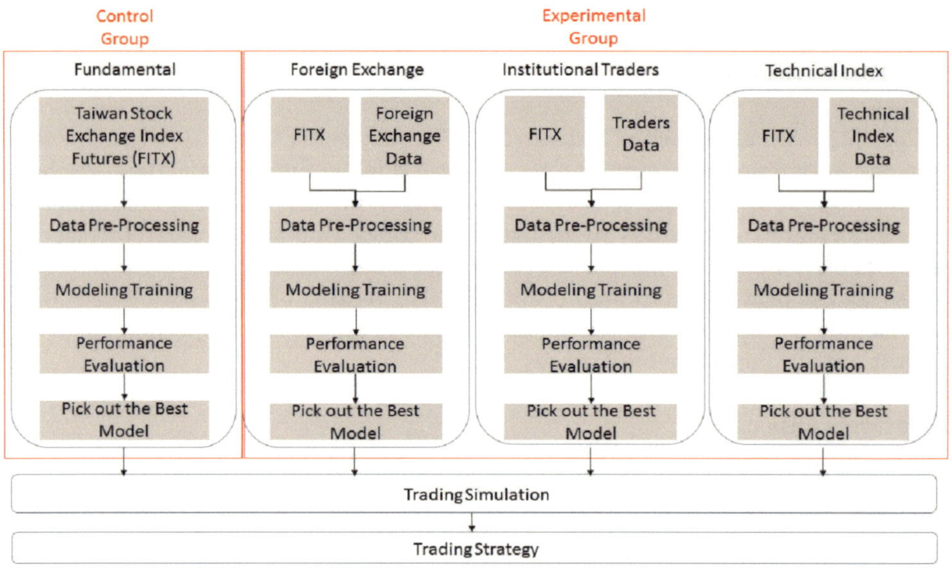

Figure 2.
The experimental design for FITX.

For the technical index, this study also applies eight parameters from KD, MACD and RSI. Jiang et al [20] and Picasso et al. [21] suggested that KD, MACD and RSI are important technical indexes. The eight parameters include RSV, K, D, EMA12, EMA26, DIF, MACD and RSI.

For the three major institutional traders, the data come from the TAIFEX, and include six variables. The three major institutional traders are defined as the dealers, the investment trusts and the foreign investors. Only the long and short trading volumes of the three institutional traders are selected as the input variables of the model. This study only selects trading volume because that the trading volume positively correlates with the contract value.

3.3 Dimensionality reduction and feature selection

All data are subject to the dimensionality reduction suggested by Noryani et al. [36] and normalization according to Cao et al. [34] before using as the inputs of the models.

To avoid decrease the accuracy of model, we adopt the stepwise regressions that for dimensionality reduction. The selection criterion is the group with the largest value of adjusted R square. In the models, we use current dependent variables, but use lagged independent variables. Finally, we select 53 variables, including 13 variables for the opening prices of the Taiwan 50 ETF, 14 variables for the closing prices of the Taiwan 50 ETF, 13 variables for the opening prices of the FITX, and 13 variables for the closing prices of the FITX.

Regarding the Taiwan 50 ETF, the variables of opening prices refer to five variables related to foreign exchanges (HKD, GBP, EUR, JPY, and CNY), two variables related to three major institutional traders (Long trading volumes of the foreign investors and short trading volumes of the dealers), and six variables related to technical indices (EMA26, MACD, EMA12, RSI, RSV, and D). This study adds USD into the variables of closing prices of the Taiwan 50 ETF, others are similar to the opening prices of the Taiwan 50 ETF.

Regarding the FITX, the variables of opening prices refer to fix variables related to foreign exchanges (HKD, GBP, EUR, JPY, CNY and USD), two variables related to three major institutional traders (Long trading volumes of the foreign investors and short trading volumes of the dealers), and five variables related to technical indices (MACD, EMA12, RSI, RSV, and D). The variables for closing prices of the FITX are the same as for opening prices of the FITX.

4. Experimental results and performance evaluation

4.1 Experimental environment

The experimental environment of this study was developed under the Windows 10 system (i7 CPU, 16G RAM); the application was programmed with the Python, while the stepwise regression analysis in the SPSS (Statistical Product and Service Solutions) was selected to perform the dimensionality reduction of the data; the free value-added open source version of Anaconda software was used to create the artificial intelligence model, under which the Tensorflow environment was established; the Keras kit was used to create the models with the ANN, the RNN and the LSTM, while the machine learning model was built with the Scikit-Learn kit to create the SVR model.

4.2 Parameters setting and performance evaluation index

This study chooses the linear kernel function with the C (cost) adjusted to 10 and the learning rate of kernel algorithm adjusted to 0.001. Except for the kernel function, the other parameters were tested by trial and error method. The ANN is divided into four layers, one of which was the input layer, two the hidden layers, and one the output layer. The number of iterations is 200. This study uses the adaptive moment estimation (ADAM) as the optimizer and the MAE in the Loss equation with the learning rate 0.001 and the activation function Linear. All the parameter settings are also tested by trial and error method.

In the RNN model, there are five layers, one of which was the input layer, two the RNN layers, one the fully connected layer, and one the output layer. The number of layers is set according to Jiang et al. [20]. The number of iterations is 200. We select the ADAM as the optimizer and the MAE in the Loss equation with the learning rate 0.001 and the time step 3. The activation function of the RNN layer is Tanh, and the activation function of the output layer is Linear. All the parameter settings are tested by trial and error method.

In the LSTM model, there are also five layers, one of which was the input layer, two the LSTM layers, one the fully connected layer, and one the output layer. The number of layers is set according to Cao et al. [34]. The number of iterations is 200. Again, we select the ADAM as the optimizer and the MAE in the Loss equation with the learning rate 0.001 and the time step 3. The activation functions of the LSTM layer are Sigmoid and Tanh, and output layer activation functions is Linear. All the parameter settings are tested by trial and error method.

This study selects the mean absolute error (MAE), the mean square error (MSE) and the mean absolute percent error (MAPE) as the evaluation indices, where the formulas are listed as follows:

$$MAE = \frac{1}{n}\sum_{i=1}^{n} |y_i - \hat{y}| \tag{1}$$

$$MSE = \frac{1}{n}\sum_{i=1}^{n} (y_i - \hat{y})^2 \tag{2}$$

$$MAPE = \frac{1}{n}\sum_{i=1}^{n} |\frac{y_i - \hat{y}}{y_i}| \tag{3}$$

Where $\boldsymbol{y_i}$ is the actual value, $\boldsymbol{\hat{y}}$ the predicted value, n the total number of data, i a certain amount of data. The smaller the values of MAE, MSE and MAPE are, the better the accuracy of the predictive model.

4.3 Experimental results

In the experimental results of this study, the mean absolute error (MAE), the mean square error (MSE) and the mean absolute percent error (MAPE) were selected as the evaluation indices of the model, where the smaller the values of MAE, MSE and MAPE are, the better the accuracy of the predictive model.

Tables 1–4 show the results of the Taiwan 50 ETF. This study gets the different results among fundamental data, foreign exchange, the technical indices and the major institutional traders. For the fundamental data, the LSTM gives the best predictive power, followed by the RNN, and finally the ANN. **Figures 3** and **4** illustrates the trend prediction for the closing price and opening price with different machine

Models	Prediction	MAE	MSE	MAPE
SVR	Closing price	1.984	4.587	2.406
ANN	Closing price	0.628	0.788	0.772

Models	Prediction	MAE	MSE	MAPE
RNN	Closing price	0.627	0.772	0.769
LSTM	Closing price	0.620	0.763	0.765
SVR	Opening price	4.696	23.298	5.699
ANN	Opening price	0.413	0.379	0.497
RNN	Opening price	0.409	0.367	0.493
LSTM	Opening price	0.403	0.378	0.488

Table 1.
The results of the fundamental data of the Taiwan 50 ETF.

Models	Prediction	MAE	MSE	MAPE
SVR	Closing price	3.306	16.054	4.032
ANN	Closing price	0.603	0.732	0.743
RNN	Closing price	0.618	0.756	0.753
LSTM	Closing price	0.610	0.743	0.751
SVR	Opening price	5.137	32.284	6.126
ANN	Opening price	0.386	0.359	0.478
RNN	Opening price	0.398	0.384	0.488
LSTM	Opening price	0.391	0.373	0.481

Table 2.
The results of the foreign exchange of the Taiwan 50 ETF.

Models	Prediction	MAE	MSE	MAPE
SVR	Closing price	3.164	10.928	3.842
ANN	Closing price	0.638	0.759	0.783
RNN	Closing price	0.674	0.829	0.832
LSTM	Closing price	0.633	0.748	0.767
SVR	Opening price	4.937	25.623	5.897
ANN	Opening price	0.421	0.380	0.512
RNN	Opening price	0.488	0.469	0.604
LSTM	Opening price	0.419	0.381	0.510

Table 3.
The results of the major institutional traders of the Taiwan 50 ETF.

Models	Prediction	MAE	MSE	MAPE
SVR	Closing price	3.934	16.596	4.796
ANN	Closing price	0.608	0.721	0.751
RNN	Closing price	0.621	0.746	0.761
LSTM	Closing price	0.611	0.829	0.776
SVR	Opening price	5.303	29.290	6.447

Models	Prediction	MAE	MSE	MAPE
ANN	Opening price	0.383	0.346	0.474
RNN	Opening price	0.393	0.368	0.491
LSTM	Opening price	0.388	0.356	0.484

Table 4.
The results of the technical indices of the Taiwan 50 ETF.

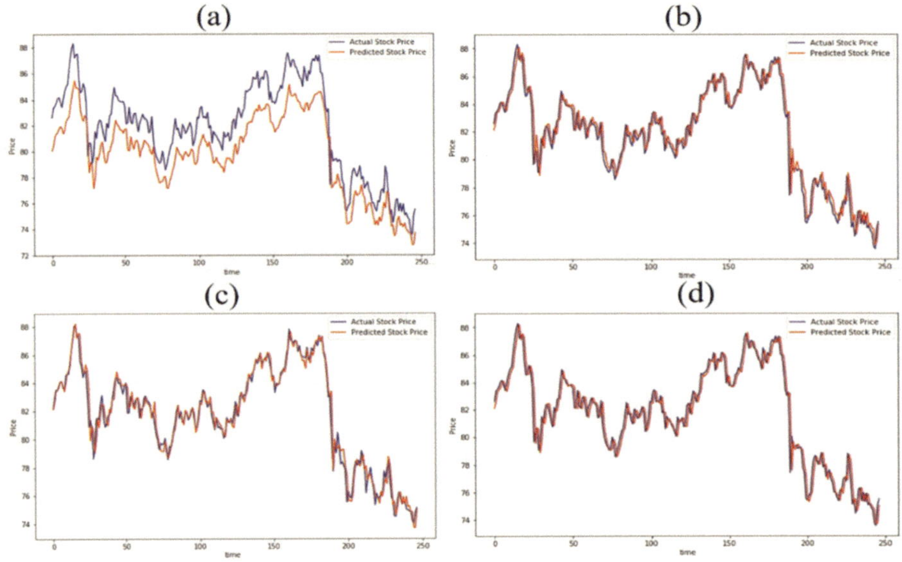

Figure 3.
The prediction of the Taiwan 50 ETF closing price of the fundamental data. (a) SVR, (b) ANN, (c) RNN and (d) LSTM.

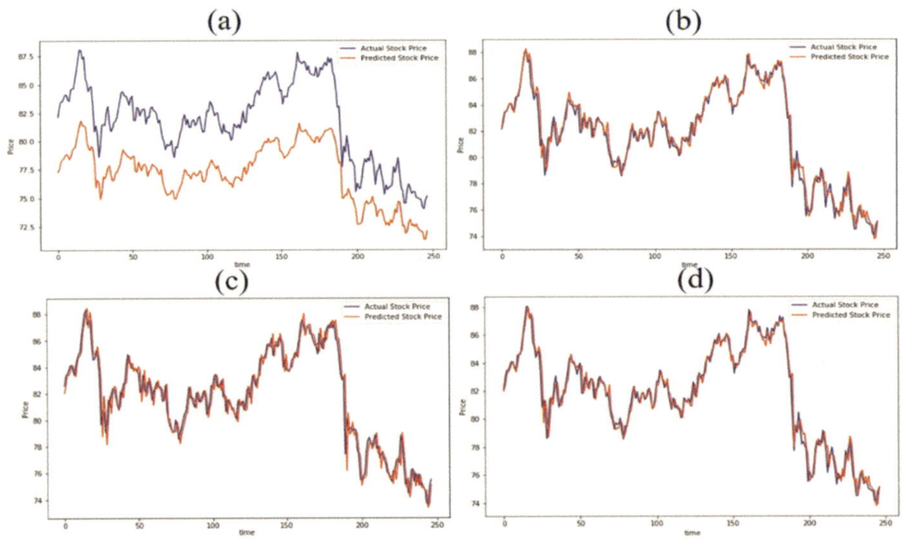

Figure 4.
The prediction of the Taiwan 50 ETF opening price of the fundamental data. (a) SVR, (b) ANN, (c) RNN and (d) LSTM.

learning and deep learning approaches, respectively. For the foreign exchange and the technical indices, the ANN exhibits the best predictive power, followed by the LSTM, and finally the RNN. **Figures 5** and **6** illustrates the foreign exchange trend prediction for the closing price and opening price with different machine learning and deep learning approaches, respectively. **Figures 7** and **8** are represented for the closing

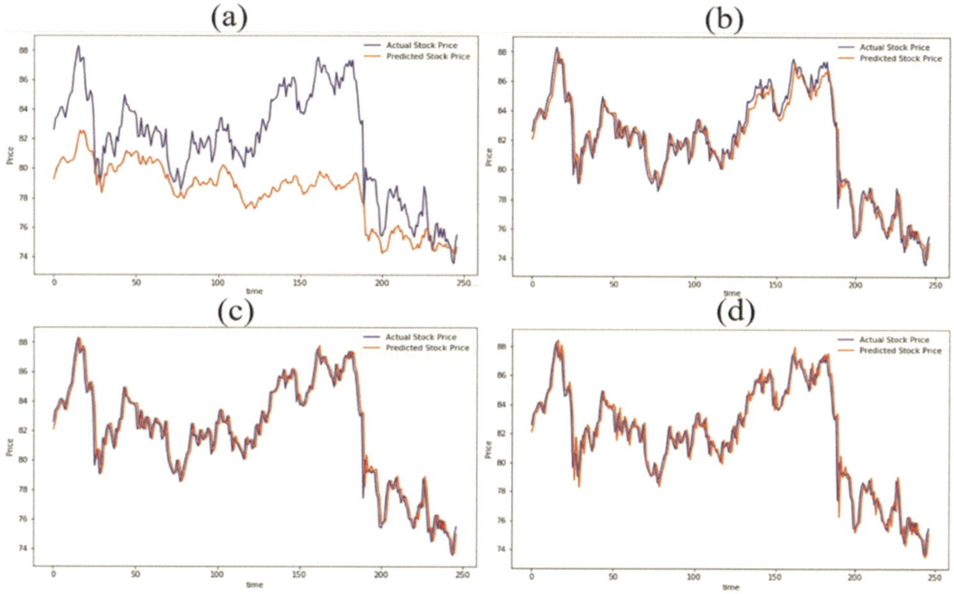

Figure 5.
The prediction of the closing price of the foreign exchange rate. (a) SVR, (b) ANN, (c) RNN and (d) LSTM.

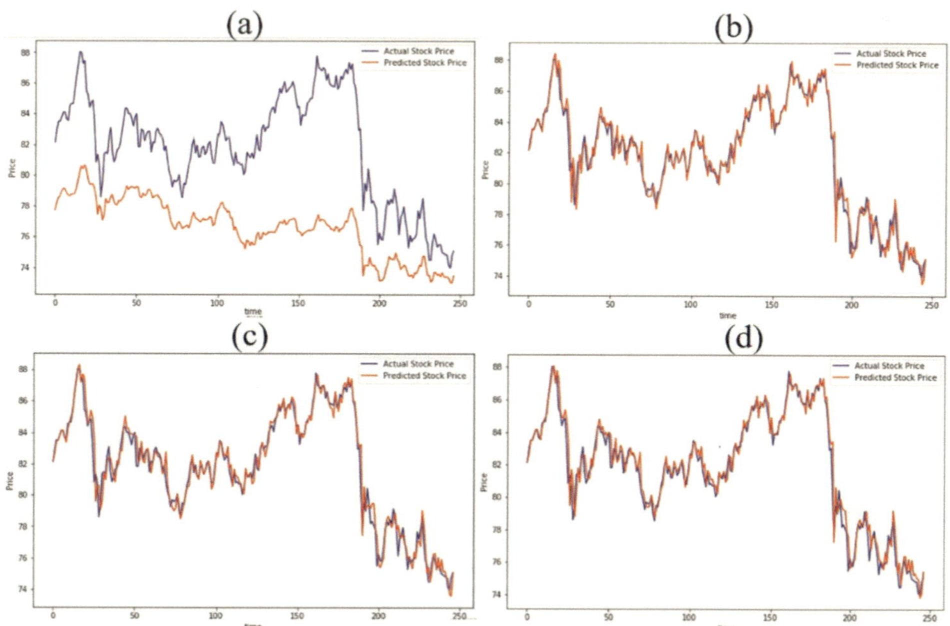

Figure 6.
The prediction of the opening price of the foreign exchange rate. (a) SVR, (b) ANN, (c) RNN and (d) LSTM.

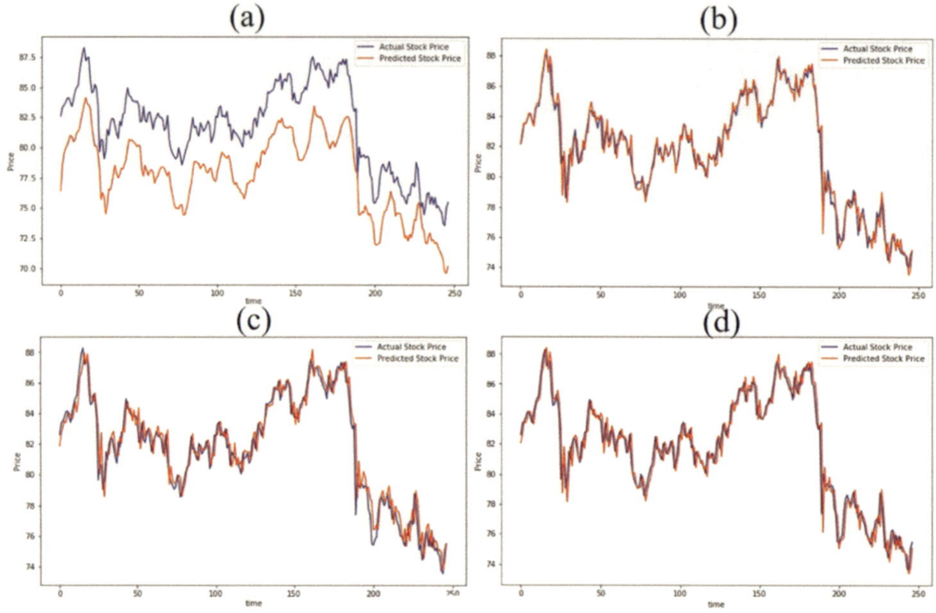

Figure 7.
The prediction of the closing price of the technical indices. (a) SVR, (b) ANN, (c) RNN and (d) LSTM.

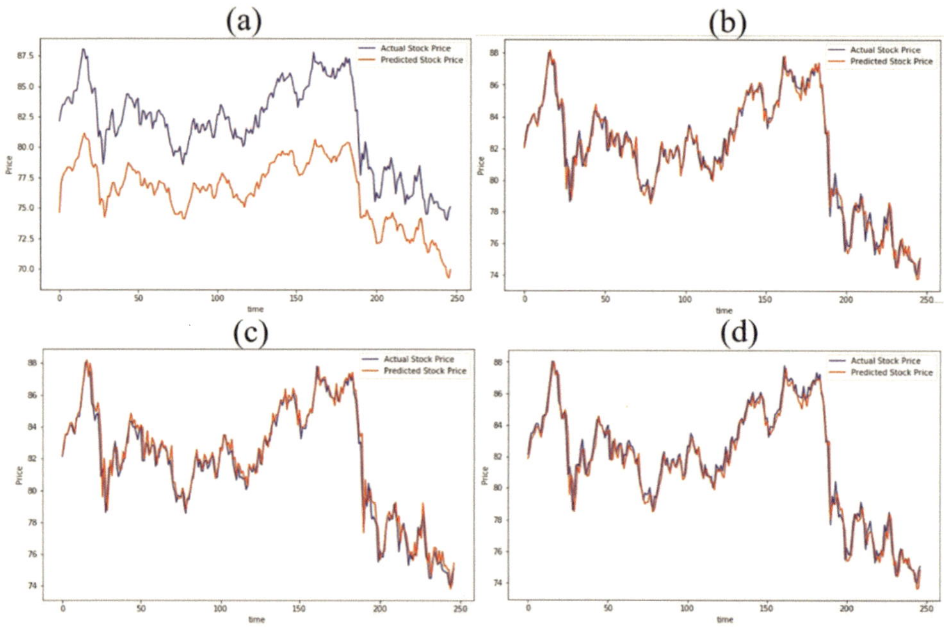

Figure 8.
The prediction of the opening price of the technical indices. (a) SVR, (b) ANN, (c) RNN and (d) LSTM.

price and opening price with technical indices. For the major institutional traders, the LSTM presents the best results, followed by the ANN, and finally the RNN. The details are also illustrated in **Figures 9** and **10**.

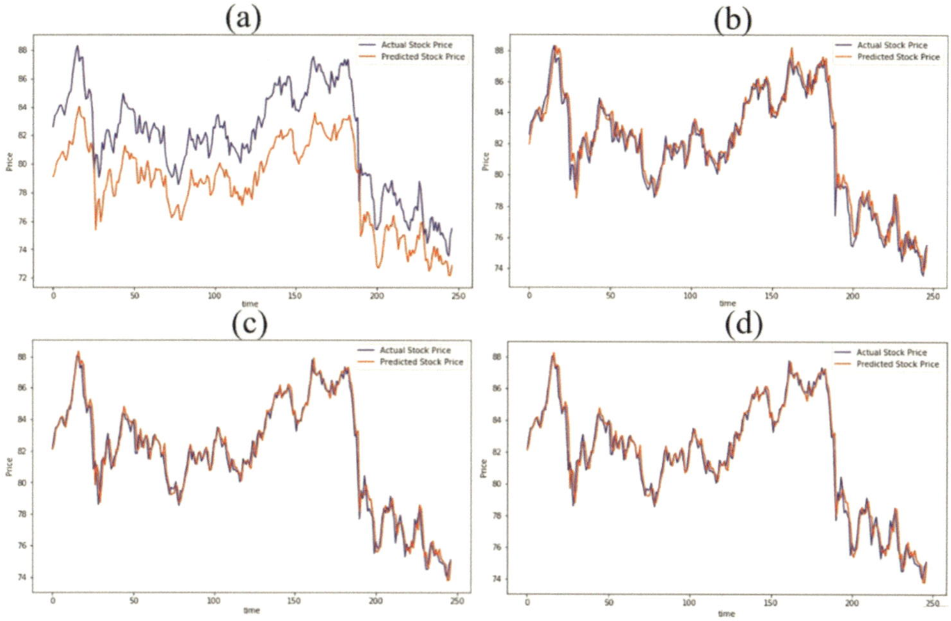

Figure 9.
The prediction of the closing price of the major institutional traders. (a) SVR, (b) ANN, (c) RNN and (d) LSTM.

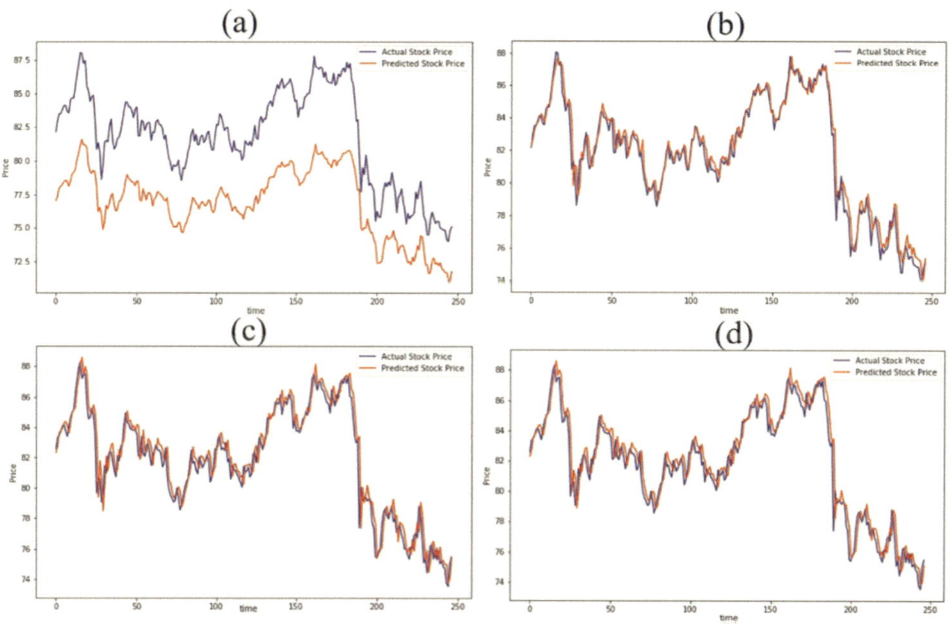

Figure 10.
The prediction of the opening price of the major institutional trader group. (a) SVR, (b) ANN, (c) RNN and (d) LSTM.

Tables 5–8 present show the results of the FITX. For the fundamental data, the LSTM gives the best predictive power, followed by the RNN, and finally the ANN. Besides, fundamental data, foreign exchange, the technical indices and the major

Models	Prediction	MAE	MSE	MAPE
SVR	Closing price	205.683	51803.42	1.925
ANN	Closing price	82.635	13881.782	0.794
RNN	Closing price	81.351	13511.3	0.786
LSTM	Closing price	80.893	13315.75	0.770
SVR	Opening price	406.140	180288.4	3.822
ANN	Opening price	55.214	6979.852	0.531
RNN	Opening price	54.520	6807.414	0.523
LSTM	Opening price	53.960	6701.942	0.518

Table 5.
The results of the fundamental data of the FITX.

Model	Prediction	MAE	MSE	MAPE
SVR	Closing price	385.580	168158.3	3.065
ANN	Closing price	79.325	12857.62	0.758
RNN	Closing price	80.150	13731.32	0.761
LSTM	Closing price	78.087	11314.08	0.743
SVR	Opening price	180.467	46233.91	1.604
ANN	Opening price	51.591	6326.661	0.483
RNN	Opening price	53.664	6724.012	0.520
LSTM	Opening price	52.117	6865.473	0.495

Table 6.
The results of the foreign exchange of the FITX.

Model	Prediction	MAE	MSE	MAPE
SVR	Closing price	199.591	49900.01	1.873
ANN	Closing price	84.654	14017.21	0.828
RNN	Closing price	85.681	14851.94	0.823
LSTM	Closing price	82.742	13731.18	0.803
SVR	Opening price	413.321	184692.3	3.903
ANN	Opening price	57.731	6659.928	0.552
RNN	Opening price	59.927	7734.202	0.621
LSTM	Opening price	55.975	6390.768	0.536

Table 7.
The results of the major institutional traders of the FITX.

Model	Prediction	MAE	MSE	MAPE
SVR	Closing price	273.919	86916.05	2.586
ANN	Closing price	79.087	12014.09	0.746
RNN	Closing price	80.301	13448.05	0.765
LSTM	Closing price	79.153	12442.942	0.748
SVR	Opening price	500.666	265107.2	4.734

Model	Prediction	MAE	MSE	MAPE
ANN	Opening price	53.546	6435.225	0.514
RNN	Opening price	53.153	6411.562	0.511
LSTM	Opening price	52.344	6433.198	0.499

Table 8.
The results of the technical indices of the FITX.

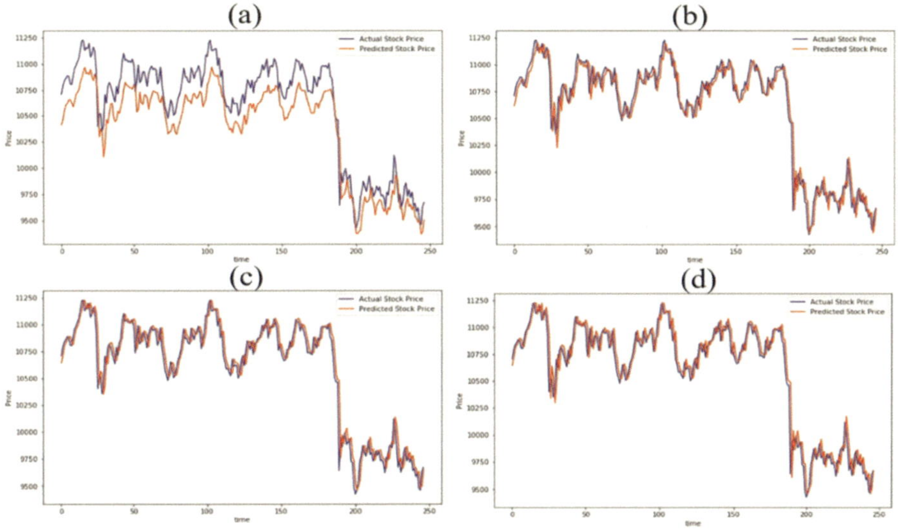

Figure 11.
The prediction of the FITX closing price of the fundamental data. (a) SVR, (b) ANN, (c) RNN and (d) LSTM.

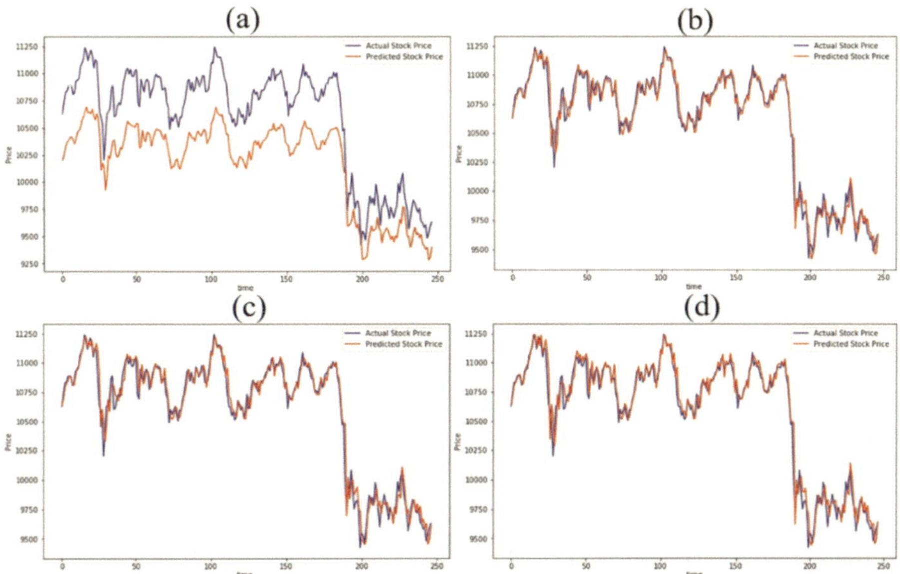

Figure 12.
The prediction of the FITX opening price of the fundamental data. (a) SVR, (b) ANN, (c) RNN and (d) LSTM.

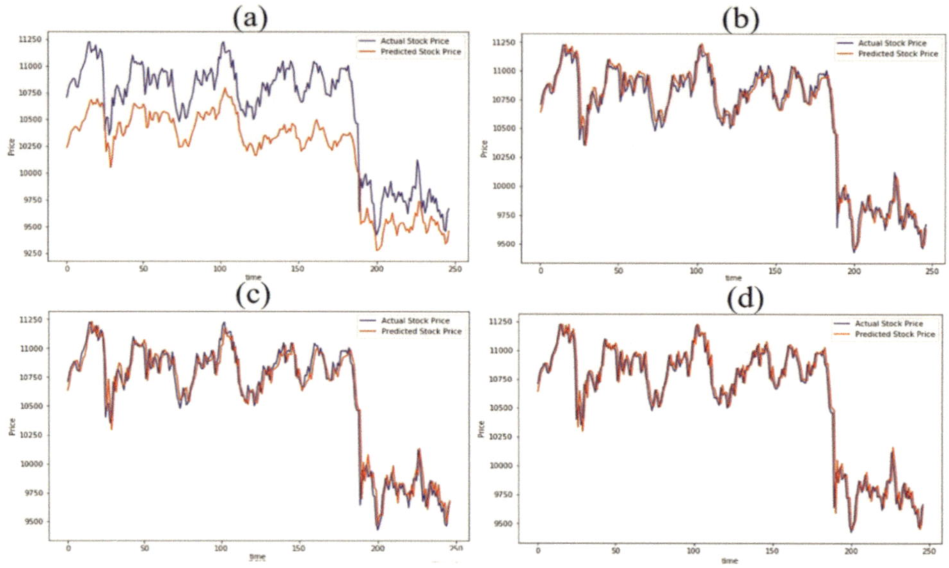

Figure 13.
The prediction of the FITX closing price of the foreign exchange rate. (a) SVR, (b) ANN, (c) RNN and (d) LSTM.

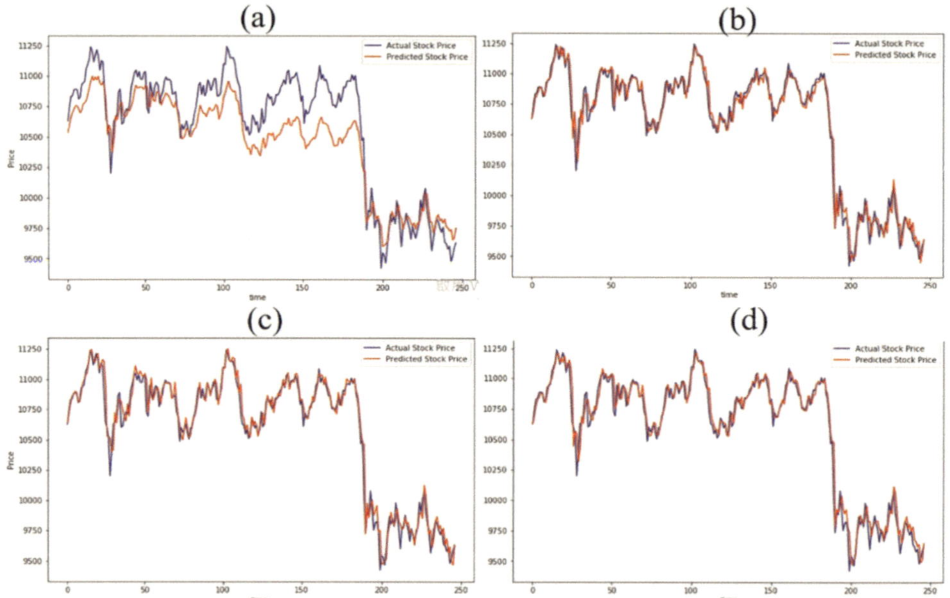

Figure 14.
The prediction of the FITX opening price of the foreign exchange rate. (a) SVR, (b) ANN, (c) RNN and (d) LSTM.

institutional traders have the same priority of predictive power. This study finds that the LSTM exhibits the best results, followed by the ANN and finally the RNN. The details are also illustrated in **Figures 11–18.**

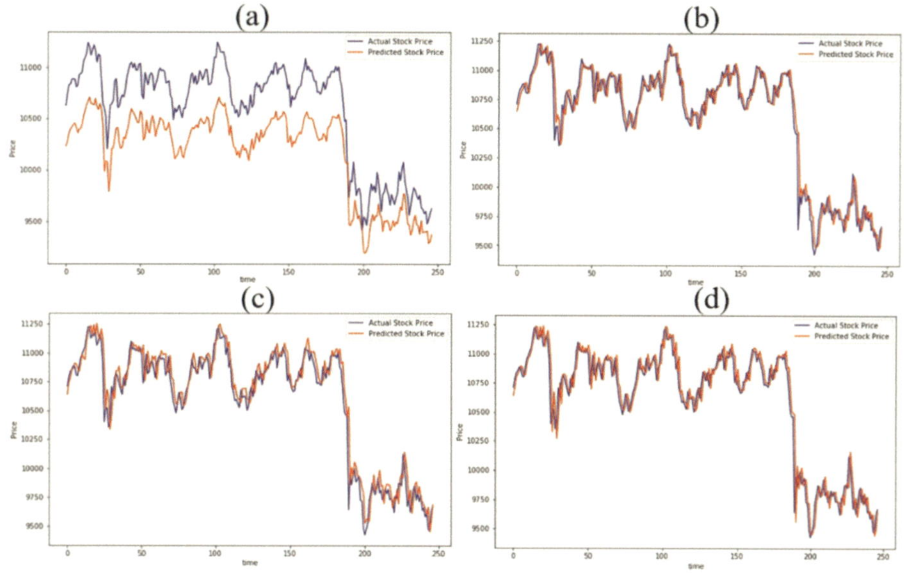

Figure 15.
The prediction of the FITX closing price of the major institutional traders. (a) SVR, (b) ANN, (c) RNN and (d) LSTM.

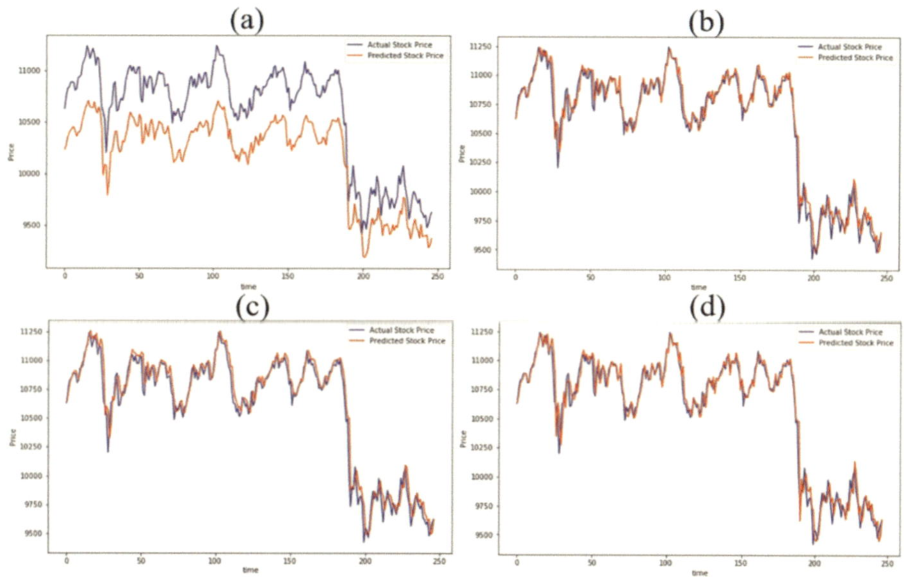

Figure 16.
The prediction of the FITX opening price of the major institutional traders. (a) SVR, (b) ANN, (c) RNN and (d) LSTM.

4.4 Prediction of the price fluctuation

Finally, this study picks out the model with the best training performance according to the above results. This study then further predicts the price fluctuation of

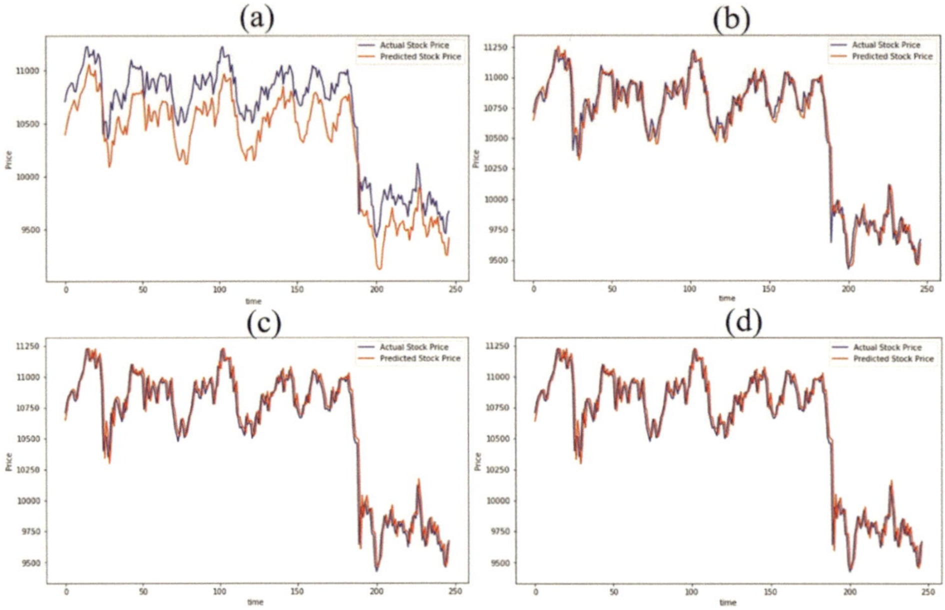

Figure 17.
The prediction of the FITX closing price of the technical indices. (a) SVR, (b) ANN, (c) RNN and (d) LSTM.

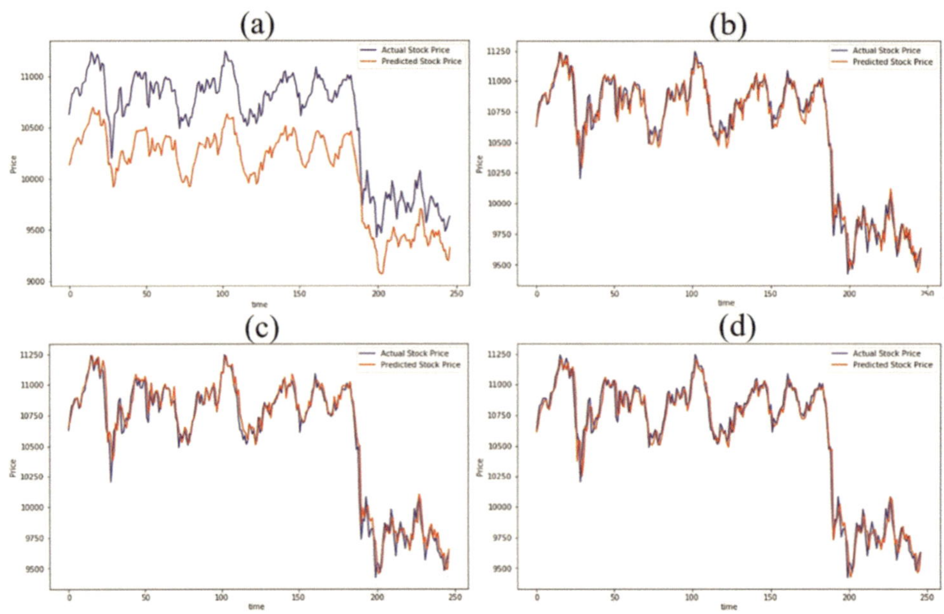

Figure 18.
The prediction of the FITX opening price of the technical indices. (a) SVR, (b) ANN, (c) RNN and (d) LSTM.

2018 for all trained models with the same parameter settings. The trading results are converted into a confusion matrix, whose equations are listed as follows:

$$Precision = TP/(TP + FP) \tag{4}$$

Group	Model	Benchmark	Precision	Recall	F1-score	Accuracy
Fundamental	LSTM	Opening price	0.733	0.687	0.709	0.707
Foreign exchange	ANN	Opening price	0.758	0.694	0.725	0.731
Major institutional trader	LSTM	Opening price	0.686	0.648	0.666	0.668
Technical index	ANN	Opening price	0.775	0.720	0.746	0.743

Table 9.
The confusion matrix of Taiwan 50 ETF.

Group	Model	Benchmark	Precision	Recall	F1-score	Accuracy
Fundamental	LSTM	Opening price	0.611	0.738	0.669	0.670
Foreign exchange	ANN	Opening price	0.664	0.773	0.714	0.711
Major institutional trader	LSTM	Opening price	0.597	0.720	0.653	0.654
Technical index	LSTM	Opening price	0.656	0.8	0.721	0.723

Table 10.
The confusion matrix of FITX.

$$Recall = TP/(TP + FN) \tag{5}$$

$$F1 - score = 2 \times TP/(2 * TP + FP + FN) \tag{6}$$

$$Accuracy = (TP + TN)/(TP + FP + TN + FN) \tag{7}$$

The TP herein is defined as True Positive, FP as False Positive, TN as True Negative, and FN as False Negative. Where TP represent that the actual value is correct and the predicted value is correct, FP the actual value wrong and the predicted value correct, TN the actual value wrong and the predicted value wrong, as well as FN the actual value correct and the predicted value wrong. The precision, the recall, the F1-score and the accuracy are the evaluation indices of the confusion matrix, where the larger the value of the evaluation index, the better the accuracy of the model.

Tables 9 and **10** show the model with the highest confusion matrix values of Taiwan 50 ETF and FITX respectively, and are further used to predict the price fluctuation of the next day. This study takes the Taiwan 50 ETF and the FITX as the targets. TP represents that the price rises actually and is predicted to rise, FP represents that the price falls actually but is predicted to rise, TN represents that the price falls actually and is predicted to fall, and FN represents that the price rises actually but is predicted to fall. In **Table 9**, the experimental results find that the prediction accuracies of fluctuation for Taiwan 50 ETF are about 70%, which proves that this prediction of the price fluctuation is successful. In **Table 10**, the experimental results also find that the prediction accuracies of price fluctuation for the FITX are about 70%, which again proves that this prediction of the price fluctuation is successful and is of certain commercial value.

5. Conclusion

In this study, there are three findings. After using the stepwise regression method for data dimensionality to reduce by select the variables, the first experimental results showed that the foreign exchange and the technical indices are superior to the fundamental data, and the major institutional traders is inferior to the fundamental data. Secondly, this study compares the results of SVR, the ANN, the RNN and the LSTM models, and then use them to predict the stock market dynamics. The experimental results find that the SVR performs the worst. Specifically, the LSTM has the highest model accuracy in the control group, and the highest accuracy is given mostly by the LSTM but partly by the ANN in the experimental group. Thirdly, this study predicts the price fluctuation and obtains the accuracy about 70%.

5.1 Dimensionality reduction and feature selection

In this study, an experimental group and a control group are distinguished. In the experiments, stepwise regression analysis is used to select important variables from each data to achieve data dimensionality reduction. In the experimental group, basic stock market information is combined with many additional variables in an attempt to improve the accuracy of the model. The control group used the basic information of the stock market to compare the results with the experimental group. The experimental results showed that the model accuracy of the foreign exchange group and the major institutional trader group was higher than that of the basic group, while the major institutional trader group was lower than that of the basic group, which means that this experiment is successful. The additional variables of the foreign exchange group and the major institutional trader group help to increase the accuracy of the model, but adding the major institutional trader group actually reduces it. According to the study Abdioglu et al. [1], it shows that the three major legal institutional trader exist among the investors. Information asymmetries may cause the legal team to be unable to learn effectively during training.

5.2 Models comparison

This study uses SVR, ANN, RNN, and LSTM models to predict the stock market dynamics. The experimental results show that SVR is the worst among all testing results. It is speculated that SVR may not be able to adapt to this data. In the control group, the LSTM in predicting the opening price and closing price, both models have the highest accuracy. The experimental results show that consistent with Fischer and Krauss [33], LSTM has the best learning effect. In the experimental group, most of the LSTM models have the highest accuracy, but partly the ANN model is the highest. Overall, except for SVR, the ANN, RNN, and LSTM all perform well in predicting prices.

5.3 Forecast of uptrend and downtrend

This study predicts the price fluctuation. The price fluctuation prediction for the fundamental data, the foreign exchange, the technical indices and the major institutional traders are all have the accuracy about 70%, which is of a certain commercial value.

According to the final experimental results of this study, it can be found that the trend of uptrend and downtrend can be grasped in 2018. In the future, this study will continue to update the dataset with different time period to see whether the accuracy of the future model is as good as now. In addition, according to the parameters setting of this study, the method of predicting the opening and closing prices of the stock market was adopted. The method can also be redesigned to directly predict the future rise and fall of the stock market to explore Taiwan's financial market. It can also be used from another deep learning methodology—CNN model in the form of pictures to predict the Taiwan's future financial market trends.

There is still the following limitation in the experiments of this study. The simulated trading set in this study is sort of simplified without considering the actual trading situations, such as the transaction fee, the change of position and the emergency conditions, leading to the final trading results which might be slightly changed. This study provides a method to predict the fluctuation of the financial market. In the future, other scholars may take into account the conditions which will be encounter during the actual investment behavior and develop a real-time trading system.

Acknowledgements

This work was supported by the Ministry of Science and Technology, Taiwan, under Grant MOST 109-2410-H-006-116-MY2, Grant MOST110-2511-H-006-013-MY3, and Grant MOST 109-2410-H-025-016-MY2; and in part by the Higher Education Sprout Project, Ministry of Education to the Headquarters of University Advancement at National Cheng Kung University (NCKU).

Conflict of interest

The authors declare no conflict of interest.

Author details

Min-Hsuan Fan[1], Jing-Long Huang[1] and Mu-Yen Chen[2,3]*

1 National Taichung University of Science and Technology, Taichung, Taiwan

2 National Cheng Kung University, Tainan, Taiwan

3 Center for Innovative FinTech Business Models, National Cheng Kung University, Tainan, Taiwan

*Address all correspondence to: mychen119@gs.ncku.edu.tw

References

[1] Abdioglu N, Bamiatzi V, Cavusgil ST, Khurshed A, Stathopoulos K. Information asymmetry, disclosure and foreign institutional investment: An empirical investigation of the impact of the Sarbanes-Oxley Act. International Business Review. 2015;**24**(5):902-915

[2] Armano G, Marchesi M, Murru A. A hybrid genetic-neural architecture for stock indexes forecasting. Information Sciences. 2005;**170**(1):3-33

[3] Atsalakis GS, Valavanis KP. Surveying stock market forecasting techniques–Part II: Soft computing methods. Expert Systems with Applications. 2009;**36**(3):5932-5941

[4] Enke D, Mehdiyev N. Stock market prediction using a combination of stepwise regression analysis, differential evolution-based fuzzy clustering, and a fuzzy inference neural network. Intelligent Automation & Soft Computing. 2013;**19**(4):636-648

[5] Rather AM, Agarwal A, Sastry V. Recurrent neural network and a hybrid model for prediction of stock returns. Expert Systems with Applications. 2015; **42**(6):3234-3241

[6] Zhu H, Jiang ZQ, Li SP, Zhou WX. Profitability of simple technical trading rules of Chinese stock exchange indexes. Physica A: Statistical Mechanics and Its Applications. 2015;**439**:75-84

[7] Chen Y, Hao Y. A feature weighted support vector machine and K-nearest neighbor algorithm for stock market indices prediction. Expert Systems with Applications. 2017;**80**:340-355

[8] Paiva FD, Cardoso RTN, Hanaoka GP, Duarte WM. Decision-making for financial trading: A fusion approach of machine learning and portfolio selection. Expert Systems with Applications. 2019;**115**:635-655

[9] Chen W, Yeo CK, Lau CT, Lee BS. Leveraging social media news to predict stock index movement using RNN-boost. Data & Knowledge Engineering. 2018;**118**:14-24

[10] Wang C, Zhang X, Wang M, Lim MK, Ghadimi P. Predictive analytics of the copper spot price by utilizing complex network and artificial neural network techniques. Resources Policy. 2019;**63**:101414

[11] Yong YL, Lee Y, Gu X, Angelov PP, Ngo DCL, Shafipour E. Foreign currency exchange rate prediction using neuro-fuzzy systems. Procedia Computer Science. 2018;**144**:232-238

[12] Henríquez J, Kristjanpoller W. A combined independent component analysis–Neural network model for forecasting exchange rate variation. Applied Soft Computing. 2019;**83**:105654

[13] Grodinsky J. Investments. New York: Ronald Press Company; 1953

[14] Bunea OI, Corbos RA, Popescu RI. Influence of some financial indicators on return on equity ratio in the Romanian energy sector-A competitive approach using a DuPont-based analysis. Energy. 2019;**189**:116251

[15] Lončarski I, Vidovič L. Sorting out the financials: Making economic sense out of statistical factors. Finance Research Letters. 2019;**31**:110-118

[16] Robert R. Dow Theory: An Explanation of Its Development and An Attempt to Define Its Usefulness as An

Aid in Speculation. New York: Baron's; 1932

[17] Elliott RN. The Wave Principle. Los Angeles: Alanpuri Trading; 1938

[18] Granville JE. A Strategy of Daily Stock Market Timing for Maximum Profit. Englewood Cliffs, N.J.: Prentice-Hall; 1960

[19] Lin Q. Technical analysis and stock return predictability: An aligned approach. Journal of Financial Markets. 2018;**38**:103-123

[20] Jiang M, Liu J, Zhang L. An improved stacking framework for stock index prediction by leveraging tree-based ensemble models and deep learning algorithms. Physica A: Statistical Mechanics and Its Applications. 2019;**541**:122272

[21] Picasso A, Merello S, Ma Y, Oneto L, Cambria E. Technical analysis and sentiment embeddings for market trend prediction. Expert Systems with Applications. 2019;**135**:60-70

[22] Patel J, Shah S, Thakkar P, Kotecha K. Predicting stock and stock price index movement using trend deterministic data preparation and machine learning techniques. Expert Systems with Applications. 2015;**42**(1): 259-268

[23] Lee TK, Cho JH, Kwon DS, Sohn SY. Global stock market investment strategies based on financial network indicators using machine learning techniques. Expert Systems with Applications. 2019;**117**:228-242

[24] Vapnik V, Chervonenkis A. Theory of Pattern Recognition. Moscow: Nauka; 1974

[25] Lahmiri S. Minute-ahead stock price forecasting based on singular spectrum analysis and support vector regression. Applied Mathematics and Computation. 2018;**320**:444-451

[26] Mishra S, Padhy S. An efficient portfolio construction model using stock price predicted by support vector regression. The North American Journal of Economics and Finance. 2019;**50**: 101027

[27] Rezaee MJ, Jozmaleki M, Valipour M. Integrating dynamic fuzzy C-means, data envelopment analysis and artificial neural network to online prediction performance of companies in stock exchange. Physica A: Statistical Mechanics and Its Applications. 2018; **489**:78-93

[28] LeCun Y, Boser B, Denker JS, Henderson D, Howard RE, Hubbard W, et al. Backpropagation applied to handwritten zip code recognition. Neural Computation. 1989;**1**(4):541-551

[29] Williams RJ, Zipser D. A learning algorithm for continually running fully recurrent neural networks. Neural Computation. 1989;**1**(2):270-280

[30] Gunduz H, Yaslan Y, Cataltepe Z. Intraday prediction of Borsa Istanbul using convolutional neural networks and feature correlations. Knowledge-Based Systems. 2017;**137**:138-148

[31] Xu B, Zhang D, Zhang S, Li H, Lin H. Stock Market Trend Prediction Using Recurrent Convolutional Neural Networks. Lecture Notes in Computer Science. LNAI 11109. 2018. pp. 166-177

[32] Hochreiter S, Schmidhuber J. Long short-term memory. Neural Computation. 1997;**9**(8):1735-1780

[33] Fischer T, Krauss C. Deep learning with long short-term memory networks

for financial market predictions. European Journal of Operational Research. 2018;**270**(2):654-669

[34] Cao J, Li Z, Li J. Financial time series forecasting model based on CEEMDAN and LSTM. Physica A: Statistical Mechanics and Its Applications. 2019; **519**:127-139

[35] Baffour AA, Feng J, Taylor EK. A hybrid artificial neural network-GJR modeling approach to forecasting currency exchange rate volatility. Neurocomputing. 2019;**365**:285-301

[36] Noryani M, Sapuan SM, Mastura MT, Zuhri MYM, Zainudin ES. Material selection of natural fibre using a stepwise regression model with error analysis. Journal of Materials Research and Technology. 2019;**8**(3):2865-2879

Chapter 3

Aspects Regarding a Deep Understanding of the Prediction for Stock Market Movements

Hu Xuemei

Abstract

It is an important puzzle in the financial market to predict stock return movement direction. In this chapter, we not only propose (group) penalized logistic regression with multiple indicators to predict up- or downtrends, but also propose group penalized trinomial logit regression with multiple indicator groups to predict stock return movement direction: uptrends, sideways trends and downtrends. For the former, we construct the corresponding coordinate descent (CD) algorithm to complete variable selection and obtain parameter estimator, and introduce two-class confusion matrix, Receiver Operating Characteristic (ROC) and the area under a ROC curve (AUC) to assess two-class prediction performance. For the latter, we develop a rapidly convergent group coordinate descent (GCD) algorithm to simultaneously complete group selection and group estimation, introduce the relatively optimal Bayes classifiers to identify class indexes, and finally adopt three-class confusion matrix, Kappa, PDI, ROC surface and hypervolume under the ROC manifold (HUM) to assess three-class prediction performance.

Keywords: technical indicators, stock return movement direction, coordinate descent algorithm, group coordinate descent algorithm, prediction accuracy, G-LASSO/G-SCAD/G-MCP estimators

1. Introduction

Forecasting the financial market is a major challenge in both academic and business. In recent decades, some methods have been proposed to forecast the future stock returns or trend direction. For example, time series analysis develops some statistical models such as ARIMA, ARCH and GARCH to study the past stock behavior and predict the future stock returns. Technical analysis developed by Murphy [1] and Edwards et al. [2] on financial market and stock trends applies statistical charts, technical indicators and historical data to forecast stock behavior. Fundamental analysis studies the economic factors that may influence market movements and applies financial methodologies with fundamental variables to predict stock market. For instance, Cavalcante et al. [3] sought economic factors influencing market trends. Nti et al. [4] summarized fundamental and technical analysis for stock market prediction. Machine learning techniques model nonstationary and nonlinear data to predict market behavior.

Henrique et al. [5] overviewed machine learning techniques on financial market prediction by the bibliometric analysis. Jiang [6] summarized stock market prediction using deep learning methods such as LSTM, Convolutional Neural Network (CNN), Deep Neural Network (DNN) and Recurrent Neural Network (RNN) [7–10].

The selection of input features plays a key role in predicting uptrends and downtrends for stock returns. The following three types of input features have been studied: A. extract-related indicators through fundamental and technical analysis [4]; B. apply text mining techniques to extract textual features from financial news or tweets [11]; C. generate candlestick charts to extract image features [12]. Recently, Jiang et al. [13] and Hu and Yang [14] combined technical indicators with (group) penalized logistic regressions to predict up- and downtrends for stock prices. Lin et al. [15] applied financial news to construct text mining-based stock prediction models. Li et al. [16] found that models including prices and news sentiments outperformed models only including either technical indicators or news sentiments. This research mainly predicted up- or downtrends. In this chapter, we not only summarize (group) penalized logistic regressions with multiple technical indicators to predict up- or downtrends, but also provide group penalized trinomial logit dynamic models with multiple technical indicator groups to predict uptrends, sideways trends and downtrends, for more details see Ref. [17].

Firstly, we propose Ridge/LASSO/ENet/SCAD/MCP penalized logistic regressions with multiple indicators to further improve the two-class prediction performance, not only apply the training set and the CD algorithm to obtain parameter estimators and probability estimators, but also employ the testing set and the learned estimators to obtain two-class confusion matrix and draw ROC curves to assess two-class prediction performance. Secondly, we propose G-LASSO/G-SCAD/G-MCP penalized logistic regressions to predict up- or downtrends, not only apply the training set to learn parameter estimators and probability estimators, but also adopt the testing set and the learned estimators to obtain confusion matrix and draw ROC curves in order to assess two-class prediction performance. Finally, we propose G-LASSO/G-SCAD/G-MCP penalized trinomial dynamic logit models to predict uptrends, sideways trends, and downtrends, not only develop the GCD algorithm to complete group selection and group estimation, but also introduce Bayes classifier to identify class labels, still adopt three-class confusion matrix, HUM, Kappa and PDI to assess three-class prediction performance to stock return movement direction.

The rest is organized as follows. Section 2 predicts uptrends and downtrends. Section 3 predicts uptrends, sideways trends and down trends. Section 4 gives conclusions and prospects. Section 5 provides discussions.

2. Predicting uptrends and downtrends

In this section, we not only propose five penalized logistic regressions with technical indicators to predict up- or downtrends, but also propose three group penalized logistic regressions to further improve two-class prediction performance.

2.1 Five penalized logistic regression prediction methods

Hu and Jiang [18] proposed logistic regression to predict up- or downtrends. Here, we propose Ridge/LASSO/ENet/SCAD/MCP penalized logistic regressions to predict up- or downtrends.

2.1.1 Five penalized logistic regressions

Introduce the direction indicator function

$$Y_t = \begin{cases} 1, & \text{if} \quad C_{t+1} > C_t, \\ 0, & \text{if} \quad C_{t+1} \leq C_t, \end{cases} \tag{1}$$

where C_t represents the closing price at the end of the t-th trading day. Then, $Y_t = 1$ represents uptrends, and $Y_t = 0$ represents downtrends. Now, we generalize [18] and introduce logistic regression with p technical indicators:

$$P(X_t; \beta_0, \beta) = P(Y_t = 1 | X_t; \beta_0, \beta) = \frac{\exp(\beta_0 + X_t^\top \beta)}{1 + \exp(\beta_0 + X_t^\top \beta)}, \tag{2}$$

$$1 - P(X_t; \beta_0, \beta) = P(Y_t = 0 | X_t; \beta_0, \beta) = \frac{1}{1 + \exp(\beta_0 + X_t^\top \beta)}, \tag{3}$$

where β_0 is an unknown intercept term, $\beta = \left(\beta_1, \beta_2, \dots, \beta_p\right)^\top$ is an unknown parameter vector, and $X_t = \left(X_{t,1}, X_{t,2}, \dots, X_{t,p}\right)^\top$ is a predictor vector whose distribution is usually unknown. To improve two-class prediction performance, we propose the five penalized logistic regressions to predict up- or downtrends.

Let $x_t = \left(x_{t,1}, x_{t,2}, \dots, x_{t,p}\right)^\top$ and y_t be the observation samples for X_t and Y_t, respectively. Given the training set $\left\{x_t, y_t\right\}_{t=1}^{n_1}$ with the sample size n_1, we obtain the negative log-likelihood function

$$l(\beta) = -L(\beta) = -\sum_{t=1}^{n_1} \{y_t(\beta_0 + x_t^\top \beta) - \log[1 + \exp(\beta_0 + x_t^\top \beta)]\}, \tag{4}$$

and its penalized version

$$Q(\beta; \lambda, \gamma) \equiv l(\beta) + p_{\lambda,\gamma}(\beta), \tag{5}$$

where $p_{\lambda,\gamma}(\beta)$ is a penalty function with a tuning parameter λ and a regularization parameter γ. **Table 1** lists the five penalties.

2.1.2 Parameter estimators and probability estimators

Suppose that the current parameter estimators are $\left(\hat{\beta}_0, \hat{\beta}(m)\right)$. For the non-differentiable function (4), we transform it into the following weighted least-squares function:

$$l_Q(\beta_0, \beta) = -\frac{1}{2n_1} \sum_{t=1}^{n_1} W_t \left(\tilde{Y}_t - \beta_0 - x_t^\top \beta\right)^2 + C\left(\hat{\beta}_0, \hat{\beta}(m)\right), \tag{6}$$

where

Penalties	Formulae
Ridge	$p_{\lambda(\beta)} = \lambda\|\beta\|_2^2.$
LASSO	$p_\lambda(\beta) = \lambda\|\beta\|_1.$
ENet	$p_{\lambda,\gamma}(\beta) = \frac{1}{2}\lambda[(1-\gamma)\|\beta\|_2^2 + \gamma\|\beta\|_1], \lambda \in (0,\infty), \gamma \in (0,1).$
MCP	$p_{\lambda,\gamma}(\beta) = \begin{cases} \lambda\beta - \dfrac{\beta^2}{2\gamma}, & \text{if } \beta \le \gamma\lambda, \\ \dfrac{1}{2}\gamma\lambda^2, & \text{if } \beta > \gamma\lambda, \end{cases} \quad \lambda \ge 0, \gamma > 1.$
SCAD	$p_{\lambda,\gamma}(\beta) = \begin{cases} \lambda\beta, & \text{if } \beta \le \lambda, \\ \dfrac{\lambda\gamma\beta - 0.5(\beta^2+\lambda^2)}{(\gamma-1)}, & \text{if } \lambda < \beta \le \lambda\gamma, \\ \dfrac{\lambda^2(\gamma+1)}{2}, & \text{if } \beta > \lambda\gamma. \end{cases} \quad \lambda \ge 0, \gamma > 2.$

Table 1.
Penalized functions.

$$\tilde{Y}_t = \hat{\beta}_0 + x_t^\top \hat{\beta}(m) + \frac{y_t - \tilde{P}_t}{\tilde{P}_t(1-\tilde{P}_t)}, W_t = \tilde{P}_t(1-\tilde{P}_t), \tilde{P}_t = \frac{\exp(x_t^\top \hat{\beta}(m))}{1 + \exp(x_t^\top \hat{\beta}(m))}, \tag{7}$$

and $C(\hat{\beta}_0, \hat{\beta}(m))$ is constant. Similarly, we replace the non-differentiable function $l(\beta)$ in (5) by the weighted least-squares function $l_Q(\beta_0, \beta)$, apply the CD algorithm to obtain the parameter estimator

Penalties	Estimators
LASSO	$\hat{\beta}_j^{LASSO}(Z_j;\lambda) = \frac{S(Z_j,\lambda)}{\nu_j}.$
MCP	$\hat{\beta}_j^{MCP}(Z_j;\lambda,\gamma) = \begin{cases} \dfrac{S(Z_j,\lambda)}{\nu_j - 1/\gamma}, & \|Z_j\| \le \nu_j\lambda\gamma, \\ \dfrac{Z_j}{\nu_j}, & \|Z_j\| > \nu_j\lambda\gamma, \end{cases} \quad \gamma > 1/\nu_j.$
SCAD	$\hat{\beta}_j^{SCAD}(Z_j;\lambda,\gamma) = \begin{cases} \dfrac{S(Z_j,\lambda)}{\nu_j}, & \|Z_j\| \le \lambda(\nu_j+1), \\ \dfrac{S(Z_j,\gamma\lambda/(\gamma-1))}{\nu_j - 1/(\gamma-1)}, & \lambda(\nu_j+1) < \|Z_j\| \le \nu_j\lambda\gamma, \gamma > 1 + 1/\nu_j. \\ \dfrac{Z_j}{\nu_j}, & \|Z_j\| > \nu_j\lambda\gamma, \end{cases}$
Symbols	$\hat{P}_t = \exp\left(x_t^\top \hat{\beta}^{\lambda,\gamma}(m)\right)/[1 + \exp(x_t^\top \hat{\beta}^{\lambda,\gamma}(m)], W_t = \hat{P}_t(1-\hat{P}_t), t = 1, \ldots, n_1,$ $W = diag\{W_1, W_2, \ldots, W_n\}, \tilde{Y} = x^\top \hat{\beta}^{\lambda,\gamma}(m) + W^{-1}(Y - \hat{P}), \hat{P} = (\hat{P}_1, \ldots, \hat{P}_n),$ $x_j = (x_{1j}, \ldots, x_{n_1 j})^\top, \nu_j = n_1^{-1} x_j^\top W x_j, j = 1, \cdots, p,$ $Z_j = n_1^{-1} x_j^\top W(\tilde{Y} - x_{\cdot -j}\beta_{-j}) = n_1^{-1} x_j^\top W r + \nu_j \hat{\beta}_j^{\lambda,\gamma}(m),$ $x_{\cdot -j} = (x_{\cdot 1}, \cdots, x_{j-1}, 0, x_{j+1}, \cdots, x_{\cdot p})^\top,$ $\beta_{-j} = (\beta_1, \cdots, \beta_{j-1}, 0, \beta_{j+1}, \cdots, \beta_p).$

Table 2.
Penalized functions and parameter estimators for penalized logistic regressions.

$$\hat{\beta}^{\lambda,\gamma} = \arg\min_{\beta} \left\{ l_Q(\beta_0, \beta) + p_{\lambda,\gamma}(\beta) \right\}. \tag{8}$$

More details refer to [18]. **Table 2** lists LASSO/SCAD/MCP estimator.

For j in $\{1, 2, \dots, p\}$, the CD algorithm partially optimizes a target function $Q(\beta; \lambda, \gamma)$ with respect to a single parameter β_j with the remaining parameters $\beta_l, l \neq j$ fixed at the updated values $\hat{\beta}_1^{\lambda,\gamma}(m+1), \dots, \hat{\beta}_{j-1}^{\lambda,\gamma}(m+1), \hat{\beta}_{j+1}^{\lambda,\gamma}(m), \dots, \hat{\beta}_p^{\lambda,\gamma}(m)$, then cycling through all the parameters until convergence or a maximum iteration number M is reached, and this process repeats over a grid of values for λ to produce a path of the solution. For Ridge/LASSO/ENet penalty, variable selection is determined by the tuning parameter λ. In order to select an appropriate λ, we apply a cross-validation method to calculate the full solution path to model parameters, select a specific solution path from the full solution path, and take the binomial deviation as the risk measure. Then. we get the mean cross-validation error curve and the one-standard-deviation band. The parameter estimators for MCP/SCAD penalized logistic regression depend on λ and the regularization parameter γ. For γ, we generally take $\gamma = 3.7$. Algorithm 1 tells us how to apply the CD algorithm to calculate MCP estimator. The other four cases are similar to Algorithm 1.

Algorithm 1: The CD algorithm for MCP logistic regression.

Require: the training set $\left\{x_t = \left(x_{t,1}, x_{t,2}, \cdots, x_{t,p}\right), y_t\right\}_{t=1}^{n}$, a grid of increasing λ values $\Lambda = \{\lambda_1, \dots, \lambda_L\}$, γ, a given tolerance limit ε and a maximum iteration number M.

1: Initialization $\hat{\beta}(0) = \hat{\beta}(\lambda_{max} = \lambda_L, \gamma = 5)$.

2: **for** each $m = 0, 1 \cdots$, each $l \in \{L, L-1, \cdots, 1\}$, **do**.

3: **repeat**.

4: $\hat{\eta}_t \Leftarrow \beta_0 + x_t^{\top} \hat{\beta}^{\lambda,\gamma}(m)$.

5: $\hat{P}_t \Leftarrow e^{\hat{\eta}_t} / \left(1 + e^{\hat{\eta}_t}\right)$.

6: $W \Leftarrow \mathrm{diag}\left\{\hat{P}_1(1 - \hat{P}_1), \cdots, \hat{P}_n(1 - \hat{P}_n)\right\}$.

7: $r \Leftarrow W^{-1}\{Y - \hat{P}\}$.

8: $\tilde{Y} \Leftarrow \eta + r$.

9: **while** not convergent **do**.

10: **for** each $j \in \{1, 2, \cdots, p\}$ **do**.

11: $\nu_j \Leftarrow n^{-1} x_{\cdot j}^{\top} W x_{\cdot j}$.

12: $$\begin{aligned} Z_j &\Leftarrow \frac{1}{n} x_{\cdot j}^{\top} W \left(\tilde{Y} - x_{\cdot -j}\beta_{-j}\right) \\ &\Leftarrow \frac{1}{n} x_{\cdot j}^{\top} W r + \nu_j \hat{\beta}_j^{\lambda,\gamma}(m) \end{aligned}.$$

13: **if** $|Z_j| \leqslant \nu_j \gamma \lambda$ **then.**

14: $\hat{\beta}_j^{\lambda,\gamma}(m+1) \Leftarrow \frac{S(Z_j, \lambda)}{\nu_j - 1/\gamma}$.

15: **else.**

16: $\hat{\beta}_j^{\lambda,\gamma}(m+1) \Leftarrow \frac{Z_j}{\nu_j}$.

17: **end if.**

18: $r \Leftarrow r - x_{\cdot j}^{\top}\left(\hat{\beta}_j^{\lambda,\gamma}(m+1) - \hat{\beta}_j^{\lambda,\gamma}(m)\right)$.

19: **end for.**

20: **end while.**

21: **until** $\left\|\hat{\beta}^{\lambda,\gamma}(m+1)-\hat{\beta}^{\lambda,\gamma}(m)\right\|_2^2 \leqslant \varepsilon$ or do a maximum iteration number M.

22: **end for.**

Ensure: $\hat{\beta}^{\lambda,\gamma}$.

Now we apply the CD algorithm to the five penalized logistic regressions to obtain the final parameter estimators $\hat{\beta}_0^{\lambda,\gamma}$ and $\hat{\beta}^{\lambda,\gamma}$, then combine them with the testing set $\{x_t, y_{t+1}^k\}_{t=n_1+1}^{n_1+n_2}$ to compute the probability estimators

$$\hat{P}\left(Y_t = 1|X_t; \hat{\beta}_0^{\lambda,\gamma}, \hat{\beta}^{\lambda,\gamma}\right) = \frac{\exp\left(\hat{\beta}_0^{\lambda,\gamma} + X_t^{\mathsf{T}}\hat{\beta}^{\lambda,\gamma}\right)}{1+\exp\left(\hat{\beta}_0^{\lambda,\gamma} + X_t^{\mathsf{T}}\hat{\beta}^{\lambda,\gamma}\right)}, \tag{9}$$

$$\hat{P}\left(Y_t = 0|X_t; \hat{\beta}_0^{\lambda,\gamma}, \hat{\beta}^{\lambda,\gamma}\right) = \frac{1}{1+\exp\left(\hat{\beta}_0^{\lambda,\gamma} + X_t^{\mathsf{T}}\hat{\beta}^{\lambda,\gamma}\right)}. \tag{10}$$

2.2 Three-group penalized logistic regression prediction methods

In this subsection, we propose G-LASSO/G-SCAD/G-MCP penalized logistic regressions with multiple technical indicators to predict up- or downtrends.

2.2.1 Three-group penalized logistic regressions

Suppose that the binary response Y_t represents the stock price movement directions, and the p-dimensional predictor vector $\mathbf{X}_t = \left(X_{t,1}, \dots, X_{t,p}\right)^{\mathsf{T}}$ represents p technical indicators influencing stock price movement direction. The training set $\{(\mathbf{X}_t, Y_t), t = 1, \dots, n_1\}$ is made up of the predictor vector $\mathbf{X}_t \in \mathbb{R}^p$ allowing both categorical and continuous predictors and the binary response $Y_t \in \{0, 1\}$. We divide the p-dimensional predictor vector $\mathbf{X}_t$ into the G different groups $\mathbf{x}_t = \left(\mathbf{x}_{t,1}^{\mathsf{T}}, \dots, \mathbf{x}_{t,g}^{\mathsf{T}}, \dots, \mathbf{x}_{t,G}^{\mathsf{T}}\right)^{\mathsf{T}}$ with $\mathbf{x}_{t,g} = \left(\mathbf{X}_{t,df_{g-1}+1}, \dots, \mathbf{X}_{t,df_g}\right)$ and the g-th group length df_g, g $= 1, \cdots, G$. Then, the group logistic regression is

$$p_\beta(\mathbf{x}_t) = P_\beta(Y_t = 1|\mathbf{x}_t) = \frac{\exp\left(\beta_0 + \sum_{g=1}^G \mathbf{x}_{t,g}^{\mathsf{T}}\boldsymbol{\beta}_g\right)}{1+\exp\left(\beta_0 + \sum_{g=1}^G \mathbf{x}_{t,g}^{\mathsf{T}}\boldsymbol{\beta}_g\right)}, \tag{11}$$

$$1 - p_\beta(\mathbf{x}_t) = P_\beta(Y_t = 0|\mathbf{x}_t) = \frac{1}{1+\exp\left(\beta_0 + \sum_{g=1}^G \mathbf{x}_{t,g}^{\mathsf{T}}\boldsymbol{\beta}_g\right)}, \tag{12}$$

where β_0 is the intercept, $\boldsymbol{\beta}_g \in \mathbb{R}^{\mathrm{df}_g}$ is the g-th parameter vector, and $\boldsymbol{\beta} = \left(\beta_0, \boldsymbol{\beta}_1^{\mathsf{T}}, \dots, \boldsymbol{\beta}_{\mathbf{G}}^{\mathsf{T}}\right)^{\mathsf{T}} \in \mathbb{R}^{p+1}$ is the whole parameter vector.

2.2.2 Parameter estimators and probability estimators

Based on the training set $\{(\mathbf{x}_t, Y_t), t = 1, \dots, n_1\}$, we obtain the log-likelihood function

$$l(\beta) = \sum_{t=1}^{n_1} \{Y_t \eta_\beta(\mathbf{x}_t) - \log[1 + \exp(\eta_\beta(\mathbf{x}_t))]\} \tag{13}$$

with $\eta_\beta(\mathbf{x}_t) = \log\left\{\frac{p_\beta(\mathbf{x}_t)}{1-p_\beta(\mathbf{x}_t)}\right\} = \beta_0 + \sum_{g=1}^{G} \mathbf{x}_{t,g}^{\top} \boldsymbol{\beta}_g$, the penalized log-likelihood function is

$$S_{\lambda,\gamma}(\boldsymbol{\beta}) = -l(\boldsymbol{\beta}) + \sum_{l=1}^{p} P(\beta_l; \lambda, \gamma), \tag{14}$$

and the group penalized log-likelihood is

$$S_{\lambda,\gamma}(\boldsymbol{\beta}) = -l(\boldsymbol{\beta}) + \sum_{g=1}^{G} P\left(\|\boldsymbol{\beta}_g\|_2; \lambda\sqrt{df_g}, \gamma\right), \tag{15}$$

where $P\left(\|\boldsymbol{\beta}_g\|_2; \lambda\sqrt{df_g}, \gamma\right)$ with a tuning parameter $\lambda \geq 0$ and a regularization parameter γ defines a family of penalty functions concave in $\|\boldsymbol{\beta}_g\|_2$. The estimator $\hat{\boldsymbol{\beta}}$ is the minimizer of the convex function $S_{\lambda,\gamma}(\boldsymbol{\beta})$. Here, we take $P(\beta_l; \lambda, \gamma)$ as $P_{SCAD}(\beta_l; \lambda, \gamma)$ or $P_{MCP}(\beta_l; \lambda, \gamma)$, and take $P\left(\|\boldsymbol{\beta}_g\|_2; \lambda\sqrt{df_g}, \gamma\right)$ as $P_{gSCAD}\left(\|\boldsymbol{\beta}_g\|_2; \lambda\sqrt{df_g}, \gamma\right)$ or $P_{gMCP}\left(\|\boldsymbol{\beta}_g\|_2; \lambda\sqrt{df_g}, \gamma\right)$. Three group penalized functions are listed in **Table 3**. According to Breheny and Huang [19] and Fan and Li [20], the Bayes risks are not sensitive to the choice of γ. In general, we take $\gamma = 3.7$ for SCAD/gSCAD (group SCAD) and $\gamma = 3$ for MCP/gMCP(group MCP). According to Hu and Liu [21], we adopt the GCD algorithm to complete group selection and group estimations listed in **Table 4**.

After applying the training set $\{(\mathbf{x}_t, Y_t), t = 1, \ldots, n_1\}$ and the GCD algorithm to obtain group estimation $\hat{\boldsymbol{\beta}}_g$, we apply the testing set $\{(\mathbf{x}_t, Y_t), t = n_1 + 1, \ldots, n\}$ and $\hat{\boldsymbol{\beta}}_g$ to obtain the predicted probabilities for up- or downtrends:

Symbols	Three-group penalized functions
gLASSO	$P_{gLASSO}(\beta; \lambda) = \lambda\sqrt{df_g}\left\|\beta_g\right\|_2.$
gSCAD	$P_{gSCAD}\left(\|\boldsymbol{\beta}_g\|_2; \lambda\sqrt{df_g}, \gamma\right) = \begin{cases} \lambda\sqrt{df_g}\left\|\beta_g\right\|_2, & \left\|\beta_g\right\|_2 \leq \lambda\sqrt{df_g}, \lambda \geq 0, \\ \frac{2\lambda\sqrt{df_g}\gamma\left\|\beta_g\right\|_2 - \left(\left\|\beta_g\right\|_2^2 + \lambda^2 df_g\right)}{2(\gamma-1)}, & \lambda\sqrt{df_g} < \left\|\beta_g\right\|_2 \leq \lambda\sqrt{df_g}\gamma, \\ \frac{\lambda^2 df_g(\gamma^2-1)}{2(\gamma-1)}, & \left\|\beta_g\right\|_2 > \lambda\sqrt{df_g}\gamma, \gamma > 2. \end{cases}$
gMCP	$P_{gMCP}\left(\|\boldsymbol{\beta}_g\|_2; \lambda\sqrt{df_g}, \gamma\right) = \begin{cases} \lambda\sqrt{df_g}\left\|\beta_g\right\|_2 - \left\|\beta_g\right\|_2^2/2\gamma, & \left\|\beta_g\right\|_2 \leq \lambda\sqrt{df_g}\gamma, \\ \lambda^2 df_g\gamma/2, & \left\|\beta_g\right\|_2 > \lambda\sqrt{df_g}\gamma, \end{cases} \quad \lambda \geq 0, \gamma > 1.$

Note: gLASSO stands for group LASSO.

Table 3.
gLASSO, gSCAD and gMCP functions.

Symbols	Three parameter estimators
gLASSO estimator	$\hat{\beta}^{gLASSO} = \frac{1}{v} S\left(vZ_g, \sqrt{d_g}\lambda\right).$
gSCAD estimator	$\hat{\beta}_g^{gSCAD} = \begin{cases} \frac{1}{v} S\left(vZ_g, \sqrt{d_g}\lambda\right), & \|Z_g\| \le 2\sqrt{d_g}\lambda, \\ \frac{\gamma-1}{\gamma-2} \cdot \frac{1}{v} S\left(vZ_g, \frac{\sqrt{d_g}\lambda\gamma}{\gamma-1}\right), & 2\sqrt{d_g}\lambda < \|Z_g\| \le \sqrt{d_g}\lambda\gamma, \\ Z_g, & \|Z_g\| \ge \sqrt{d_g}\lambda\gamma, \end{cases} \gamma > 2.$
gMCP estimator	$\hat{\beta}_g^{gMCP} = \begin{cases} \frac{\gamma}{\gamma-1} \cdot \frac{1}{v} S\left(vZ_g, \sqrt{d_g}\lambda\right), & \|Z_g\| \le \sqrt{d_g}\lambda\gamma, \\ Z_g, & \|Z_g\| \ge \sqrt{d_g}\lambda\gamma, \end{cases} \gamma > 1.$
Labels	$v_j = n_1^{-1} X_j^\top W X_j, j = 1, \cdots, p, Z_j = n_1^{-1} X_j^\top W\left(\tilde{Y} - X_{-j}\beta_{-j}\right),$
	$\tilde{Y} = X^\top \beta^{(m)} + W^{-1}(Y - P), X_{-j} = (X_1, \cdots X_{j-1}, 0, X_{j+1}, \cdots, X_p),$
	$\beta_{-j} = \left(\beta_1, \cdots, \beta_{j-1}, 0, \beta_{j+1}, \cdots, \beta_p\right);$
	$v = \max_t \sup_\eta \{\Delta^2 L_t(\eta)\}, L_t(\eta) = Y_t \eta_t - \log(1 + e^{\eta_t}), \eta_t = \beta_0 + \sum_{g=1}^G X_{t,g}^\top \beta_{(g)}, t = 1, \cdots, n_1,$
	$Z_g = X_g^\top\left(\overline{Y} - \mathrm{x}_{-g}\beta_{-(g)}\right), g = 1, \cdots, G, \overline{Y} = \mathrm{x}^\top \beta^{(m)} + W^{-1}(Y - P),$
	$\mathrm{x}_{-g} = \left(X_{(1)}^\top, \cdots X_{(g-1)}^\top, 0^\top, X_{(g+1)}^\top, \cdots, X_{(G)}^\top\right),$
	$\beta_{-(g)} = \left(\beta_{(1)}^\top, \cdots, \beta_{(g-1)}^\top, 0^\top, \beta_{(g+1)}^\top, \cdots, \beta_{(G)}^\top\right).$

Note: $\boldsymbol{X} = (\boldsymbol{X}_1, \ldots, \boldsymbol{X}_{n_1})^\top$ is a $n_1 \times p$ *matrix,* $\boldsymbol{x} = (\boldsymbol{x}_1, \ldots, \boldsymbol{x}_{n_1})^\top$ *is a* $n_1 \times p$ *matrix,* $\boldsymbol{Y} = (Y_1, \ldots, Y_{n_1})^\top$ *is a* $n_1 \times 1$ *vector, W is a* $n_1 \times n_1$ *weighted diagonal matrix, P is the estimated probability of the m-th iteration,* $\beta^{(m)}$ *is the parameter estimator of the m-th iteration.*

Table 4.
The iterative parameter estimators for gLASSO, gSCAD and gMCP.

$$\hat{p}_\beta(\mathbf{x}_t) = \hat{\mathbb{P}}_\beta(Y_t = 1|\mathbf{x}_t) = \frac{\exp\left(\hat{\beta}_0 + \sum_{g=1}^G \mathbf{x}_{t,g}^\top \hat{\boldsymbol{\beta}}_g\right)}{1 + \exp\left(\hat{\beta}_0 + \sum_{g=1}^G \mathbf{x}_{t,g}^\top \hat{\boldsymbol{\beta}}_g\right)}, \tag{16}$$

$$1 - \hat{p}_\beta(\mathbf{x}_t) = \hat{\mathbb{P}}_\beta(Y_t = 0|\mathbf{x}_t) = \frac{1}{1 + \exp\left(\hat{\beta}_0 + \sum_{g=1}^G \mathbf{x}_{t,g}^\top \hat{\boldsymbol{\beta}}_g\right)}, \tag{17}$$

where n represents the sample size of the entire dataset. G-lasso estimators can be computed by R package grplasso. Now we estimate the predicted value $\hat{Y}_t$ according to the following rules:

$$\text{If} \quad \hat{P}_t > c, \text{ then } \hat{Y}_t = 1, \text{ else } \hat{Y}_t = 0, \tag{18}$$

where c is a given threshold. Raghavan et al. [22] tell us how to select the optimal threshold.

2.3 Two-class prediction performance

We introduce the two-class confusion matrix listed in **Table 5** to assess two-class prediction performance.

True \ Predicted class	$\hat{Y}_t = 1$	$\hat{Y}_t = 2$	*Total*
$Y_t = 1$	$V(1, 1)$	$V(1, 2)$	$V(1, \cdot)$
$Y_t = 2$	$V(2, 1)$	$V(2, 2)$	$V(2, \cdot)$
Total	$V(\cdot, 1)$	$V(\cdot, 2)$	$V(\cdot, \cdot)$

Table 5.
Two-class confusion matrix.

$V(k, \overline{k})$ is the number of items that truly belong to class k and are predicted as class $\overline{k}$.

According to **Table 5**, one can compute

$$\text{Accuracy} = \frac{TP + TN}{TP + TN + FP + FN}, \text{Precision} = \frac{TP}{TP + FP}.$$

In fact, accuracy cannot reflect the losses from two types of errors. However, a ROC curve can clearly assess two-class prediction performance. For a given threshold c, $TPR(c) = P(Y_t < c)$ is true-positive rate, and $FPR(c) = P(1 - Y_t < c)$ is false-positive rate. Given the different threshold c, we can calculate $\{(TPR(c), FPR(c))\}$ or (Sensitivity, 1-Specificity) and draw a ROC curve, where

$$\text{Sensitivity(True positive rate, TPR)} = TP/(TP + FN) \tag{19}$$

measures the ability of classifiers to correctly identify positive samples, and

$$\text{Specificity(1-False positive rate, 1-FPR)} = TN/(TN + FP) \tag{20}$$

measures the ability to correctly identify negative labels. ROC is a graphical method to evaluate the performance of the binary classifier. Here, we choose ggplot2 to draw the ROC curve and compute the corresponding AUC (the area under the ROC curve).

3. Predicting uptrends, sideways trends and downtrends

3.1 Three-group penalized trinomial logit prediction methods

Let C_t be the closing price at the end of the t-th trading day, $Z_t = C_t - C_{t-k}$ be the k period stock excess return, and

$$Y_t(c) = \begin{cases} 1, & \text{if} \quad Z_t > c, \\ 2, & \text{if} \quad -c \leq Z_t \leq c, \\ 3, & \text{if} \quad Z_t < -c. \end{cases} \tag{21}$$

be an unordered three-category response variable. Then, $Y_t(c) = 1$ represents uptrends, $Y_t(c) = 2$ represents sideways trends, and $Y_t(c) = 3$ represents downtrends. When $c = 0$, $Y_t(c)$ is an indicator for positive returns. When $c = 0.1C_{t-1}$, $Y_t(c)$ is an indicator for "large" positive returns. When $c = -0.1C_{t-1}$, $Y_t(c)$ is an indicator for "large" negative returns. More details on how to choose c may refer to [23]. Suppose that the predictive vector $\mathbf{X}_t = (X_{t,1}, \dots, X_{t,p})^{\top}$ allowing both categorical and continuous predictors can represent the factors influencing stock return movement direction. One main goal is to predict stock return movement direction $Y_{t+1}(c)$ using the available information set $I_t = \sigma\{X_t, X_{t-1}, \cdots\}$ at time t. If $Y_{t+1}(c)$ only depend on $\mathbf{X}_t$, then we can predict $Y_{t+1}(c)$ based on $\mathbf{X}_t$. Trinomial logit dynamic model for stock return movement direction is

$$\begin{aligned} P(Y_{t+1}(c) = 1|x_t;\beta) &= \frac{\exp\left(\beta_0^1 + \sum_{g=1}^{G} \mathbf{x}_{t(g)} \boldsymbol{\beta}_{(g)}^1\right)}{\sum_{k=1}^{3} \exp\left(\beta_0^k + \sum_{g=1}^{5} \mathbf{x}_{t(g)} \boldsymbol{\beta}_{(g)}^k\right)}, \\ P(Y_{t+1}(c) = 2|x_t;\beta) &= \frac{\exp\left(\beta_0^2 + \sum_{g=1}^{G} \mathbf{x}_{t(g)} \boldsymbol{\beta}_{(g)}^2\right)}{\sum_{k=1}^{3} \exp\left(\beta_0^k + \sum_{g=1}^{5} \mathbf{x}_{t(g)} \boldsymbol{\beta}_{(g)}^k\right)}, \\ P(Y_{t+1}(c) = 3|x_t;\beta) &= \frac{\exp\left(\beta_0^3 + \sum_{g=1}^{G} \mathbf{x}_{t(g)} \boldsymbol{\beta}_{(g)}^3\right)}{\sum_{k=1}^{3} \exp\left(\beta_0^k + \sum_{g=1}^{5} \mathbf{x}_{t(g)} \boldsymbol{\beta}_{(g)}^k\right)}, \end{aligned} \tag{22}$$

where the parameter vector $\beta = \left(\beta_0^1, (\beta^1)^{\top}, \beta_0^2, (\beta^2)^{\top}, \beta_0^3, (\beta^3)^{\top}\right)$ with the k-th class intercept $\beta_0^k \in R$ and the g-th group parameter vector from the k-th class $\boldsymbol{\beta}_{(g)}^k = \left(\beta_{df_{g-1}+1}, \dots, \beta_{df_g}\right)^{\top}$, $g = 1, \cdots, 5$. The k-th class parameter vector is $\beta^k = \left(\left(\beta_{(1)}^k\right)^{\top}, \cdots, \left(\beta_{(G)}^k\right)^{\top}\right)^{\top}$, $k = 1,2,3$. According to the training set $\{(\mathbf{X}_t, Y_{t+1}(c)), t = 1, \dots, n_1\}$ and $y_{t+1}^k = I(Y_{t+1}(c) = k)$, we obtain the group trinomial logit log-likelihood function

$$l(\beta) = \sum_{t=1}^{n_1} \left\{ \sum_{k=1}^{3} y_{t+1}^k \left(\beta_0^k + \mathrm{x}_t \beta^k\right) - \log\left[\sum_{k=1}^{3} \exp\left(\beta_0^k + \mathrm{x}_t \beta^k\right)\right] \right\} \tag{23}$$

and the corresponding group penalized trinomial logit log-likelihood function

$$Q^{\lambda,\gamma}(\beta) \equiv R_{n_1}(\beta) + \sum_{k=1}^{3} \sum_{g=1}^{G} \mathbf{P}\left(\|\beta_{(g)}^k\|; \lambda\sqrt{p_g}, \gamma\right), \tag{24}$$

where $R_{n_1}(\beta) = \frac{1}{n_1} \sum_{t=1}^{n_1} \gamma_\beta\left(x_t, y_{t+1}^k\right) = -\frac{1}{N} \sum_{t=1}^{n_1} \left\{ \sum_{k=1}^{3} y_{t+1}^k \left(\beta_0^k + x_t \beta^k\right) - \log\left[\sum_{k=1}^{3} \exp\left(\beta_0^k + x_t \beta^k\right)\right] \right\}$ is the empirical risk to $R(\beta) = E\gamma_\beta(x, y)$ with $y = (y^1, y^2, y^3)$ and the loss function

$$\gamma_\beta(x, y) = -\left\{ \sum_{k=1}^{3} y^k \left(\beta_0^k + x\beta^k\right) - \log\left[\sum_{k=1}^{3} \exp\left(\beta_0^k + x\beta^k\right)\right] \right\}, \tag{25}$$

$\mathbf{P}\left(\|\beta_{(g)}^k\|; \lambda\sqrt{p_g}, \gamma\right)$ defines a family of penalty functions. Next, we introduce the three group penalized criterions:

a. *G-LASSO penalized function*

$$Q^{\lambda,\gamma}_{G-LASSO}(\beta) \equiv R_{n_1}(\beta) + \sum_{k=1}^{3}\sum_{g=1}^{G}\lambda\sqrt{p_g}\|\beta^k_{(g)}\|; \tag{26}$$

b. G-SCAD penalized function

$$Q^{\lambda,\gamma}_{G-SCAD}(\beta) \equiv R_{n_1}(\beta) + \sum_{k=1}^{3}\sum_{g=1}^{G}\mathbf{P}_{G-SCAD}\left(\|\beta^k_{(g)}\|;\lambda\sqrt{p_g},\gamma\right) \tag{27}$$

for $\lambda \geq 0$ and $\gamma > 2$, where

$$\mathbf{P}_{G-SCAD}\left(\|\beta^k_{(g)}\|;\lambda\sqrt{p_g},\gamma\right) = \lambda\sqrt{p_g}\int_0^{\|\beta^k_{(g)}\|}\min\left\{1,\left(\gamma-\lambda\sqrt{p_g}x\right)_+/(\gamma-1)\right\}dx$$
$$= \begin{cases} \lambda\sqrt{p_g}\|\beta^k_{(g)}\|, & \text{if } \|\beta^k_{(g)}\| \leq \lambda\sqrt{p_g}, \\ \dfrac{2\lambda\sqrt{p_g}\gamma\|\beta^k_{(g)}\| - \left(\|\beta^k_{(g)}\|^2 + \lambda^2 p_g\right)}{2(\gamma-1)}, & \text{if } \lambda\sqrt{p_l} < \|\beta^k_{(g)}\| \leq \lambda\sqrt{p_g}\gamma, \\ \dfrac{\lambda^2 p_g(\gamma^2-1)}{2(\gamma-1)}, & \text{if } \|\beta^k_{(g)}\| > \lambda\sqrt{p_g}\gamma \end{cases}$$

and $x_+ = x1_{\{x\geq 0\}}$ represents the nonnegative part of x.

c. *G-MCP penalized function*

$$Q^{\lambda,\gamma}_{G-MCP}(\beta) \equiv R_{n_1}(\beta) + \sum_{k=1}^{3}\sum_{g=1}^{G}\mathbf{P}_{G-MCP}\left(\|\beta^k_{(g)}\|;\lambda\sqrt{p_g},\gamma\right) \tag{28}$$

for $\lambda \geq 0$ and $\gamma > 1$, where

$$\mathbf{P}_{G\text{-}MCP}\left(\|\beta^k_{(g)}\|;\lambda\sqrt{p_g},\gamma\right) = \lambda\sqrt{p_g}\int_0^{\|\beta^k_{(g)}\|}\left(1 - x/\left(\lambda\sqrt{p_g}\gamma\right)\right)_+ dx$$
$$= \lambda\sqrt{p_g}\cdot\left(\|\beta^k_{(g)}\| - \|\beta^k_{(g)}\|^2/\left(2\lambda\sqrt{p_g}\gamma\right)\right)I\left(\|\beta^k_{(g)}\| < \lambda\gamma\right) + \lambda^2 p_g\gamma/2\cdot I\left(\|\beta^k_{(g)}\| \geq \lambda\gamma\right)$$
$$= \begin{cases} \lambda\sqrt{p_g}\|\beta^k_{(g)}\| - \|\beta^k_{(g)}\|^2/2\gamma, & \text{if } \|\beta^k_{(g)}\| \leq \lambda\sqrt{p_g}\gamma, \\ \lambda^2 p_g\gamma/2, & \text{if } \|\beta^k_{(g)}\| > \lambda\sqrt{p_g}\gamma. \end{cases}$$

3.2 GCD algorithm completes group selection and group estimations

For g in $\{1, 2, \ldots, G\}$, GCD partially optimizes the target function

$$Q^{\lambda,\gamma}(\beta) \equiv -\frac{1}{n_1}\sum_{t=1}^{n_1}\left\{\sum_{k=1}^{3} y^k_{t+1}\left(\beta^k_0 + x_t\beta^k\right) - \log\left[\sum_{k=1}^{3}\exp\left(\beta^k_0 + x_t\beta^k\right)\right]\right\}$$
$$+\sum_{k=1}^{3}\sum_{g=1}^{G}\mathbf{P}\left(\|\beta^k_{(g)}\|;\lambda\sqrt{p_g},\gamma\right)$$

for a single group $\beta_{(g)}$ with the other groups $\beta_{(\overline{g})}, \overline{g} \neq g$ fixed at the updated values $\tilde{\beta}^k_{(1)}(m+1), \ldots, \tilde{\beta}^k_{(g-1)}(m+1), \tilde{\beta}^k_{(g+1)}(m), \ldots, \tilde{\beta}^k_{(G)}(m)$, then iteratively cycling through all the groups until convergence or a maximum iteration is reached. Now, we develop the GCD algorithm for G-LASSO/G-SCAD/G-MCP penalized trinomial logit dynamic models. We perform partial Newton steps by forming the partial quadratic approximation

$$R_{Qk}\left(\beta_0^k, \left(\beta^k\right)^\top\right) = \frac{1}{2n_1}\sum_{t=1}^{n_1}\omega_t^k\left(\zeta_t^k - \beta_0^k - x_t^\top\beta^k\right)^2 - C\left(\left\{\tilde{\beta}_0^{\bar{k}}, \tilde{\beta}_1^{\bar{k}}\right\}_{\bar{k}=1}^3\right)$$

to the empirical risk $R_{n_1}(\beta) = -\frac{1}{n_1}\sum_{t=1}^{N}\left\{\sum_{k=1}^3 y_{t+1}^k\left(\beta_0^k + x_t\beta^k\right) - \log\right.$ $\left.\left[\sum_{k=1}^3 \exp\left(\beta_0^k + x_t\beta^k\right)\right]\right\}$ or Taylor expansion about current estimates $\left\{\tilde{\beta}_0^{\bar{k}}, \tilde{\beta}_1^{\bar{k}}\right\}_{\bar{k}=1}^3$, allowing only $\left(\beta_0^k, \left(\beta^k\right)^\top\right)^\top$ to vary for a single class at a time, where $\omega_t^k = \hat{P}_t^k\left(1 - \hat{P}_t^k\right)$, $\hat{P}_t^k = \exp\left(\tilde{\beta}_0^k + x_t\tilde{\beta}^k\right)/\left[\sum_{k=1}^3 \exp\left(\tilde{\beta}_0^k + x_t\tilde{\beta}^k\right)\right]$, and $\zeta_t^k = \tilde{\beta}_0^k + x_t^\top\tilde{\beta}^k + \left(y_{t+1}^k - \hat{P}_t^k\right)/\omega_t^k$. For each given (λ, γ), we create an outer loop which cycles over k and compute $R_{Qk}\left(\beta_0^k, \left(\beta^k\right)^\top\right)$ about current estimates $\left\{\tilde{\beta}_0^{\bar{k}}, \tilde{\beta}_1^{\bar{k}}\right\}_{\bar{k}=1}^3$. Then, we apply the GCD algorithm to solve the negative group penalized weighted least-squares problem

$$\min_{\left(\beta_0^k, \left(\beta^k\right)^\top\right) \in R^{\sum_{g=1}^G p_l + 1}} \left\{R_{Qk}\left(\beta_0^k, \left(\beta^k\right)^\top\right) + \sum_{g=1}^G \mathbf{P}\left(\|\beta_{(g)}^k\|; \lambda\sqrt{p_l}, \gamma\right)\right\}.$$

The main four steps are as follows:

Step 1. Set $m = 0$ and $\tilde{\beta}^k(0) = \left(\tilde{\beta}_0^k(0), \left(\tilde{\beta}_{(1)}^k(0)\right)^\top, \dots, \left(\tilde{\beta}_{(G)}^k(0)\right)^\top\right)^\top$ be the initial value. Calculate $\hat{P}^k(0) = \left(\hat{P}_1^k(0), \hat{P}_2^k(0), \dots, \hat{P}_{n_1}^k(0)\right)^\top$ with

$$\hat{P}_t^k(0) = \frac{\exp\left(\tilde{\beta}_0^k(0) + \sum_{g=1}^G x_{t(g)}\tilde{\beta}_{(g)}^k(0)\right)}{\sum_{k=1}^3 \exp\left(\tilde{\beta}_0^k(0) + \sum_{g=1}^G x_{t(g)}\tilde{\beta}_{(g)}^k(0)\right)}, W^k(0) = \mathrm{diag}\left(\omega_1^k(0), \omega_2^k(0), \dots, \omega_{n_1}^k(0)\right)$$

with $\omega_t^k(0) = \hat{P}_t^k(0)\left(1 - \hat{P}_t^k(0)\right)$, and obtain the initial residual vector $r^k(0) = \left(r_1^k(0), r_2^k(0), \dots, r_N^k(0)\right)^\top$ with $r_t^k(0) = \left(y_{t+1}^k - \hat{P}_t^k(0)\right)/w_t^k(0)$..

Step 2. At the g-th step of $m + 1$ iterations, $g = 1, \dots, G$, carry out (A)-(C):

A. Calculate $\omega_t^k(m) = \hat{P}_t^k(m)\left(1 - \hat{P}_t^k(m)\right), \hat{P}^k(m) = \left(\hat{P}_1^k(m), \hat{P}_2^k(m), \dots, \hat{P}_{n_1}^k(m)\right)^\top, W^k(m) = \mathrm{diag}\left(\omega_1^k(m), \omega_2^k(m), \dots, \omega_{n_1}^k(m)\right)$ with

$$\hat{P}_t^k(m) = \frac{\exp\left(\tilde{\beta}_0^k(m) + \sum_{\bar{g}=1}^{g-1} x_{t(\bar{g})}\tilde{\beta}_{(\bar{g})}^k(m) + \sum_{\bar{g}=g}^{G} x_{t(\bar{g})}\tilde{\beta}_{(\bar{g})}^k(m-1)\right)}{\sum_{k=1}^3 \exp\left(\tilde{\beta}_0^k(m) + \sum_{\bar{g}=1}^{g-1} x_{t(\bar{g})}\tilde{\beta}_{(\bar{g})}^k(m) + \sum_{\bar{g}=g}^{G} x_{t(\bar{g})}\tilde{\beta}_{(\bar{g})}^k(m-1)\right)},$$ and obtain the m-th iterations' residual vector $r^k(m) = \left(r_1^k(m), r_2^k(m), \dots, r_N^k(m)\right)^\top$ with

$$r_t^k(m) = \left(y_{t+1}^k - \hat{P}_t^k(m)\right)/w_t^k(m).$$

Then, compute the $p_l \times p_l$ matrix $\nu^k_{(g)}(m) = n_1^{-1} x^{\top}_{(g)} W^k(m) x_{(g)}$, $g = 1, 2, \dots, G$, and the $p_l \times 1$ vector $z^k_{(g)}(m) = n_1^{-1} x^{\top}_{(g)} W^k(m) r^k(m) + \nu^k_{(g)}(m) \tilde{\beta}^k_{(g)}(m)$, $g = 1, 2, \dots, G$.

B. Update the g-th group estimator $\tilde{\beta}^k_{(g)}(m+1)$:

a. *G-LASSO estimator*

$$\tilde{\beta}^k_{(g)}(m+1) \leftarrow \frac{S\left(z^k_{(g)}(m), \lambda\sqrt{p_g}\right)}{\nu^k_{(g)}(m)}, \tag{29}$$

where the soft-thresholding operator

$$S\left(z^k_{(g)}(m), \lambda\sqrt{p_g}\right) = S\left(\|z^k_{(g)}(m)\|, \lambda\sqrt{p_g}\right) \frac{z^k_{(g)}(m)}{\|z^k_{(g)}(m)\|} = \left(1 - \lambda\sqrt{p_g}/\|z^k_{(g)}(m)\|\right)_+ z^k_{(g)}(m).$$

b. *G-SCAD estimator*

$$\tilde{\beta}^k_{(g)}(m+1) \leftarrow \begin{cases} \dfrac{S\left(z^k_{(g)}(m), \lambda\sqrt{p_g}\right)}{\nu^k_{(g)}(m)}, \text{if } \; \|z^k_{(g)}(m)\| \le \lambda\sqrt{p_g}\left(\|\nu^k_{(g)}(m)\| + 1\right), \\ \dfrac{S\left(z^k_{(g)}(m), \lambda\sqrt{p_g}\gamma/(\gamma-1)\right)}{\nu^k_{(g)}(m) - 1/(\gamma-1)}, \text{if } \; \lambda\sqrt{p_g}\left(\|\nu^k_{(g)}(m)\| + 1\right) < \|z^k_{(g)}(m)\| \le \|\nu^k_{(g)}(m)\|\lambda\sqrt{p_g}\gamma, \\ \dfrac{z^k_{(g)}(m)}{\nu^k_{(g)}(m)}, \text{if } \; \|z^k_{(g)}(m)\| > \|\nu^k_{(g)}(m)\|\lambda\sqrt{p_g}\gamma, \gamma > 1 + 1/c_*\left(\beta^k_{(g)}\right), \end{cases} \tag{30}$$

where $c_*\left(\beta^k_{(g)}\right)$ denotes the minimum eigenvalue of $N^{-1} x^{\top}_{(g)} W^k(m) x_{(g)}$.

c. *G-MCP estimator*

$$\tilde{\beta}^k_{(g)}(m+1) \leftarrow \begin{cases} \dfrac{S\left(z^k_{(g)}(m), \lambda\sqrt{p_g}\right)}{\nu^k_{(g)}(m) - 1/\gamma}, \text{if } \; \|z^k_{(g)}(m)\| \le \|\nu^k_{(g)}(m)\|\lambda\sqrt{p_g}\gamma, \\ \dfrac{z^k_{(g)}(m)}{\nu^k_{(g)}(m)}, \text{if } \; \|z^k_{(g)}(m)\| > \|\nu^k_{(g)}(m)\|\lambda\sqrt{p_g}\gamma, \gamma > 1/c_*\left(\beta^k_{(g)}\right). \end{cases} \tag{31}$$

(C) update $r^k(m+1) \leftarrow r^k(m) - x^{\top}\left(\tilde{\beta}^k_{(g)}(m+1) - \tilde{\beta}^k_{(g)}(m)\right)$.

Step 3. Update $m \leftarrow m+1$.

Step 4. Repeat steps 2–3 until convergence or the maximum iteration number is reached, the iterations stop and the final estimators are obtained.

For λ depending on the sample size, the group number, and the degree of freedom within each group, we can apply the grid search method to λ on a grid $\{\lambda_0, \dots, \lambda_{K+1}\}$. Let $\lambda_{min} = \lambda_0 > \lambda_1 > \dots > \lambda_K > \lambda_{K+1} = \lambda_{max} = \max_{1 \le g \le s} \|z^k_{(g)}(m)\|$, where $z^k_{(g)}(m) =$

$N^{-1}x_{(g)}W^k(m)r^k(m) + \nu^k_{(g)}(m)\tilde{\beta}^k_{(g)}(m)$ and $W^k(m), r^k(m), \nu^k_{(g)}(m)$ and $\tilde{\beta}^k_{(g)}(m)$. For any given γ, the algorithm starts at λ_{min} and proceeding toward λ_{max}. Each time sets the initial value of $\beta^k_{(g)}$ to be $\tilde{\beta}^k_{(g)}(m)$ estimated from the previous grid point to ensure that the initial values will never be far from the solution. To find the optimal λ on a grid $\{\lambda_0, \dots, \lambda_{K+1}\}$, we divide the stock dataset into S subsets $\{S_k\}_{k=1}^S$ with the same sample size and apply the S-fold cross-validation procedure to choose the optimal λ.

3.3 Three-class prediction performance

We firstly combine the GCD algorithm with the training set $\{x_t, y^k_{t+1}\}_{t=1}^{n_1}$ to learn G-LASSO/G-SCAD/G-MCP penalized trinomial logit dynamic models, then combine group estimators

$$\tilde{\beta} = \left(\tilde{\beta}^1_0, \left(\tilde{\beta}^1\right)^{\mathsf{T}}, \tilde{\beta}^2_0, \left(\tilde{\beta}^2\right)^{\mathsf{T}}, \tilde{\beta}^3_0, \left(\tilde{\beta}^3\right)^{\mathsf{T}}\right)^{\mathsf{T}}$$

with the testing set $\{x_t, y^k_{t+1}\}_{t=n_1+1}^{n_1+n_2}$ to compute class probability estimations

$$\tilde{P}(y^k_{t+1} = k | X_t; \tilde{\beta}) = \frac{\exp\left(\tilde{\beta}^k_0 + x_t\tilde{\beta}^k\right)}{\sum_{\bar{k}=1}^3 \exp\left(\tilde{\beta}^{\bar{k}}_0 + x_t\tilde{\beta}^{\bar{k}}\right)}, k = 1,2,3, \tag{32}$$

and finally introduce the *Bayes classifier* to predict class indexes

$$\hat{Y}_{t+1}(c) = k \quad \text{if} \quad \tilde{P}(y^k_{t+1} = k|X_t; \tilde{\beta}) = \max_{\bar{k} \in \{1,2,3\}} \tilde{P}(y^k_{t+1} = \bar{k}|X_t; \tilde{\beta}). \tag{33}$$

Table 6 lists three-class confusion matrix for assessing the prediction performance. $V(k, \bar{k})$ is the number of items that truly belong to class k and are predicted as class $\bar{k}$. $V(k, \cdot)$ is the number of items that truly belong to class k. $V(\cdot, \bar{k})$ is the number of items that were predicted as class $\bar{k}$.

From **Table 1**, one can compute Accuracy. For unordered multi-category response variables, some traditional accuracy measures such as AUC are not applicable, a few important statistical concepts for assessing multi-category classification accuracy have been proposed. For example, **Kappa coefficient**(**Kappa**) $= \left(\sum_{k=1}^K p_{kk} - \sum_{k=1}^K p_{k+}p_{+k}\right) / \left(1 - \sum_{k=1}^K p_{k+}p_{+k}\right)$ with $p_{kk} = P(Y_t = k, \hat{Y}_t = k), p_{k+} = P(Y_t = k), p_{+k} = P(\hat{Y}_t = k)$ measures multi-category classification accuracy, and **Kappa** $\in (0, 0.2)$, $(0.2, 0.4)$, $(0.4, 0.6)$, $(0.6, 0.8)$, $(0.8, 1.0)$ represent no consistency, slightly consistency, mild consistency, reasonably consistency, strong consistency, almost identical, respectively. PDI evaluates the probability of an event related to simultaneously classifying n subjects from K categories. For a fixed category k, define the class-specific PDI to be $\text{PDI}_k = P(p_{kk} > p_{jk}, j \neq k Y_t = k)$ with p_{ij} be the probability of placing a subject from category i into category j. The overall PDI is $\text{PDI} = \sum_{k=1}^K \text{PDI}_k / K$.

According to the three-class confusion matrices and the three testing sets, we compute sensitivity and specificity for class 1–3. Plotting true classification rates in

True \ Predicted class	$\hat{Y}_t = 1$	$\hat{Y}_t = 2$	$\hat{Y}_t = 3$	*Total*
$Y_t = 1$	$V(1,1)$	$V(1,2)$	$V(1,3)$	$V(1,\cdot)$
$Y_t = 2$	$V(2,1)$	$V(2,2)$	$V(2,3)$	$V(2,\cdot)$
$Y_t = 3$	$V(3,1)$	$V(3,2)$	$V(3,3)$	$V(3,\cdot)$
Total	$V(\cdot,1)$	$V(\cdot,2)$	$V(\cdot,3)$	$V(\cdot,\cdot)$

Table 6.
Three-class confusion matrix.

three dimensions (3D) obtains the 3D ROC surface in the unit cube. HUM is a reflection of the intrinsic accuracy of three-class classifier. Here, we choose R package mcca to draw the ROC surfaces. The HUM value is higher, and the prediction performance is better. More details see Refs. [24, 25].

4. Conclusions and prospects

In this chapter, we combine different technical indicators with five penalized logistic regressions, three-group penalized logistic regressions and three-group penalized trinomial logit regressions to predict stock return movement direction. The future research focuses on adding more variables such as fundamental factors, specific news, national policies and market sentiment to the proposed regressions, and further improves the prediction performance to stock return movement direction.

5. Discussions

In the aforementioned methods, it is very important to select important (group) variables by tuning two parameters λ and γ. The different tuning parameters will bring the different prediction performance. However, after we choose the relative optimum tuning parameters λ and γ by some model selection criterion such as cross-validation and BIC, the proposed methods perform very robust in terms of accuracy, AUC or HUM, Kappa and PDI. In addition, the proposed CD or GCD algorithm converges very rapidly. They can be generalized to high-dimensional or super high-dimensional cases by containing more variables influencing stock movement directions. From Refs. [13–15], we can found that the proposed methods outperform some classical machine learning or deep learning methods in terms of robustness and effectiveness and calculation. Therefore, these prediction methods are worth of further promotion.

Author details

Hu Xuemei
School of Mathematics and Statistics, Chongqing Technology and Business University, Chongqing, China

*Address all correspondence to: huxuem@163.com

References

[1] Murphy JJ. Technical Analysis of the Financial Markets. New York: Prentice Hall Press; 1999

[2] Edwards RD, Magee J, Bassetti WC. Technical Analysis of Stock Trends. Florida: CRC Press; 2018

[3] Cavalcante RC, Brasileiro RC, Souza VLF, Nobrega JP, Oliveira ALI. Computational intelligence and financial markets: A survey and future directions. Expert Systems with Applications. 2016; **55**(15):194-211. DOI: 10.1016/j.eswa.2016.02.006

[4] Nti IK, Adekoya AF, Weyori BA. A systematic review of fundamental and technical analysis of stock market predictions. Artificial Intelligence Review. 2020;**53**(4):3007-3057. DOI: 10.1007/s10462-019-09754-z

[5] Henrique BM, Sobreiro VA, Kimura H. Literature review: Machine learning techniques applied to financial market prediction. Expert Systems with Applications. 2019;**124**:226-251. DOI: 10.1016/j.eswa.2019.01.012

[6] Jiang WW. Applications of deep learning in stock market prediction: Recent progress. Expert Systems with Applications. 2021;**184**:115537. DOI: 10.1016/j.eswa.2021.115537

[7] Nelson DMQ, Pereira ACM, De Oliveira RA. Stock market's price movement prediction with LSTM neural networks. In: 2017 International Joint Conference on Neural Networks (IJCNN). IEEE; 2017. pp. 1419-1426. DOI: 10.1109/IJCNN.2017.7966019

[8] Chen W, Jiang MR, Zhang WG, Chen ZS. A novel graph convolutional feature based convolutional neural network for stock trend prediction. Information Sciences. 2021;**556**:67-94. DOI: 10.1016/j.ins.2020.12.068

[9] Long J, Chen Z, He W, Wu T, Ren J. An integrated framework of deep learning and knowledge graph for prediction of stock price trend: An application in Chinese stock exchange market. Applied Soft Computing. 2020; **91**:106205. DOI: 10.1016/j.asoc.2020.106205

[10] Zhao J, Zeng D, Liang S, Kang H, Liu Q. Prediction model for stock price trend based on recurrent neural network. Journal of Ambient Intelligence and Humanized Computing. 2021;**12**:745-753. DOI: 10.1007/s12652-020-02057-0

[11] Xing FZ, Cambria E, Welsch RE. Natural language based financial forecasting: A survey. Artificial Intelligence Review. 2018;**50**(1):49-73. DOI: 10.1007/s10462-017-9588-9

[12] Lee J, Kim R, Koh Y, Kang J. Global stock market prediction based on stock chart images using deep Q-network. IEEE Access. 2019;**7**:167260-167277. DOI: 10.1109/ACCESS.2019.2953542

[13] Jiang HF, Hu XM, Jia H. Penalized logistic regressions with technical indicators predict up and down trends. Soft Computing. 2022;**27**:1-12. DOI: 10.1007/s00500-022-07404-1

[14] Hu XM, Yang JW. G-LASSO/G-SCAD/G-MCP penalized trinomial logit dynamic models predict up trends, sideways trends and down trends for stock returns. Expert Systems with Applications. 2024;**249**:123476. DOI: 10.1016/j.eswa.2024.123476

[15] Lin WC, Tsai CF, Chen H. Factors affecting text mining based stock

prediction: Text feature representations, machine learning models, and news platforms. Applied Soft Computing. 2022;**130**:109673. DOI: 10.1016/j.asoc.2022.109673

[16] Li XD, Wu PJ, Wang WP. Incorporating stock prices and news sentiments for stock market prediction: A case of Hong Kong. Information Processing and Management. 2022;**57**(5): 102212. DOI: 10.1016/j.ipm.2020.102212

[17] Yang YL, Hu XM, Jiang HF. Group penalized logistic regressions predict up and down trends for stock prices. The North American Journal of Economics and Finance. 2022;**59**:101564. DOI: 10.1016/j.najef.2021.101564

[18] Hu XM, Jiang HF. Logistic regression model with technical indicators predicts ups and downs for Google stock prices. Journal of Systems Science and Mathematical Sciences (in Chinese). 2021;**41**(3):1-22

[19] Breheny P, Huang J. Coordinate descent algorithms for nonconvex penalized regression, with applications to biological feature selection. Annals of Applied Statistics. 2011;**5**(1):232. DOI: 10.1214/10-AOAS388

[20] Fan JQ, Li RZ. Variable selection via non-concave penalized likelihood and its oracle properties. Journal of American Statistical Association. 2001;**96**(456): 1348-1360. DOI: 10.1198/016214501753382273

[21] Hu XM, Liu F. Estimation Theory and Model Recognition for High-Dimensional Statistical Models. Beijing: Higher Education Press; 2020

[22] Raghavan R, Ashour FS, Bailey B. A review of cutoffs for nutritional biomarkers. Advances in Nutrition. 2016;**7**(1):112-120

[23] Hong Y, Chung J. Are the directions of stock price changes predictable? In: Statistical Theory and Evidence. Cornell University; 2006

[24] Li JL, Gao M, D'Agostino R. Evaluating classification accuracy for modern learning approaches. Statistics in Medicine. 2019;**38**(13):2477-2503. DOI: 10.1002/sim.8103

[25] Li JL, Fine JP. ROC analysis with multiple classes and multiple tests: Methodology and its application in microarray studies. Biostatistics. 2008; **9**(3):566-576. DOI: 10.1093/biostatistics/kxm050

Section 2

Specific Strategies in Emerging and Frontier Markets – Toward a New Agenda

Chapter 4

Alternative Investment Vehicles Adapted for Entrepreneurial and Innovative Firms Financing in Emerging Markets

Gabriela Prelipcean and Mircea Boscoianu

Abstract

Alternative investment vehicles (AIVs) are an innovative organizational form of financing providers that provide opportunities for developed markets. The objective of this chapter is to deeply understand both the capabilities of different types of AIVs (crowdfunding, business angels, venture capital/private equity funds, and hedge funds) and the possibility of being efficiently integrated within the frontier or emerging markets, with a special focus on venture capital funds (VCFs). This topic is very important in the actual context of market turbulences and multiple crises. Following the medical COVID-19 crisis, institutional interferences have proved to be efficient in balancing the short-term situation. Nevertheless, long-term imbalances have manifested as such following the supply chain turmoil as a result of the increased inflation especially after the outbreak of the war in Ukraine. The present turbulent setting has become even more complicated due to both the energy crisis and the recent banking crises and by high and persistent inflation. The financing of innovative and entrepreneurial firms is significantly influenced by the current context. Therefore, the VCFs could have a major contribution in identifying new strategies in adjusting the financing mechanisms and the nature of governance to the ongoing markets' dynamics.

Keywords: entrepreneurial and innovative firms, alternative investment vehicles (AIVs), venture capital funds (VCFs), investment decisions, emerging markets

1. Introduction

In the actual turbulent global context, which has a major impact on both the financial and capital Romanian markets, the entrepreneurial investment process has been also influenced. The need for finance is increasing alongside the negative impact of the restrictions and access barriers on the entrepreneurial processes. The entrepreneurial investments have become more complex and opaque while the understanding of the movement of the markets and the reconfiguration of the opportunities and of the risks require new research strategies and solutions.

The actual context of the entrepreneurial investment processes is extremely uncertain and the decision processes are more complex because investors focus on not only the way to achieving success but also on how to achieve success as well as on the surviving strategies during critical situations. The high number of data that is necessary for the decision-making process fails to enable a deep understanding of the relevant information (i.e. the data on the investment factors, criteria, and risk elements) given the fact that the majority of decisions need to be taken fast and live. The entrepreneurial decision-making process is linked both to intuiting process, System 1 (with fast speed processing and significantly biased based on emotions), and to System 2 (i.e. which is a slower and analytical one given the lack of relevant data or their processing capacity) [1]. The spectral nature of the existing opportunities combined with the lack of a meaningful database call for the latest version of trade-off that manifests between the speed of decision-making and the accuracy of the analyzes. Both the time pressure and the uncertainty level are warning signs against the test jam hazard, which is counterbalanced by the key role of a fast intuiting process as such. The new frame of the intuiting process incorporates cognitions and emotions. In this case, it is both analytical and subjective. The underlying idea is that investors capture and manage an extended set of information in cvasi-real time. Consequently, the trade-off between System 1 and System 2 will no longer be valid in this particular instance. They will both work in parallel and they will complement each other synergistically. The design of an analytical strategy is cvasi-impossible. However, the whole point is to understand the way new ways of entrepreneurial investment approach works with special attention to identifying the optimal financing solution based on understanding the relationship between entrepreneurs and investors. The distinction between the retail investors, professional investors, and fund managers will also be part of the analytical processes.

Section 2 is devoted to presenting the aspects regarding the role of VCFs in emerging markets by highlighting the VC-cycle within the actual market context.

Section 3 presents the evaluation models of the VCFs portfolios. Technically speaking, based on the existence of the classical evaluation models that are already set in place, we have suggested the use of the MBU models (i.e. modified bottom-up) comprising a set of historical data (i.e. the VCF placement memorandum, the portfolio's evolution, a series of estimated financial multiples) and MCA (i.e. modified comparable approach) in which the valuation is based on a grading strategy. The means through which this particular grading contributes to the bias reduction needs to be examined, too. The monitoring process is constantly revised and adjusted. The two models are complementary because MBU provides more precision for both older portfolios and the short-term evaluations whereas MCA is more geared toward the new funds and the long-term approaches.

Section 4 presents three paradigms that help understand the evolutionary mechanisms and dynamics characterizing the VCF as well as their implications in terms of reconciling the partnership between the fund manager and the fund's investors.

In the paradigm of complex adaptive systems (VCF-CAS), the focus is on the means by which VCFs incorporate the vectors of innovation. The configuration mechanism of the specific set of opportunities is being explained, too. As far as the paradigm of evolutionary theory in VCFs (VCF-ET) is concerned, the focus is on capitalizing on the way the VCF portfolio management strategies benefit from learning and adjusting to change, namely configuring an adaptive situation which is continuously reshaped based on fitness (survival and competition) processes.

As far as the paradigm of dynamic capabilities in VCF portfolio management (VCF-DC) is concerned, the focus is on capitalizing on getting a sustainable competitive advantage in fast-paced changing environments as a result of a deeper understanding of the management of the resources and of the abilities to keep pace with this kind of dynamics as such [2, 3]. Based on the use of organizational resilience, the strategic actions for adjusting an organization to unexpected and turbulent situations can be improved. It is an extremely useful concept in itself especially in terms of the management of the VCFs portfolios. Both the dynamic capabilities and the organizational resilience can be hybridized (refer to the DCOR concept) by starting from the use of the reconfiguring cycle of the operating capabilities (i.e. discovery-learning-integration-coordination). This fact will enable deciphering a series of implications in terms of the relationship between managers and investors in terms of the VCFs.

Section 5 comprises three analyzes of the portfolio investment decisions from three distinct angles, which are useful for understanding the means of formulating the strategies for harmonizing the investors with entrepreneurial finance in Romania. It is also imperative to focus on understanding the (retail and professional) investors' preferences in terms of the selection of the assets and the management strategies of the VCF portfolios.

The first case study is based on the CAWI method (Computer Assisted Web Interviewing) and the data have been collected over a 2-week period (16–27 January 2023) based on two distinct questionnaires which were used on a sample of 110 retail investors (investors medium age 45 years, medium investment experience 12 years, medium investment per transaction 9000 Euros) and on 30 professional investors (investors medium age 42 years, medium investment experience 14 years, medium investment per transaction 45,000 Euros). The questionnaire included three introductory questions referring to education and professional background, two questions to general features of investing behavior, two questions to experience in investment decisions, and the main part with six questions, which focused mainly on understanding the attitudes, opinions, and behavior of both the retail and the professional investors.

The second study focuses on understanding the problems related to entrepreneurial investment decisions and the means of shaping up the relevant database for taking advantage of the investment opportunities given the actual inflation context, the understanding of the interactions between the entrepreneurs and the investors. Six entrepreneurs (medium age 48 years, medium entrepreneurial experience 18 years, medium financing amount per transaction 115,000 Euros) who benefited from financing within the VCF partnerships in Romania were interviewed.

The third case study was based on short interviews with three fund managers (medium age 42 years, medium experience in asset management 12 years, medium assets under management 1,552,000 Euros) with the aim to understand the new trend of professional investment approach and portfolio management and the specific strategies adapted for this complicated inflationary environment.

In the final part of the chapter, conclusions and contributions are presented.

2. Venture capital funds – Particularities in the case of frontier and emerging markets

VCF are alternative investment vehicles (AIVs) investing one's own funds as well as the investors' funds in long-term opportunities, private or publicly listed companies functioning based on a contract or on a general partnership agreement or on an investment contract for the portfolio management [4–9]. The VCF partnership focuses on the fund manager (GP-general partner, responsible for operations and portfolio management) and the passive/semi-passive investors (LP-limited partners who provide the capital), the alignment of interests (discouraging the moral hazard, adverse selection and opportunism) based on the confluence of the dual role in which managers are also investors and, as the case may be, investors can participate more actively in the management of the fund [10]. VCFs are usually long-term investments (7–10 years) while the other types are based on close-end investment funds (CEFs) or exchange-traded notes (ETNs) structures [11, 12]. Access to the VCF is limited to retail investors, being usually allowed only to institutional or professional investors. However, there are also distribution options for retail investors, which can be achieved through IPOs of LVCF (listed Venture Capital Funds), LPEFoF (Listed Private Equity Fund of Funds), or ETF (Exchange Traded Funds), usually for large funds and superior financing rounds. It should be mentioned that the main problems of the VCF start from the long life of the fund, the low liquidity especially in the CEIF organization, and the difficult exit especially in the case of distressed situations where investors are affected by the discount compared to the unitary value of the net asset or even worse, situations of self-liquidating funds (with portfolio sell-off). The share capital distributions are fully managed by the fund manager who, in turn, faces difficult exits from companies not listed on organized markets [13, 14].

Unlike VCFs that have a long-term orientation, hedge funds (HFs) aim at a more complex, short-term investment philosophy, based not only on conventional asset opportunities but also on an extended set of strategies (short, leverage, derivatives). Moreover, the HFs are architecturally organized in the form of open-end investment funds (OEIFs) thus providing both an easier liquidity and exit in comparison with the VCFs. It should be mentioned that the evolution of the markets has enabled the creation of hybrid strategies and structures that allow the combination of specific characteristics of the two alternative vehicles, VCFs and HFs. Thus, VCFs can invest in listed companies (a strategy also called PILF - private investments in listed firms), and HFs in private companies, mezzanine-finance, or companies in difficulty and undervalued, prepared for restructuring or subsequent resale [15–17].

The VC-cycle concept [12, 18] highlights the harmonization of fund placements with its objectives, management based on the rotation of portfolio holdings or carrying out new financing rounds, respectively the periodic liquidations of cash flows or of portfolio holdings. The key elements for the investors refer to the understanding of the general operating model of the VCF, and how to set investment programs and exit strategies.

VCFs are vehicles of great complexity, in which the processes of evaluation and financing of entrepreneurial and innovation opportunities are characterized by insufficient understanding, lack of transparency and often being perceived as having a strictly speculative character [19]. The understanding, the means of evaluating/measuring the portfolio elements, the management, and the long-term diversification of the portfolio involves professional experience and flexibility in continuously adjusting to the evolution of the industrial sectors of which the portfolio elements are part and of the economy in general [20]. In the VCF financing processes, there is an insufficiency or even a lack of clarity regarding the business model, the solutions proposed by the portfolio companies, and the exit processes [21, 22]. Thus, the role and importance of the intuition of the fund manager in the decision-making process can be essential in the successful crossing of some undesirable developments in which the transition from optimism to pessimism creates the perception of a strictly speculative character [23–25].

Despite the fact that the specialty literature highlights those periods of time when the VCFs have proved to be quite inefficient in terms of investment opportunities, there are examples of excellent collaboration among managers and investors. Investors aim to strengthen their long-term relationships to have access to recognized management funds, whereas managers focus on collaborating with investors whose main priority is the market itself and the long-term strategies, who understand market terms and conditions, with reduced sensitivity to immediate liquidity. Their goal alignment contributes both to the VCF ecosystem itself and to its resilience in uncertain times.

3. VCF portfolio assessment models

When evaluating both the value of the portfolios and of the overall fund it is essential to report the findings and the performances alike. The communication with investors and the setting up of the administration fees are because in terms of the VCF strategies there are usually more funding rounds. These events need to be geared toward specific situations (especially because there are possible entry barriers for new investors). This process should ensure precision irrespective of the evaluation process of the VCF portfolios' consistency and quality of information [13, 14, 26].

At a very early stage, the net asset value (NAV) was calculated by the fund manager himself by taking into account the evaluation of the portfolio possession as well as other listed firms for which the recent market quotes have been reduced by a liquidity risk factor or by a long-term risk. There are no similarities as far as the emerging markets are concerned. The estimation models based on discounted future cash flows (DCF methodology) are used. DCF commences with the cash flow forecast. Nonetheless, there are also permanent adjustments to the unexpected movements in the outside environment. DCF needs to be put in place in several scenarios.

The performance of VCF is metaphorically represented by the *J-curve* which is defined by the curve of different measures of performances generated by the fund on the entire lifecycle [27]. In the case of returns, the J-curve (IRR-J-curve) points at an initial period with negative returns ("the valley of tears"). The IRR internal rate of return is a relevant estimator only after this initial period of the fund itself. There are also other J-curves that can be expressed by the cash flow (i.e. CF-J-curve), namely NAV (i.e. NAV-J-curve). In terms of these quantitative indicators, one cannot make clear distinctions during the first development stage of VCF, too. Most of the time the relevant information is also based on qualitative indicators.

The NAV estimation represents a simple evaluation in itself, which fails to take into account the role of the manager in the development processes of the portfolio elements for start-ups. This evaluation is useful only for those firms that have already grown significantly. The precision and accuracy of the estimations is extremely sensitive for the unlisted portfolio elements which cannot be tested as such.

In practice, due to the obvious limitations of the VAV evaluation models the MBU (i.e. modified bottom-up) models have been suggested. They are based on setting a rating and on MCA (i.e. modified comparable approach) in which evaluation is based on a grading strategy. MBU provides extra precision for both the older portfolios and the short-term evaluations while MCA is more geared toward the new funds and the long-term approaches.

3.1 The MBU model

The MBU model is based on the understanding of the added values factors (e.g. the quality of the management, the structure of the fund, the portfolio, and the existing strategies in terms of the portfolio elements) as well as on combining them in a group based mainly on cash flow streams. The result is the target rate of return, the cost of capital, or the net present value of NPV-VCF.

Investors are not aware of the existing scenarios from the portfolio elements. The initial data comprises historical trends, the VCF manager's historical suggestions, and the stocks' progression on the secondary market. The idea of the MBU originated from the understanding of the specific metrics and the structural elements and even comprises those aspects from the memorandum or the VCF prospectus. The undertaking focuses on providing transparency in terms of the accurate value of VCF given the use of certain upgrading factors corresponding to the secondary market.

The MBU steps refer to:

- The management's historical analysis, the terms of the VCF placement memorandum as well as the portfolio's actual condition;
- The percentage of the liquidities waiting to be placed; the use of a benchmarking for the return;
- The understanding of the multiples which are expected to correspond to the elements or the portfolio possessions as well as the timeline and the strategies to exist the fund;
- The estimation of the future cash flows (in several scenarios) of the VCF;
- The identification of NPV-VCF based on the update at an appropriate rate.

3.2 Valuation model based on grading MCA

The MCA relative evaluation model is based on the examination of certain comparable or similar elements or funds. The value of the fund stems from comparing it with the values pertaining to similar funds or funds, which have been scaled to the size of the fund itself and adjusted to the qualitative differences. The actual model does not comprise the values of the individual elements but an overall estimation starting from the analogy with the previous performances of similar funds. The expected performance level (i.e. the P level, for example, a rank based on four quartiles such as P-A, P-B, P-C, and P-D) emerges from a hierarchy that refers to the following elements: the qualitative score, the quantitative score, the combination of the two elements based on the weighting with the age of the fund itself (i.e. the inclusion of the J-curve mechanism), the review and the adjustment of the hierarchies. The present rating system is based on the analogy with the rating techniques that have been used for the credit risk (bonds).

The comparables which serve as a basis for the multiples of performance have been modified based on the benchmarking data filtering according to the expected performance score (which is similar to the ratings of the bonds) by using both the qualitative and the quantitative criteria.

The steps of the evaluation methodology of the fund are as follows:

- Setting up a qualitative score which will comprise the qualitative aspects (the skills of the fund's management, the motivation and the stability of the management team, possible conflicts of interest, architectures, costs, and the validation of the investors);

- Selecting the set of comparable funds in order to suggest a quantitative score that has been calculated based on the use of IRR (and possibly on NAV or cash flow timing) of a benchmarking (a linear score between 1 and 4);

- Combining the qualitative and quantitative scores together in a performance score in order to rank the fund to be evaluated as part of the comparable set of (P-A, P-B, P-C, and P-D) funds;

- Reviewing (and adjusting) the expected performance grade based on the set of quality elements such as the portfolio's diversity level; overexposures on certain sectors; the liquidity that is needed for the support along the way of the elements that make up the VCF portfolio;

- Estimating the IRR-VCF investment return (based on the current grade of the fund, the internal age of the fund);

- Forecasting cash flows starting from the comparison of the cash flow with the historical data of other funds or by using the (Yale) scenario method based on IRR, the age of the fund, NAV (the method is useful for the understanding of certain possible future events and is being used for long-term analyzes);

- Computing NPV-VCF.

This grading system does not eliminate biases. The monitoring process is revised and adjusted continuously. The grading scale is essential when making comparisons, which inevitably can be biased.

4. Paradigms for understanding the mechanism and the evolving dynamics characterizing VCF – Implications for adapting the partnership between the fund manager and investors

There are no clearly defined theoretical concepts in the VCF literature. The authors have resorted to creating comparative metaphors or analyzing certain parallels among organizations, markets and sectors.

4.1 The complex adaptive system paradigm in VCFs (VCF-CAS)

In the first paradigm, VCF could be considered as a CAS (i.e. complex adaptive system) with a huge number of components and interactions. In this particular representation, there are mechanisms that are responsible for the behavior of the entrepreneurs and the financiers (managers and investors) alike. Schumpeter has demonstrated the spontaneous and discontinuous nature of the economic development mechanisms for which innovation plays a crucial role (credit destruction mechanism). VCF comprises innovation in multiple and extensive meanings (i.e. technical, technological, and managerial). He has highlighted a comprehensive set of factors, which interact and create elements of discontinuity (i.e. technological evolution, the change of the customers' options for products, manufacture and marketing innovation, and multiple changes in terms of mindset and social behavior). All these elements customize the set of opportunities characterizing the VCF.

Venture capital funds (VCF) stands for an interesting niche in the alternative asset market, which has to do with the technological build-ups characterizing the innovative processes that are inherently nonlinear and serve as a basis of the dynamics of the range of new opportunities. Given these complex adaptive systems, one can take notice of the manifestation of the oscillations and punctual balance. The specific aspects characterizing the innovation can be understood based on the use of the scale-free power–law distributions. VCF also represents closely coupled systems in which the movements of the participants will trigger chain reactions of the market players and nonlinear behaviors. The VCF-CAS paradigm could provide a better understanding of certain aspects characterizing the emerging markets that lack the data that are necessary to conduct quantitative analyzes.

4.2 The evolutionary theory paradigm in VCFs (VCF-ET)

The VCF uncertainty limits the possibilities for planning the flashes of portfolio whereas the management will take on improvised actions (i.e. intuiting processes). This fact represents a different approach in comparison with the classical mutual funds. Thus, Chen [28] suggested the analogy with the evolution of natural or biological phenomena in which the evolution of the species contributes to the reduction of the side effects of the changes in the environment. Nature has to deal with extreme situations in a resilient way. In the same metaphorical sense, Beinhocker [29] has stated that the evolutionary theory has a very broad meaning and that, based on learning and resilience; there will always be innovative solutions that will be available to solve problems. Therefore, the portfolio strategy could benefit from the evolutionary theory.

The VCF managers search and experience new strategies and solutions that change the rules of this particular market and bring about spectacular changes. The suggested rules are part of an evolutionary process, which is free of inferior performances and makes room for other rules in order to bring about a performance boost. This kind of adaptive scenario is continuously reshaped based on fitness processes (i.e. survival and competition). Natural selection combined with survival will forge the emerging within the fitness environment. We believe that this is the most appropriate way of understanding the possible itineraries of the set of risks corresponding to the multiple strategic scenarios. Diamond [30] suggested the landscape amnesia concept when he defined the situations when there are long periods of change and the perceptions are missed out. Although investors monitor and analyze the market, the speeds of change are difficult to anticipate (i.e. the anticipation of sectorial speculative bubbles, the differences in identifying the lifetime of the funds by the managers versus the investors, the oversubscription of the sub-optional IPOs).

The VCFs have robust adjusting structures and are thus able to cope with the change and innovation pace. Moreover, the success stories reveal genetic strategy and expertise models to the next fund generations. However, biologists have drawn attention to the frailty of the biological systems facing severe extinctions during certain periods. By analogy, there is no guarantee in terms of maintaining the VCF structures in their actual format. The main survival strategies are differentiation and specialization. Furthermore, in order to obtain long-term returns that are superior to the market benchmark portfolios one has to take into account the critical mass for the VCF value, which is essential in terms of diversification, the long-term architecture as well and its relationship with the investors as such.

4.3 The paradigm of dynamic capabilities for portfolio management-contributions in VCFs (VCF-DC) adjustment and resilience

The understanding of the competitive advantage sustainability for the fast-paced change can provide the VCF managers with strategies and solutions for adjusting to turbulent conditions and crises. In spite of the fact that the resilience concept includes strategic actions for an organization's adjustment to the current situation, there are very few applicative approaches in terms of the issue of the portfolios' management. As far as the VCF portfolios are concerned, the concepts of resilience and dynamic capabilities could provide a new approach. The fast adjustment strategies and reconfiguration of the resources together with the capabilities ensure a better understanding and a more adequate answer to the issue of the present-day markets. The sustainability of the competitive advantage for the dynamic markets refers to the reconfiguration of both the resources and the corporate capabilities.

The DCP dynamic capabilities paradigm provides a means of understanding the sustainability of the competitive advantage in fast-paced environments, namely the deepening of understanding the resources management as well as the capabilities in order to react to rapid environmental changes [31]. The dynamic capabilities support organizations not only to adjust to the environment but also in order to adjust structurally based on innovation and the partnership with other organizations and markets. The Dynamic capabilities are related to the organizational reshaping and reconfiguration according to the adequate adjustment to the environmental conditions. Organizations need to be flexible and innovative due to the fact that the competition dynamics are difficult to anticipate. The dynamic capabilities start from abilities, processes, procedures, organizational structures, and decision-making rules which promote the detection and the size of the opportunities in order to transform and adjust continuously the capabilities as such [32]. The dynamic capabilities refer to designing the resource combinations, which create value and are difficult to imitate including the coordination of the inter-organizational relationships which can provide a competitive advantage by thus representing a genuinely sustainable advantage resource for the fast-paced changing Schumpeterian regimes [33].

The implementation of the dynamic capabilities is based on the configuration of the cognition processes. However, exploring the opportunities needs to be fast and ensure the ability to learn, innovate, and integrate. The efficient use of the external knowledge needs to be accomplished based on internalization (i.e. identifying the opportunities and the learning from the acquired knowledge) and the combination (the integration) of the information together with the latest knowledge, namely the coordination with the existing understanding. The turmoil, the instabilities as well and the crises will decrease the growth potential and the organizations' survival chance, which stands for a critical aspect in terms of the VCFs. The consequence is to identify the routes and the understanding of the means to combine the existing knowledge with their capturing and processing in order to adjust efficiently to new opportunities. Furthermore, one needs to enhance these capabilities in order to take advantage of opportunities, to understand the amplification mechanisms of those capabilities in order to set up businesses that will be more resilient to the impact caused by turmoil and crises.

Organizational resilience refers to the need of an organization to deal with the rapid changes of the business environment based on the understanding of the environment's dynamic nature [34]. Organizational resilience is a universal concept that is used for the strategic actions of making an organization adjust to unexpected situations and turmoil. This concept could be extremely useful for the VCFs management [35, 36].

Organizations need to take into account behaviors and strategies such as agility, integration, leadership, change, and communication. Resilience has to do with the forecast and the prevention of unexpected threats [37]. However, certain elements such as sensitivity, the perception of change, and the management of flexible decision-making need to be incorporated, too. In the given context, resilience has become a key strategy that allows the establishment of the trends that unbalance a business from the point of view of understanding the impact and anticipating the moment of acceleration of the process of change. Having in view the present-day uncertainty context as well as the rapid changes, one needs to design a way of creative action that will be efficient in the most difficult situations, too. Consequently, a resilient organization will be able to estimate the opportunities and will be able to take advantage of the situation.

Resilience focuses on the system's ability to compensate for the distortions and the shocks, which are a result of an external phenomenon. Resilient firms are capable of facing these challenges. Survival during turmoil stems from understanding and anticipating the changing mechanisms from the point of view of the turmoil and crisis scenarios [38]. In other words, resilience is the ability to maintain the system's functionality when it experiences severe turmoil and makes it possess the ability to maintain its functionality. In the event the distortion/shock affects the system's functions significantly, it will be able to adjust itself by making use of renewal or reorganization processes.

The resilience together with the organizational resilience can be used for the VCFs portfolios' management based on the following issues:

- The ability to absorb the shocks as well as the quality of the restructuring processes of the VCF portfolio;
- The renewal ability in the event the distortions/shocks will alter or even block the portfolio's liquidity;
- The ability to evaluate, acknowledge, adjust, and absorb the variations, changes, shocks, and unexpected events [39] is essential for the VCFs portfolios, too where shakes of the portfolio are being anticipated and have a spectral nature.

Within the following theoretical development, the two paradigms—the dynamic capabilities and the organizational resilience-can be hybridized (the DCOR concept) starting from the reconfiguration stage of the operational capabilities (i.e. discovery-learning-integration-coordination) [40]. DCOR refers to designing new products and processes and implementing new organizational forms and entrepreneurial business models. Dynamic capabilities enable the understanding of the mechanisms based on which the opportunities once identified can be made to reconfigure the business when both the market and the technologies change, too. Dynamic capabilities have an indirect impact on performance based on changing the operational; capabilities into new capabilities that will blend with the environment. The organizational performance is tightly linked with the portfolios'resilient nature. In order to maintain long-term sustainable competitiveness the VCF management needs to engage in a continuous process of searching for new opportunities of interest. The understanding of the survival strategies as a critical endeavor for small funded businesses, VCF is even more important in those situations when the uncertainty on the market, the turmoil, and crises will make this endeavor more difficult to accomplish.

4.4 Implications in terms of the relationship between managers and investors

The understanding of the relationship between managers and investors differs significantly for VCF in comparison with one of the classic mutual funds. As far as emerging markets are concerned, these aspects should be more carefully studied. Irrespective of their (retail, professional, investment) nature, investors are inclined to consolidate their long-term relationships with the fund managers based on their access (through invitation or IPO) to the recognized management funds whereas the managers, on the other hand, look for investors that are concerned with understanding the market mechanisms as part of a long-term approach lacking the sensitivity for the immediate liquidity [41]. The alignment of the managers' and the investors' interests will ensure both the progress of the VCF ecosystem and the resilience in uncertain times.

5. Analyzes for portfolio investment decisions – A strategy for matching with entrepreneurial finance in Romania

5.1 Studies regarding the understanding of the investors' preferences for selecting the assets and the portfolios' management strategies

The research methodology for the portfolios' active management strategy starts from the understanding of the investors' motivation and from the possible alignment of the objectives with the offers that have been suggested by the fund managers together with the criteria used by investors to make asset valuations and the mechanisms for perceiving the investment opportunities. The given context of the research is extremely interesting due to the fact that it is an evaluative crossroads which refers to: crossing 2022 which was an extremely difficult and turbulent year for all the markets; the impact of the dynamics of the interest rates (both a direct and an indirect effect on the risk premiums); the bank crisis in the USA and its contagion effects in Europe. The present study has been done by using the CAWI (computer-assisted web interviewing) methods. The data were collected during 2 weeks (16–27th January) based on two separate questionnaires which were given to 110 retail investors (of average 45 years old, 12 years average investment experience, average investment per transaction of 9000 euros) and to 30 professional investors (of average 42 years old, 14 years average investment experience, average investment per transaction of 45000 euros). The questionnaire comprised three introductory questions referring to the educational and professional background, two questions referring to the general features of the investing behavior, and six questions that focused on understanding the retail investors' and the professional investors' attitudes, opinions, and behavior.

1. What kind of investment strategies do retail and professional investors prefer (portfolios' passive management vs. portfolios' active management)?

2. What types of investment strategies do retail and professional investors (direct investments or investments based on mutual funds or other alternative tools, which are managed by a professional)?

3. What kind of direct investments did investors prefer (at the Bucharest Stock Exchange, investments on international stock exchange, ETFs, alternative investment)?

4. What types of alternative investments were preferred (real estate; cryptocurrencies, business angels, crowdfunding; venture capital/private equity VCF/PEF funds)?

5. How do you rank the management performances of the mutual funds, which are offered by the Romanian market (satisfactory, good, very good)?

6. What solutions for improving the performances do you suggest (cutting down on the administration fees, simplified access to ETFs, easy access to the discretionary individual portfolios, speeding up the access to the alternative tools)?

After the centralization of the results it was established that:

- There are significant disparities between the two types of investors. The retail investors are 84% in favor of the passive management as compared to 9% of the professional investors;

- Eighty one percent (81%) of the retail investors are in favor of professional management, which is ensured by the mutual funds as compared with 4% of the professional investors;

- As far as the direct investments are concerned, retail investors are in favor of including equity investments at Bucharest Stock Exchange (75%), investments on international exchanges (35%), ETF exchange-traded funds (11%), alternative investments (9%) in their portfolios while professional investors prefer joint-stock investments at Bucharest Stock Exchange (67%), investments on international exchanges (65%), ETFs (41%), alternative investments (9%);

- As far as the alternative investments are concerned, retail investors prefer the context of diversification real estate investments (65%), cryptocurrencies (32%), and crowdfunding (8%) while professional investors have access to the context of the diversification of the real estate investments (48%), cryptocurrencies (43%), crowdfunding (18%) and the venture capital/private equity VC/PE (19%);

- The retail investors have considered the performances of the mutual funds on the Romanian market as follows: low (15%), good (19%), and very good (66%) while the professional investors have manifested a decreased interest in these performances based on the big commissions as low (35%), good (30%), very good (35%);

- As far as the means of enhancing the performances, investors have identified the limited possibilities of diversifying their portfolios. The retail investors have suggested cutting down on the administration fees (65%), designing a simplified access mechanism to the discretionary individual portfolios (27%), speeding up the access to the alternative tools (10%) while the professional investors have suggested the reduction of the administration fees (65%), simplified access to the ETFs (45%), a more convenient way to use the individual discretionary portfolios (4%), speeding up the access to the alternative tools (10%).

5.2 Short-interviews with entrepreneurs

The interviews were conducted with 12 entrepreneurs (of average 48 years old, 18 years of average entrepreneurial experience, and average investment per transaction of 115,000 euros) and there were six entrepreneurs who benefited from financial support within the VCF partnerships. The goal of having of this set of short- interviews with entrepreneurs was as follows:

- To understand the issues related to entrepreneurial investment decisions and the means of setting up the relevant database in order to take full advantage of the set of investment opportunities during the present-day inflationary circumstances;

- To understand the interplay between the entrepreneurs and the investors (i.e. accessibility, knowledge, communication) given the present-day situation.

After the centralization of the results it was established that:

- There are significant disparities among the investment decisions during the turbulent circumstances (the actual situation of the inflationary environments) as compared with instances of normality;

- Entrepreneurs are sometimes focused on overcoming inflation through investing in new opportunities;

- In the present circumstances the relationships between the entrepreneurs and the investors suffer from communication issues and alignment given the fact that sometimes investors over-appreciate the risk premiums in regard to the actual funding of certain opportunities.

5.3 Short-interviews with fund managers

There have been eight fund managers who have been invited to take part in the interview and only three fund managers actually responded to the questionnaire (of average 42 years old, 12 years average management experience, average investment per transaction of 1,552,000 euros).

The goal of the set of short-interviews with fund managers was to understand:

- The new trend of professional investment approach and portfolio management in the context of a limited set of market opportunities;

- The specific strategies adjusted to the present-day high inflationary environment.

After the centralization of the results it was established that:

- The present-day possibilities of diversifying the professional management portfolios continue to have a low value in our country due to the small number of transactions on the BSE stock exchange;

- Even though nowadays there are still legislation distinctions on the alternative investment funds (AIFs) and a surge of interest for these tools, access to alternative assets is still limited while investors search for innovative liquidity and scalable solutions (e.g. crowdfunding, crypto-assets) as they are not that educated and motivated by the long-term investments such as the VCFs.

6. Conclusions

Starting from the understanding of the set of actual issues characterizing the investment portfolios focusing on alternative investment vehicles (AIVs) for entrepreneurial and innovative firm financing, Section 2 provides certain peculiarities regarding the role of venture capital funds (VCFs) in emerging markets by highlighting the change of the VC-cycle countenance in the actual context of volatile and turbulent markets.

Section 3 focuses on the comparative analysis of some of the latest evaluation models of the VCF portfolios. The research had in view the MBU (modified bottom-up) models emerging from a set of historical data (i.e. the VCF placement memorandum, the portfolios' evolution, the estimated financial multiples) as well as the MCA (the modified comparable approach) in which the valuation is based on a grading strategy. It has been shown that this grading contributes to the reduction of biases, which is an interesting aspect in terms of the VCF portfolios. The role of grading in terms of VCF portfolio management is spectacular and offers new practical perspectives for the VCFs in Romania as an emergent country. The grading is used not only for valuation but also for portfolio management by offering indications of the risk, especially for the turbulent markets. These are additional models because MBU ensures extra accuracy for the stable VCF portfolios and short-term evaluations whereas MCA is geared toward both the newly founded portfolios (in which the J-curve effects can be significant) and the long-term approaches.

In Section 4 three paradigms are presented that are useful for the understanding of the VCF mechanisms and dynamics. In the paradigm of complex adaptive systems (VCF-CAS) the means in which VCFs comprise the innovation vectors is capitalized and the mechanism of setting up of the set of specific opportunities is explained. The paradigm of evolutionary theory in VCFs (VCF-ET) capitalizes on the way the VCF portfolio management strategies benefit from learning and adjusting to change as well as the creation of a responsive setting that is continuously reshaped based on fitness processes (i.e. survival and competition). The paradigm of dynamic capabilities in VCF portfolio management (VCF-DC) capitalizes on those mechanisms of getting a sustainable competitive advantage in the fast-paced changing environments based on a thorough understanding of resource management and of the abilities to respond to these dynamics. The strategic actions of maintaining and adjusting the organization to the unexpected and turbulent situations can be accomplished based on the introduction of organizational resilience. It is a very useful concept in terms of the VCFs portfolio management. The dynamic capabilities and the organizational resilience can be hybridized (the DCOR concept) starting from the reconfiguration cycle of the operational capabilities (i.e. discovery-learning-integration-coordination). These paradigms can be used for analyzing the VCF portfolios. However, there is also an impact on the means of adjusting the partnership between the fund manager and the fund investors during the volatile and turbulent periods. Investors intend to take part in recognized management funds based on IPOs while managers intend to work with investors that have long-term approaches and who are somewhat not affected by possible immediate liquidity issues.

The different ways of considering (the short-term vs. long-term) investments make room for certain discrepancies whereas the correspondence between the interests of the management investors and entrepreneurs has become a crucial goal in terms of the progress of the VCF ecosystem as well as for ensuring the critical resiliency given the volatility and the turmoil on the market.

In Section 5 we have suggested three case studies related to the decision-making process of investors, entrepreneurs, and fund managers. Based on the design of the research methodology, we have focused on highlighting the effect of joining the three approaches. The result can be traced out in understanding the shaping up of the strategies of aligning investors with entrepreneurial finance in Romania. We took into account the negative evolution of the markets in 2022 given the rise of inflation and interest rates as a result of the war in Ukraine, the energy crisis, and the recent bank crisis in the USA. The analysis of the findings has led to a series of very interesting elements.

The deepening understanding of the (retail and professional) investors' preferences for the selection of the assets and the management strategies of the VCF portfolios are based on the use of the CAWI (computer-assisted web interviewing) method whereas the data has been collected during 2 weeks (16–27th January) as a result of using two distinct questionnaires that have been used on 110 retail investors (investors of average 45 years old, 12 years average investment experience, average investment per transaction of 9000 euros) and 30 professional investors (investors of average 42 years old, 14 years of average investment experience, average investment per transaction of 45,000 euros). The questionnaire comprised three introductory questions referring to education and professional background, two questions referring to general features of investment behavior, and two questions referring to experience in investment decisions. The main part consisted of six questions aimed at understanding the retail and professional investors' attitudes, opinions, and behavior given the present-day volatility and turmoil in the market which is significantly influenced by the high inflation rates.

The first study has shown that there is a very high confidence and openness among the investors for the latest tools and creative performance strategies. There are major differences between the retail and the professional investors (i.e. the preference for active management, the acceptance of externally managed elements based on the mutual funds of VCFs in the individual portfolios, an openness toward the inclusion of a sub-portfolio for alternative investment within the actual portfolios). However, there are certain common features characterizing our country (both categories of investors are interested in short-term treasury bonds as well as in crypto-assets and real estate investments).

Another aspect has to do with the interest in the active management of the portfolios and the inclusion of in some sub-portfolios of the alternative assets in which the interest for the VC/PE funds is diminished while there is an incredible interest for crowdfunding and crypto-assets.

The second case study focused on the issue related to entrepreneurial investment decisions and the means of designing the relevant database for a deeper understanding of the set of investment opportunities given the present-day inflationary circumstances, namely the understanding of the relationships between entrepreneurs and investors. The interview was conducted with six entrepreneurs (of average 48 years old, 18 years of average entrepreneurial experience, average investment per transaction of 115,000 euros) who were the beneficiaries of funding within the VCF partnerships in Romania.

Romanian entrepreneurs are very rigid when it comes to business control and they are reluctant to involve the VCF in the funding processes. We have even identified significant evaluation disparities in our relationship with the investors.

The third case study referred to short- interviews with three fund managers (of average 42 years old, 12 years average in the field of asset management, and average assets per transaction of 1,552,000 E). The goal was to understand the new trend of professional investment approach and portfolio management together with the specific strategies adjusted to this complicated inflationary environment.

The main contributions of the present research are as follows

- To understand the adjustment of the VC cycle for a better alignment of the fund's placements with its goals as well as the means of designing certain flexibility solutions for the portfolio management issues (i.e. the rotation of the sub-portfolios, the management of the latest rounds of financing, namely the regular liquidations of the cash flows or of holdings of portfolios);

- To design the comparative analysis of the valuation models of the VCF portfolios in emerging markets with a special focus on grading methodology which fails to have a predictive power and an early possible warning tool;

- To design the means of putting into practice those three paradigms for the understanding of the evolutionary mechanisms and dynamics characterizing the VCF as well as to formulate the implications for adjusting the partnership between the fund manager and the investors;

- To use the dynamic capabilities and organizational resilience paradigms within a hybridized concept starting from the reconfiguration cycle of the operational capabilities (i.e. discovery-learning-coordination) which will have an impact both on the internal VCFs processes and on the means of implementing the latest organizational solutions in order to partner fund investors with entrepreneurs.

- To put in practice the investigations from Section 5 from a triple perspective (i.e. investors-entrepreneurs- fund managers).

The limits and future research are:

In spite of the fact that BSE was inaugurated only in 1996 in Romania, investors have adjusted and have focused on understanding the market mechanisms. As far as Romania is concerned, investment opportunities remain low, whereas the actual communication among investors, fund managers, and entrepreneurs is limited. Database shortage has restricted the development of some relevant qualitative research, yet our suggested case studies have provided extra knowledge in the field under discussion.

Future research could focus on the following issues: the use of the assessment methodologies of the portfolios, a deeper understanding of the interactions between entrepreneurs and investors (starting from issues such as accessibility, knowledge, and communication), finding solutions for the reduction of the obstacles in making VCF investment partnerships, highlighting the means of dealing with the investment biases characterizing the VCFs.

Author details

Gabriela Prelipcean[1*] and Mircea Boscoianu[2]

1 Stefan cel Mare University of Suceava, Romania

2 Transilvania University of Brasov, Romania

*Address all correspondence to: gprelipcean@yahoo.com

References

[1] Kahneman D, Tversky A, editors. Choices, Values, and Frames. Cambridge University Press; 2000

[2] Prelipcean G, Boscoianu M. Risk analysis of a hedge fund oriented on sustainable and responsible investments for emerging markets. Amfiteatru Economic. 2020;**22**(55):653-667

[3] Pohoata I, Bostan I, Prelipcean G, et al. Equity, intra/inter-generation equalization and profit, in the context of the right to a healthy life and a clean environment. Revista Română de Bioetică. 2014;**12**(2):58-69

[4] Amit R, Brander J, Zott C. Why do venture capital firms exist? Theory and canadian evidence. Journal of Business Venturing. 1998;**13**(6):441-466

[5] Bradley DJ, Jordan BD, Roten IC, Yi HC. Venture capital and IPO lockup expiration: An empirical analysis. Journal of Financial Research. 2001;**24**(4):465-493

[6] Cochrane JH. The risk and return of venture capital. Journal of Financial Economics. 2005;**75**(1):3-52

[7] Dimov D, Murray G. The determinants of the incidence and scale of seed capital investments by venture capital firms. Small Business Economics. 2008;**30**(2):127-152

[8] Gompers PA. Optimal investment, monitoring, and the staging of venture capital. Journal of Finance. 1995;**50**(5):1461-1489

[9] Hisrich RD, Jankowitz AD. Intuition in venture capital decisions: Exploratory study using a new technique. Journal of Business Venturing. 1990;**5**:49-62

[10] Dushnitzky G, Lenox MJ. When do incumbents learn from entrepreneurial ventures? Corporate venture capital and investing firm innovation rates. Research Policy. 2005;**34**(5):615-639

[11] DeAngelo H. The capital-structure puzzle: What are we missing? Journal of Financial and Quantitative Analysis. 2022;**57**(2):413-454

[12] Gompers P, Kovner A, Lerner J, Scharfstein D. Venture capital investment cycles: The impact of public markets. Journal of Financial Economics. 2008;**87**(1):1-23

[13] Kaplan SN, Stromberg P. Characteristics, contracts, and actions: Evidence from venture capitalist analyses. Journal of Finance. 2004;**59**(5):2177-2210

[14] Kaplan SN, Schoar A. Private equity performance: Returns, persistence, and capital flows. Journal of Finance. 2005;**60**(4):1791-1823

[15] Lhabitant F-S. Hedge Funds–Quantitative Insights. Chichester: John Wiley & Sons; 2004

[16] Lhabitant F-S, Learned M. Hedge fund diversification: How much is enough. The Journal of Alternative Investments. 2002;**5**(3):23-49

[17] Prelipcean G, Boscoianu M, Lupan M, Nastase CE. Innovative financing solutions based on venture capital and private equity to support the development of entrepreneurship in Romania. Transformation in Business and Economics. 2014;**13**(3C):331-347

[18] Gompers PA, Lerner J. The Money of Invention–How Venture Capital Creates New Wealth. Harvard; 2001

[19] Prado TS, Bauer JM. Big Tech platform acquisitions of start-ups and venture capital funding for innovation. Information Economics and Policy. 2022;**59C**:S0167624522000129

[20] Bingham CB, Eisenhardt KM. Rational heuristics: The simple rules that strategist learn from process experience. Strategic Management Journal. 2011;**32**:1437-1464

[21] Weidig T, Mathonet PY. The risk profiles of private equity. Risk Management eJournal. 2004

[22] Boscoianu M, Prelipcean G. Flexible adaptation of innovative investment funds architectures dedicated for technological SMEs. In: Proceedings of the STRATEGICA International Academic Conference-Eighth Edition; 15-16 October 2020; Bucharest, Romania. Preparing for Tomorrow, Today. 2020. pp. 421-432

[23] Li Y, Mahoney JT. When are venture capital projects initiated? Journal of Business Venturing. 2001;**26**(2):239-254

[24] Li Y. Duration analysis of venture capital staging: A real options perspective. Journal of Business Venturing. 2008;**23**(5):497-512

[25] Wang S, Zhou H. Staged financing in venture capital: Moral hazard and risks. Journal of Corporate Finance. 2004;**10**(1):131-155

[26] Mathonet P-Y, Monjanel G. Valuation guidelines for private equity and venture capital funds: A survey. Journal of Alternative Investments. 2006

[27] Meyer T, Mathonet P-Y. Beyond the J Curve: Managing a Portfolio of Venture Capital and Private Equity Funds. Willey; 2005

[28] Chen J. An analytical theory of project investment: A comparison with real option theory. International Journal of Managerial Finance. 2006;**2**(4):354-363

[29] Beinhocker ED. The Origin of Wealth: Evolution, Complexity, and the Radical Remaking of Economics. Harvard: Harvard Business Press; 2006

[30] Diamond J. Collapse: How Societies Choose to Fail or Survive. New York and London: Viking Penguin/Allen Lane; 2005

[31] Wang CL, Ahmed PK. Dynamic capabilities: A review and research agenda. International Journal of Management Reviews. 2007;**9**(1):31-51

[32] Rindova VP, Kotha S. Contiuous "morphing": Capabilities, form, and function. Academy of Management Journal. 2011;**44**(6):1263-1280

[33] Zahra SA, Sapienza HJ, Davidsson P. Entrepreneurship and dynamic capabilities: A review, model and research agenda. Journal of Management Studies. 2006;**43**(4):917-955

[34] Hamel G, Välikangas L. The quest for resilience. Harvard Business Review. 2003;**81**:52-63

[35] Bhamra RS, Dani S, Burnard KJ. Resilience: The concept, a literature review and future directions. International Journal of Production Research. 2011;**49**(18):5375-5393

[36] Huang L, Knight A. Resources and relationships in entrepreneurship: An exchange theory of the development and effects of the entrepreneur-investor relationship. Academy of Management Review. 2017;**42**:80-102

[37] Conger RD, Donnellan MB. An interactionist perspective on the

socioeconomic context of human development. Annual Review of Psychology. 2007;**58**:175-199

[38] Breen B, Hamel G. The Future of Management. Harvard Business School Press; 2007

[39] Hollnagel E. Resilience: The challenge of the unstable. In: Hollnagel E, Woods DD, Leveson N, editors. Resilience Engineering: Concepts and Precepts. Aldershot: Ashgate; 2006

[40] Pavlou PA, El Sawy OA. Understanding the elusive black box of dynamic capabilities. Decision Sciences. 2011;**42**(1):239-273

[41] Lerner J, Schoar A. The illiquidity puzzle: Theory and evidence from private equity. Journal of Financial Economics. 2002;**72**(1):3-40

Chapter 5

Investment Indicators and Economic Growth in Nigeria: A Systematic Review

Abdulkarim Yusuf

Abstract

Most developing countries, including Nigeria, are stuck in a vicious cycle of low investment caused by insufficient domestic savings, resulting in inadequate capital formation and a large savings-investment gap. Given the significance of investment in poverty alleviation and economic growth, the study conducted a disaggregated analysis of various measures of investment in economic growth in Nigeria from 1981 to 2020. Using the conventional and structural break stationarity tests, as well as the Autoregressive Distributed Lag (ARDL) approach, the epistemological findings confirm a compelling co-integrating relationship among the study variables and show that credit to the private sector, domestic investment, economic liberalization, foreign portfolio investment, and interest rate have a significant positive impact on long-term growth, whereas foreign direct investment, capital expenditure, and inflation have a significant negative impact. Furthermore, the short-run results revealed that economic liberalization, private-sector credit, and portfolio investment all correlate positively with growth. In contrast, foreign direct investment, infrastructure spending, and inflation rate are profoundly negative. The study, therefore, advocated for effective fiscal and monetary policy coordination to lower the cost of doing business, incentivize and open up opportunities for domestic and foreign investors, increase infrastructure spending to create jobs, reduce poverty and sustain growth.

Keywords: ARDL co-integration, domestic investment, economic growth, foreign direct investment, foreign portfolio investment, unit root test

1. Introduction

Investment entails the purchase or acquisition of new capital equipment such as machines, buildings, and other means of production that boost the economy's productive capacity. It encourages long-run economic growth by producing new capital goods and expanding countries' production efficiency. The level of growth in any economy is a reliable predictor of the country's ability to invest and allocate resources effectively [1]. Countries see investment as a major element in increasing productivity by advancing technological progress and reducing unemployment as they advance

 IntechOpen

toward economic growth. Investment is regarded as the engine of dynamic economic growth, which in turn contributes to the achievement of political and socioeconomic goals. Fluctuations in investment have a significant impact not only on aggregate demand, but also on an economy's factor productivity and long-term economic growth [2]. This has prompted several countries to concentrate on improving favorable investment conditions.

Investment comprises both domestic and foreign components that can be broadly classified into four key components: the private domestic investment (private investment), public domestic investment (government investment), Foreign Direct Investment (FDI), and Foreign Portfolio Investment (FPI). Government and public corporations invest in social infrastructure, real estate, and tangible assets through public domestic investment [3]. Public investment is needed to construct the infrastructure and social capital necessary for private sector investments in sectors of the economy that provide higher returns on investments [4]. Because private initiative and resources are limited in developing countries, the government must create an enabling environment through fiscal stimulus sufficient to encourage the growth of private investment. Public investment in key sectors of the economy should thus serve as a catalyst for economic growth. However, public investment is usually made for political reasons and thus lacks economic justification [5].

Private investment may be complemented by public investment in goods that improve the productivity of private capital, such as infrastructure. Economic growth is boosted by public investment because it encourages new private investment to benefit from the higher productivity it generates. When the government invests in public goods like physical infrastructures or services, it offers companies a chance to invest, which creates an economic cycle of opportunity [2]. Public investment boosts output, attracts private investment, and reduces unemployment. Furthermore, governments can encourage private investment through public spending by creating an appropriate political and institutional setting that minimizes uncertainty. Governments can implement public incentives like tax cuts or subsidizing policies that motivate private firms to invest in projects [6].

According to the traditional Keynesian model, an increase in government spending will lead to an increase in total demand, which will lead to an increase in total investment and employment. Keynesians frequently cite the multiplier effect as proof that government spending can effectively boost private sector investment. Neoclassical economists, on the other hand, reject this notion and contend that government spending can suppress consumer spending and private investment through interest rates or the tax structure [6]. Crowding-out effects result from two investments competing for the same resources and from a decline in private sector productivity as a result of a larger public sector. As a result of competition for limited material and financial resources, a larger fiscal deficit brought on by increased public investment may also drive away private investment through high interest rates, credit restrictions, and increased current or future tax burdens on households. In other words, countries are unable to convert additional public investment into consistently high output growth when there is a lack of absorptive capacity [7].

According to Kumo [8], private investment refers to investments made in the private sector with the intention of making a profit. It is a fundamental economic operating principle in a market-based economy where physical and financial resources are frequently privately owned and production choices are motivated by the pursuit of profit. Private investment has the potential to increase the economy's productivity and efficiency by leveraging resources and making smart investment decisions [9]. Thus, private investment is a crucial precondition for economic growth because it enables business owners to launch economic activity by effectively allocating resources to produce goods and services. According to conventional wisdom, private investment affects growth more significantly and positively than public investment. Productivity in the private sector is typically higher than that of the public sector due to the relative lower level of corruption there [6].

The ability of the private sector to allocate and use resources effectively, as well as its contributions to the volume of gross domestic investment, are both critical. The provision of infrastructure and social services, as well as the creation of jobs and income, have all been fueled by private sector investment. The private sector has the potential to produce equitable and sustainable growth in developing nations, according to the European Commission (EU) [10]. According to the International Finance Corporations (IFC) [11], the private sector plays a significant role in addressing the developmental challenges faced by emerging nations by providing contributions in a variety of areas, such as growth, employment, poverty reduction, service provision, food security, climate change mitigation, environmental sustainability, and tax contributions. This means that at the very least, the existence of the private sector can encourage economic growth and the eradication of poverty.

Private investment involves making wise investment decisions, whereas public investment is frequently perceived as being politically motivated and lacking in economic reason. Countries see increased private investment as a crucial factor in boosting productivity levels by expediting technological advancement and bringing down the unemployment rate as they move toward economic expansion. By producing new capital assets and boosting countries' production efficiency, it encourages long-term capital accumulation [7]. Since the private sector has continued to be one of the primary drivers of growth in contemporary economies all over the world, developing countries have given it more attention [12]. As a result, there is currently a paradigm shift from government to private sector-led growth policies, emphasizing the dominance of market forces in the economy and the reduction of the role of the public sector in production. The public sector needs to re-evaluate its part in the growth process in light of the new paradigm. The rule states that public-sector spending must be focused on initiatives that complement rather than supplant private-sector investment [13].

Gitahi et al. [14] argued that developing countries should aim for and maintain a level of private investment of at least 25% of GDP in order to sustain growth and poverty reduction. They noted the significance of private investment in contributing to economic growth, including its capacity to efficiently allocate and employ resources. Bage [15] came to the conclusion that investment rates between 20% and 25% could lead to growth rates between 7% and 8% based on the experiences of Asian nations. Between 1999 and 2019, Nigeria's average private investment as a percentage of GDP was less than 15% [16]. This percentage is lower than that obtainable in most Sub-Saharan African economies and that needed to achieve higher growth rates [17]. Despite a significant increase in government fiscal operations in recent years aimed at increasing private sector-led growth, the stylized reality in Nigeria demonstrates that private investment growth has been noticeably unacceptable and has continued to decline [18].

Foreign capital inflows are important mechanisms for moving resources from developed to developing nations, where they are typically more productive. To close the savings and foreign exchange gap, capital inflows are required from countries with low wealth creation. Given that those economies rely so heavily on foreign sources for their productivity expansion, these foreign capitals augment domestically sourced capitals [19]. The consistent rise in international financial trades is what has led to a considerable boost in capital inflows into economies around the world. The increased globalization of investors seeking greater rates of return on investment over time and the chance to diversify risk globally has also been a fundamental factor underlying this experience. As a result, many economies have removed restrictions that hinder capital inflows in order to promote the inflow of globally mobile capital.

Foreign portfolio investments, foreign direct investments (or foreign aids and grants), foreign remittances, Official Development Assistance (ODA), and foreign loans are all examples of this inflow of foreign capital. The main benefit of the influx of foreign capital is that it promotes growth, especially in the nations that attracted it. For least developed countries (LDCs), FDI is regarded as a significant source of capital formation, technological know-how, employment creation, and trade opportunities [20]. The widely acknowledged benefits of FDI include filling the gap between domestically mobilized savings and desired investment, increasing tax revenues, and enhancing management, technology, and labor skills in host countries. These might assist the nation in breaking the cycle of underdevelopment [21]. The reduction of poverty in the host economies may be affected directly or indirectly by foreign direct investment.

By indirect impact, we mean that FDI may encourage the reduction of poverty through economic growth, which elevates living standards as a result of rising GDP, advances in technology and productivity, and changes in the business climate. On the other hand, FDI may directly contribute to the reduction of poverty through the creation of jobs and the generation of income as a result of the rise in the demand for jobs among foreign investors [22]. Because foreign investors typically have better investment arrangements and an understanding of the economic dynamics of the host country, FDI is also thought to be less vulnerable to crises. As a result, parties involved in developing economies typically assume that FDI inflow will bring the much-needed capital, new technologies, marketing strategies, and management skills.

Due to the overwhelming significance of FDI, governments in developing nations, including Nigeria, are paying more attention to the potential benefits of attracting significant FDI. Even though it seems reasonable to claim that FDI can increase knowledge spill overs to host economies, a host country's ability to capitalize on and profit from these externalities might be constrained by its own domestic economic circumstances, which include an underdeveloped financial market and unregulated domestic industries. Additionally, since a sizable portion of FDI enters the country through mergers and acquisitions, a healthy stock market is better for the host economy. This has the potential to expand the sources of financing available to businesses, and consequently, play a significant role in fostering connections between domestic and international investors [20].

Foreign Portfolio Investment (FPI) refers to foreign investments in stocks, bonds, and other securities. FPI is a subset of global capital flows that include the transfer of financial assets like cash, stocks, and bonds across international borders in an effort to increase profits [23]. It includes transfers and financial assets like stocks or bonds that take place when investors buy non-controlling stakes in foreign corporations or government bonds, short-term securities, or notes, or buy foreign corporate or government securities. When foreigners deposit money in a nation's banks or make purchases on its stock and bond markets, sometimes for speculative reasons in search of a profit, that nation's financial system has received foreign funds. Debt and equity financial assets are included in portfolio investments in this way [19].

For foreign investors, Nigeria's government has opened up a number of economic sectors and provided a number of incentives. Foreign portfolio flows have been promoted through liberalization with the primary goal of enhancing market activity and access to foreign capital [24]. Given that emerging markets have a low correlation to developed ones, foreign investors have been motivated to diversify their holdings, protect themselves against risk, and earn higher returns in these markets. By elevating foreign portfolio investment to a significant source of investible funds to support investment in both developed and developing nations, these developments have increased the variety of investment opportunities available. As trade flows result from people, businesses, and nations taking advantage of their own comparative advantages, capital and accumulated assets also move to the areas which are likely to be most productive [23].

Even a casual observer of Africa is likely to be aware that very few African nations have Nigeria's level of economic potential. The nation is abundantly endowed with both natural and human resources. With a GDP of over USD 420 billion and an estimated population of over 211 million (National Population Commission, [25] estimate), Nigeria provides investors with a cheap labor pool, a wealth of natural resources, and perhaps the largest domestic market on the African continent. The nation has a large amount of arable land and favorable environmental factors that support agricultural activities. Nigeria has the second-largest oil reserves in Africa. Along with having abundant oil and gas reserves, the nation also has about 37 solid mineral types that are commercially available but have not yet been fully utilized. These minerals can be used in a variety of fields, including construction, pharmaceuticals, food processing, and other manufacturing processes [20]. Nigeria has a vast resource base, but the nation has not been able to grow its economy significantly or draw in foreign or portfolio investment on a par with its economic potential [19]. This is due to a lack of strong capital and money markets, poor infrastructure, corruption, an ineffective system for registering properties, an inconsistent regulatory environment, restructured trade policies, and slow and ineffective courts and dispute resolution procedures [12].

Nigeria has been categorized as an economy with low savings and even lower investment [7]. The government implemented a number of policies and reform initiatives, including the National Economic Empowerment and Development Strategy (NEEDS), privatization, and commercialization of federal and state-owned enterprises, to escape this low savings and low investment trap. Access to credit instruments offered by financial institutions has been made easier thanks to Nigeria's foreign investment regime being liberalized by the Nigerian Investment Promotion Commission Decree of 1995. The lack of investable funds or their low availability, particularly in the productive sectors of the economy, has in turn been blamed for the unfavorable investment environment. Evidently, promoting balanced investment in physical and financial assets as well as human, natural, and environmental capital is necessary for the promotion of sustained economic growth [9].

The difference between the current rate of savings in LDCs and the required rate of investment is enormous. The Brussels Declaration set 30 global development objectives for LDCs, including a 25% investment to GDP ratio and a minimum 7% annual GDP growth rate for LDCs to achieve sustainable development and poverty reduction [26]. In order to achieve the desired level of economic growth, which is essential for achieving the Sustainable Development Goals (SDGs) and reducing poverty, the Nigerian government must figure out how to encourage both domestic and foreign investment. The current study, which takes into account the importance of time horizons in econometric modeling, offers insightful information to policymakers worried about the expansion of domestic and foreign investment by robustly evaluating the long- and short-term effects of disaggregated investment measures on Nigeria's economic buoyancy and prosperity using annual data from 1981 to 2020 and the Autoregressive Distributed Lag (ARDL) methodology. Following is the format for the remaining section of the paper: The study's theoretical foundation is covered in Section 2, and the methods and procedures that were used to conduct the study are covered in Section 3. Following section five, which wraps up the study and offers policy recommendations, section four discusses the empirical findings.

2. Theoretical background of the research

Theoretical research on the relationship between investment and economic growth is quite extensive and has produced a class of well-defined theories, including but not limited to the accelerator theory, Jorgensen's neoclassical or user cost theory, and Tobin's Q theory of investment, which provided the theoretical underpinning for this study.

2.1 The accelerator theory of investment

Although it gained popularity after Keynes, the accelerator theory can be traced at least as far back as Clark [27]. The theory is based on the investment philosophies of Keynes [28], Samuelson [29], and Chenery [30]. According to Clark [27], the demand for capital varies more with the acceleration of that demand than with the volume of demand for the finished good. The model is known as the simple accelerator model of investment and is thought to have Keynesian roots due to Clark's emphasis on quantity rather than price. The basic accelerator model only considers output growth when explaining investment and presupposes that the desired level of capital is reached every time period. According to the accelerator principle, a company's increased output rate will necessitate a corresponding increase in its capital stock.

According to the accelerator theory, investment will be impacted by changes in the variables affecting national income. The relationship between increases in investment and income growth is represented numerically by the accelerator. If national income rises, it would typically be positive; if national output or income stays the same, it might be zero [29]. Based on the acceleration theory, a change in output directly affects how much demand there is for capital goods. The relationship between the capital-output ratio and the change in output level determines how much the demand for capital goods has changed. Since changes in aggregate output are dependent on changes in aggregate expenditure or aggregate demand, which themselves equal changes in the level of equilibrium income, we can say that total investment in the economy is dependent on changes in aggregate demand at any given time period, which in equilibrium equals increases in the national income plus replacement investment, which is frequently assumed constant [14].

According to the accelerator theory, investment changed as a linear function of output changes. It highlights the importance of demand conditions as the primary factor influencing investment. The demand for factories and machinery is deduced from the demand for the company's goods. So, as demand or profits increase in an economy, so do business investments. It suggests that businesses have two options for meeting demand when supply levels result in excess demand. To balance demand, they either increase investment or raise prices to reduce demand [30]. According to the theory, most companies choose to boost output and profits. In addition, the theory explains how this expansion draws in more investors, which invigorates growth. The model, however, has over time been retooled into several versions used in scientific inquiry, including the simple and flexible accelerator model, the partial adjustment model, and the crowding-out and crowding-in accelerator model, since it neglects the impact on investment of uncertainty, expectations, profits, financial factors, and capital cost [30–33].

2.2 Jorgensen's neo-classical/user cost of capital theory of investment

The user cost of capital theory, proposed by Jorgensen [34] and Jorgensen [35], states that a firm weighs the costs and benefits of investment and invests when the benefits outweigh the costs [36]. The theory is founded on the neoclassical theory of optimal capital accumulation, which is determined by the relative prices of production factors. The model attempts to assess the benefit and cost of capital ownership. The model, which is based on Keynes' original approach, attempts to relate the level of investment to the Marginal Efficiency of Capital, the interest rate, and the tax rules that affect firms.

If a perfect capital market exists, the firm will maximize its present value by investing in all projects with positive total expected returns at the current market rate of interest. According to Irving Fisher [37], all productive projects can be ranked based on their rate of return over cost. Firms will continue to invest as long as the rate of return exceeds the market rate of interest because doing so increases capital accumulation or investment. The theory held that because consumption is a function of disposable income, and savings is income not spent, while investment is income spent. This means that savings and investment are also determined by disposable income. This theory contends that savings determine investment and is primarily concerned with market equilibrium and economic growth at full employment rather than resource underutilization [38].

2.3 Tobin's Q theory of investment

According to Tobin's [39] Q theory of investment, investment is made until the market value of assets equals the replacement cost of assets. The Tobin average q is calculated using stock market data on the value of the firm's share price. The theory identified a link between investment fluctuations and stock market fluctuations. When firms have many opportunities, stock/share prices in the stock market tend to be high (as it entails high investment and high returns to shareholders). As a result, stock prices demonstrate the incentive to invest [40]. The theory is a positive function of q, which is defined as the ratio of the market value of existing capital to the cost of capital replacement. Q is a barometer for investors because it evaluates a company's prospects. Q can be defined as.

2.4 Stock value of firms/replacement cost of investment

When q is greater than one, the firm will increase its investment because the profits generated will exceed the cost of the firm's assets. If Q is less than one, the firm would be better off selling its assets rather than attempting to use them because the firm's value is less than the cost of reproducing their capital. The ideal state is when Q is close to one, indicating that the firm is in equilibrium [41]. An unstable political climate may also discourage investment or lead to high levels of inflation, which would lower the rate of national growth. For investors, inflation volatility breeds uncertainty regarding the viability of potential projects. It is an established fact that fiscal deficits can discourage private investment. Political instability is also likely to reduce policymakers' time horizons, which will result in less-than-ideal macroeconomic short-term policies. Additionally, it might cause policy changes to occur more frequently, which would increase volatility and harm economic growth [42].

The assumptions underlying the widespread optimizing investment models typically are not met in developing nations like Nigeria because of institutional and structural factors like the absence of well-functioning financial markets, the relative larger role of the government in capital formation, distortions brought on by foreign exchange restrictions, and other market imperfections [9]. Besides, when attempts are made to apply the standard models empirically, severe data limitations arise even if they could be directly adjusted to the Nigerian situation. For instance, most developing nations lack data on factors like the stock of capital, the labor force, and wages, and without knowledge of real financing rates (debt and equity), it is difficult to determine the service price or user cost of capital. In economies like Nigeria where independent public institutions play a relatively important role, there are also serious conceptual issues with defining private investment; it is frequently questionable whether such enterprises should be classified as part of the public sector or part of the private sector [43]. Overall, it is probably reasonable to assume that these various issues have historically tended to make it difficult to model investment for developing countries along conventional theoretical lines.

3. Data and methodology

In order to offer empirical solutions to the research problems, this study used the quantitative approach and a descriptive research design. Answering who, what, when, where, and how questions about a research problem is made easier by descriptive research designs [9]. Secondary data sourced from the Central Bank of Nigeria (CBN), the National Bureau of Statistics (NBS), and the statistical database for the World Development Indicators were used for this study. The subjects of the data collection included the Real Gross Domestic Product (RGDP), various components of investment disaggregated into Foreign Direct Investment Inflow as a percentage of GDP (FDI), Foreign Portfolio Investment (PINV), Gross Fixed Capital Formation as a percentage of GDP (GFCF) (proxy for private investment), and Government Capital Expenditure (CAPEX) (proxy for public investment), and control variables such as Domestic Credit to Private Sector (CPS), Inflation rate (INFR), Effective Interest rate (INTR) and Economic Liberalization (ELB) adopted as a dummy variable, respectively. Economic liberalization was included in the model as a dummy variable and measured with the value of 1 in years 1986–1993 and 2007–2020 when major attempt at economic liberalization started in Nigeria. All variables were taken on annual basis in nominal and percentage terms from 1981 to 2020. Data on RGDP, CAPEX, CPS and PINV taken in nominal forms were log-transformed to stabilize the variance of the series and make interpretation in proportionate terms while the GFCF, INFR and INTR retained their percentage form. E-views 12 statistical package was utilized for data analysis.

Following the lead of Omojolaibi et al. [44], Kengdo et al. [45] and Babu et al. [9], the study modeled economic growth proxy by RGDP as a function of disaggregated forms of investment and the afore-mentioned control variables. In accordance with the literature and the study's objectives, an Autoregressive Distributed Lag (ARDL) model with modifications, presented in its general form as an unrestricted error-correction model (UECM) regression from which all tests and estimations are conducted was devised and specified as follows:

$$\begin{aligned}\Delta Ln\ RGDP_t &= \propto_0 + \propto_1 \mathrm{LnRGDP}_t + \propto_2 \mathrm{ELB}_{t+} \propto_3 \mathrm{FDI}_t + \propto_4 \mathrm{GFCF}_t + \propto_5 \mathrm{INFR}_t \\ &+ \propto_6 \mathrm{INTR}_t + \propto_7 \mathrm{LnCAPEX}_t + \propto_8 \mathrm{LnCPS}_t + \propto_8\ \mathrm{PINV}_t + \sum_{i=0}^{n} \beta_1 \Delta \mathrm{LnRGDP}_t \\ &+ \sum_{i=0}^{n} \beta_2 \Delta ELB_t + \sum_{i=0}^{n} \beta_3 \Delta FDI_t + \sum_{i=0}^{n} \beta_4 \Delta GFCF_t + \sum_{i=0}^{n} \beta_5 \Delta \mathrm{INFR}_t + \sum_{i=0}^{n} \beta_6 \Delta \mathrm{INTR}_t \\ &+ \sum_{i=0}^{n} \beta_7 \Delta \mathrm{Ln\ CAPEX}_t + \sum_{i=0}^{n} \beta_8 \Delta LnCPS_t + \sum_{i=0}^{n} \beta_9 \Delta Ln\mathrm{PINV}_t + ECT_{t-1} + \mathcal{E}_t,\end{aligned} \tag{1}$$

where $\propto_0$ = Intercept and i is the lag indicator. $\propto_2$, $\propto_3$, $\propto_4$, $\propto_5$, $\propto_6$, $\propto_7$, $\propto_8$, and $\propto_9$ represent the long-run multipliers which show the long-run effects of the identified determinants of investment on economic growth to be calculated. Δ =Denotes the first difference operator, t = deterministic time trend consisting of years from 1981 to 2020. β_2, β_3, β_4, β_5, β_6, β_7, β_8 and β_9 are the short-run dynamic coefficients which help to estimate the error correction mechanism and the model's convergence to equilibrium. k is the number of explanatory variables, and ξ is the disturbance term that is uncorrelated with the x's. while ECT_{t-1} is the error correction term's one-period lag value and the speed adjustment parameter that gauges how quickly the variables, in the event of a disturbance, returned from short-run disequilibrium to long-run equilibrium. The coefficient must be negative, less than one and statistically significant in order to achieve long-run equilibrium. The coefficient's value provides the long-run annual path to equilibrium GDP. A test of the disturbance term, $\mathscr{E}_t$, can confirm that the regression includes an adequate lag length. If the error series is serially uncorrelated and indicative of a white noise process, the lag lengths included are sufficient.

3.1 Estimation procedure

The co-integration relationship between the variables, which must first be established before the long-run and short-run relationships are ascertained, was examined using the ARDL bounds test developed by Pesaran and Shin [46]. One of the most important characteristics of co-integrated variables, according to Pesaran and Shin [46], is that they have a propensity to react to any shock that could require a break from long-run predictability. As a result, the ARDL method's error correction model illustrates the degree to which the variables are vulnerable to short-run shocks on the one hand, as well as the measure of such variations caused by the shocks that are adjusted within a year. The ARDL has been widely used in recent empirical analysis due to its robustness, reliability, and statistical properties, which are thought to be superior to other long-run analytical techniques in the literature. When compared to other previous and traditional co-integration methods of Engle and Granger [47] and the maximum likelihood method postulated by Johansen; Johansen and Juselius [48] which call for a lengthy sample period and all variables to be I (1), the ARDL methodology has a number of advantages.

The first is that the ARDL approach does not require that all variables under study be integrated in the same order and can be used whether the underlying variables are integrated in order one, order zero, or a combination of both. This model, however, cannot be used when the underlying variables are integrated of order I. (2). None of the variables in this study were integrated of order I. (2). As a result, the econometric methodology is eased of the burden of deciding the order of integration among variables and pre-testing for unit roots [49]. However, Pesaran and Shin [46] clarified that the dependent variable should be first difference stationary to ensure the validity of the co-integrating relationship.

According to Rahman and Islam [50], the presence of any I(2) variable(s) may cause the system to crash. As a result, performing some efficient unit root tests to ensure that no I(2) variable(s) is/are present in the model is desirable. Second, when the ARDL technique is used, unbiased estimates of the long-run and short-run parameters of the study variables can be estimated simultaneously, as can the speed of adjustment to long-run equilibrium precipitated by any short-run exogenous shocks. The ARDL approach to co-integration was chosen for its suitability, particularly in studies with relatively small samples, such as the present study. Pesaran and Shin [46] asserted that in the presence of small and finite sample data sizes, the short and long-run parameters calculated using the ARDL technique are relatively more efficient, robust, and better. Furthermore, in comparison to vector autoregressive (VAR) models, the ARDL model can accommodate a greater number of variables and is more adaptable in terms of lag structure because it can incorporate various optimal lag structures for distinct variables in the model. The use of lag variables protects against the conundrum of serial correlation. The ARDL technique is also more user friendly and simple than other multivariate co-integration methods since it allows the co-integration relationship to be estimated by OLS once the model's lag order is determined. Another advantage of the ARDL method is that it accounts for potential endogeneity among the explanatory variables. The ARDL approach is expected to correct the endogeneity problem because the macroeconomic variables used in this study are disposed to have an endogenous effect on each other [13].

Despite the advantages of ARDL technique outlined above, the ARDL also suffers from some drawbacks including expressly believing that the relationship between various measures of investment and economic growth is linear and symmetrical. These two assumptions are too restrictive and impractical, particularly for economic variables that have become increasingly unstable in view of globalization where economies are now more interconnected. Similarly, the error correction term of this method is assumed to linearly respond to economic volatilities and at constant speed. However, this might not be the case if time series respond asymmetrically, implying that they react differently to economic forces pooling positively or negatively away from the equilibrium. Also, application of linear ARDL would result in inconsistent and non-robust estimates, resulting in the wrong policy conclusions [51]. The nonlinear ARDL method specified by Shin et al. [52] however, evades such an unrealistic assumption by decomposing the changes in the measures of investment into their partial sum of positive and negative deviations and estimating the nonlinear version of the ARDL model.

4. Results and discussions

4.1 Preliminary analysis of study variables

This preliminary analysis provided a general idea of the nominal data set by describing the main attributes of the study variables in our model to establish if the

Variables	RGDP	CAPEX	CPS	FDI	GFCF	INFR	INTR	PINV
Mean	36,182,298	509,505.1	6,245,879	1.50	35.72	19.14	17.64	315,207.5
Median	24,477,911	315,196.9	725,500.4	1.13	32.05	12.95	17.25	17,798.1
Maximum	84,064,364	2,289,000	29,890,460	5.79	89.39	72.84	31.66	2,687,233
Minimum	13,779,258	4100.1	96,705	0.20	14.17	5.39	8.92	151.60
Std. dev.	21,874,515	572,049.4	49,050,394	1.25	19.19	16.83	4.75	669,079.7
Skewness	0.723	1.334	1.232	1.72	1.064	1.81	0.281	2.677
Kurtosis	2.077	4.369	3.118	5.996	3.823	5.15	3.826	9.231
J. Bera	4.905	14.982	10.147	34.62	8.683	29.63	1.663	112.53
J.B Prob.	0.144	0.114	0.173	0.000	0.013	0.00	0.436	0.104
Obs.	40	40	40	40	40	40	40	40

Table 1.
Descriptive statistics of the examined variables in nominal form.

data series are normally distributed and suitable for running the OLS regression. The summary of descriptive statistics of the study variables in their nominal form are presented in **Table 1**.

The level of volatility in the variables is depicted by the standard deviation in **Table 1**. It shows how far away from the mean each variable deviates. The data's asymmetry is shown by the data's skewness. All of the variables under investigation are positively skewed, which indicates a somewhat heavy-right tail, according to the data in **Table 1**. The sharpness of a normal distribution curve's peak is assessed by kurtosis. A platykurtic distribution is evident in RGDP with kurtosis values under 3, suggesting that the variable produce outliers that are less frequent and less extreme than those found in the normal distribution. However, all the explanatory variables show evidence of leptokurtic distribution with kurtosis value greater than 3. This indicates that these variables are with higher-than-normal kurtosis and the weight in the tail of their population density function is larger than normal. The Jarque-Bera statistics measures how well sample data fit a normal distribution in terms of skewness and kurtosis. The null hypothesis is firmly accepted for these observations, as demonstrated by the probability values of the Jarque-Bera statistics for INTR, LOGRGDP, LOGCAPEX, LOGCPS, and LOGPINV series. As a result, these variables can be said to have a normal distribution since their corresponding Jarque-Bera probability values have a significance level of larger than 5%. The FDI, GFCF, and INFR series, on the other hand, display substantial Jarque-Bera probability values of less than 0.05, which clearly confirm a lack of normalcy in their residuals. This suggests that these variables are highly susceptible to shocks and other fluctuations in the economy which may have caused outliers, resulting in residual non-normality. The Jarque-Bera probability for all the logged variables showed that they are normally distributed for the purpose of our regression analysis. However, normality of data distribution is not required to apply the ARDL co-integration method used in this study [50].

Researchers often rely on correlation coefficient and Variance Inflation Factor (VIF) test among pairs of predictors to measure the severity of multi-collinearity on the accuracy of estimated regression coefficients [9, 53]. The study therefore evaluated the degree of linear dependency and level of multi-collinearity problems among

Correlation	CAPEX	CPS	FDI	GFCF	INFR	INTR	PINV
CAPEX	1.00						
CPS	0.70	1.00					
FDI	−0.16	−0.25	1.00				
GFCF	−0.65	−0.61	−0.14	1.00			
INFR	−0.32	−0.27	0.45	0.20	1.00		
INTR	−0.07	−0.14	0.56	−0.32	0.37	1.00	
PINV	0.41	−0.51	−0.11	−0.49	−0.20	−0.06	1.00

Table 2.
Pearson's correlation coefficients for explanatory variables.

the explanatory variables specified in the empirical model using the Pearson's Product Moment correlation coefficient. The correlation analysis does not however infer any measure of causality or causal relationship between the examined variables. The Pearson's Product Moment correlation coefficient of the explanatory variables in their nominal form are displayed in **Table 2**.

From **Table 2**, multi-collinearity among the study variables explicitly stated in the model does not pose a serious challenge since the correlation coefficients of these variables were detected to be within the acceptable threshold limit of ± 0.80 [13, 50]. Nevertheless, one should be cautious in interpreting high correlation coefficient or high VIF values of the variables as evidence of high degree of multi-collinearity. Robert [53] emphasize that it is important to compare VIF (and tolerance) threshold values to other factors affecting the variance of the regression coefficient. Values of the VIF of 10, 20, 40, or even greater do not, by themselves, discredit the conclusions of regression studies, suggest the use of ridge regression, or support the integration of two or more independent variables into one new variable to address multi-collinearity complications. Similarly, many recent studies have suggested that multi-collinearity may not necessarily be a problem and the frequently used method of resolving multi-collinearity issues in regression analysis may sometimes create bigger problems than the ones they seek to correct [9, 51, 53].

4.2 Test of stationarity of study variables

Time series analysis requires that the data be checked for stationarity. The literature on time series econometrics has made it clear that test results can be misleading if the estimated variables are non-stationary and/or not co-integrated. When time series data is not stationary, shocks in the data will disintegrate rather than be amplified, whereas shocks are neutralized and the data returns to its mean value when time series data is stationary. Because time series data are vulnerable to unit root problems, all study variables are pre-tested for them to ensure accurate estimation and effective time series appraisal. To ensure the validity of the co-integration bounds test, the time series' stationarity must be checked to ensure that none of the variables are integrated beyond one (I (1)). The sequence of integration of the variables under investigation was checked for this purpose using both conventional—The Augmented Dickey-Fuller (ADF) and Phillips-Perron (PP)—tests and structural breakpoint methods. This is important because econometric analysis of non-stationary variables affects the

	ADF		PP Test			Zivot-Andrews			
Variables	**Level**	**1st diff.**	**Level**	**1st diff.**	**Remark**	**Break date**	**Level**	**1st diff**	**Rmk**
RGDP	-1.319^{n}	-3.335^{b}	1.411^{n}	-2.695^{a}	I(1)	2002	−2.0653	$11/2507^{a}$	I(1)
CAPEX	4.007^{n}	-6.592^{a}	1.411^{n}	-6.030^{a}	I(1)	2016	-0.6117^{n}	-7.2387^{a}	I(1)
CPS	5.397^{n}	-5.751^{a}	4.991^{n}	-3.218^{a}	I(1)	2006	0.6076^{n}	-7.6604^{a}	I(1)
ELB	-2.038^{n}	-6.053^{a}	-2.079^{n}	-6.053^{a}	I(1)	2011	-6.6963^{a}	-7.5044^{a}	I(0)
FDI	-3.832^{a}	-5.451^{a}	-3.766^{a}	-14.34^{a}	I(0)	1995	-4.8842^{b}	-10.0321^{a}	I(0)
GFCF	-3.711^{a}	-4.584^{a}	-3.711^{a}	-4.610^{a}	I(0)	2017	-4.1190^{n}	-5.0928^{a}	I(1)
INFR	-2.978^{b}	-2.934^{a}	-2.847^{c}	-10.14^{a}	I(0)	2004	-6.3718^{a}	-11.1946^{a}	I(0)
INTR	-2.858^{c}	-2.707^{a}	-2.497^{n}	-6.973^{a}	I(1)	1995	-3.2059^{n}	-5.7041^{a}	I(1)
PINV	3.107^{n}	-3.210^{a}	-3.224^{b}	-10.28^{a}	I(0)	2018	−4.0011	-9.8706^{A}	I(1)

a, b, and c denote the rejection of the null hypothesis at 1%, 5%, and 10% significance levels, respectively, while n denotes not significant.

Table 3.
ADF, PP, and Zivot-Andrews stationarity tests results.

accuracy and reliability of empirical results. While ADF tests use parametric autoregression to approximate the ARMA structure of the errors in the test regression, PP tests help to correct the bias caused by ADF tests due to omitted autocorrelation. Thus, the Phillips-Perron (PP) unit root tests differ from the ADF tests primarily in how they handle serial correlation and heteroscedasticity in the errors [54].

The Augmented Dickey and Fuller (ADF) and Phillips-Perron (PP) unit root tests of stationarity, which are the norm, are typically ineffective in the presence of structural break. A break is a recurring shock that affects a time series over an extended period of time. The ability to veto a false unit root null hypothesis will be limited if this break is not explicitly addressed during the unit root review process [55]. The Zivot-Andrews [56]) unit root test was used to fully account for unobserved heterogeneity in the variables under study and demonstrate how susceptible the estimated results are to structural changes. The Zivot and Andrews test uses an endogenous sequential test to discover each potential break in the entire sample by using several dummy variables. The results of the conventional and structural breakpoint unit root tests are presented in **Table 3.**

The conventional and structural breakpoint unit root tests yielded similar results, as shown in **Table 3**. The variables under consideration were stationary at levels and first difference, but not at second difference. The dependent variable (RGDP) was also stationary at first difference, indicating that the necessary and sufficient condition for implementing the ARDL method were fulfilled.

4.3 Bounds test to co-integration

After the order of integration of the variables is established by unit root testing and the optimal lag length is determined using the appropriate criteria, such as Akaike Information Criterion (AIC), Schwarz Bayesian Criterion (SBC), and Hannan-Quinn Criterion (HQC), the F-test at its ideal lag length was used to test the joint significance of the lagged level variables stipulated in the model. It tested the null hypothesis that there is no long run relationship between the variables against the alternative

Model	F-statistics	K	%	Lower Bound I(0)	Upper Bound 1(1)	Decision
LOGRGDP = f (ELB, FDI, GFCF, INFR, INTR, LOGCAPEX, LOGCPS, LOGPINV)	9.0222	8	1%	2.79	4.10	Reject H_0 and accept H_A. Series are co-integrated
			2.5%	2.48	3.70	
			5%	2.22	3.39	
			10%	1.95	3.06	

Table 4.
ARDL bounds test for co-integration results.

hypothesis that the variables have long run relationship. Using Narayan [57] upper and lower bounds F-statistics for a small sample size (30–80 observations), it is possible to determine whether the variables are co-integrated or not. The guideline is to reject the null hypothesis if the calculated F-Statistic exceeds the upper bound critical value at 5% level of significance confirming a long-run relationship among the variables and accept the null hypothesis if the computed F-statistic is below the lower bound critical value. The optimal lag length was determined using the Akaike Information Criterion (AIC) as the relevance of the F-test results is highly dependent on the choice of the correct lag length.

The study's observations are annual, with a sample size of 40 and 8 parameters. Considering the small number of observations and the need to keep degrees of freedom, an ideal lag length of 1, 2 was chosen and imposed on the dependent variable and dynamic regressors. This ensured that the model dynamics were not constrained by too few lags and that the chosen model did not suffer from serial correlation. The study therefore estimated Eq. (1) with the lag structure (1, 1, 0, 2, 0, 2, 2, 2, 1) being the most efficient of the estimated models. **Table 4** provides a summary of the results from the estimated F-test and the ARDL bounds testing approach.

Table 4 shows that the calculated F-statistic value of 9.0222 is greater than the upper bound critical value of 4.10 at the 1% significance level, indicating the existence of a long-run relationship between economic growth and the various investment determinants explicitly stated in the model. This means that in the long run, these variables move together, and any short-run divergence in their interplay will revert to equilibrium.

4.4 Long-run effects of investment determinants on economic growth in Nigeria

The study estimated the conditional ARDL long-run model for Eq. (1) to determine the long-run effects of determinants of investment on economic growth in Nigeria. **Table 5** contains the long-run estimated results.

The long-run coefficient of Economic Liberalization (ELB) is positively correlated with economic growth and statistically significant at 1% level. According to the findings in **Table 5**, increased liberalization of the Nigerian economy is expected to boost economic growth by 15.29%. The result is consistent with the findings of Gitahi et al. [14] who reported a significant positive impact of economic liberalization on private investment growth in Kenya.

Variables	Coefficients	Std. error	t-statistic	*P*-value
ELB	0.1529	0.0379	4.0388	0.0008***
FDI	−0.0195	0.0129	−1.5139	0.1474^{NS}
GFCF	0.0073	0.0022	3.3134	0.0039***
INFR	−0.0025	0.0010	−2.4387	0.0254**
INTR	0.0141	0.0041	3.4045	0.0032***
LOGCAPEX	−0.1957	0.0481	−4.0709	0.0007***
LOGCPS	0.3451	0.0299	11.5161	0.0000***
LOGPINV	0.0396	0.0182	2.1811	0.0427**

Table 5.
ARDL long-run estimated results.

From **Table 5**, the long-run coefficient of Foreign Direct Investment Inflow (FDI) showed evidence of an inconsequential negative effect on economic growth in Nigeria during the review period. The negative sign of the coefficient indicates that FDI is displacing or crowding-out domestic investment and limiting growth in Nigeria during the review period. Nigeria needs significant inflows of foreign direct and portfolio investment to propel growth because it is a developing nation with weak domestic capital formation and a shortage of necessary infrastructure. Due to rising insecurity, a lack of essential infrastructure, and the displacement of multinational corporations to nearby nations, the country has lost its appeal to foreign investors.

The long run coefficient of Domestic Investment (GFCF) displays a positive effect on private investment that is significant at 1% level, suggesting that increased domestic capital formation is required to engender growth. The findings indicate that a percentage increase in domestic investment, all else being equal, stimulated an increase in economic growth of about 0.7%. Domestic investment, also known as gross fixed capital formation, is a critical determinant of economic growth. It is vital in growing the supply side of the economy's production capacity, which results in higher output and exports. The result validates prior expectations, Solow's [58] growth theory, which explains the relationship between savings, capital accumulation, investment, and economic growth, as well as current studies by Apanisile and Okunlola [59], Babu et al. [9], and Daniel [60], which reported a significant positive relationship between domestic capital formation and long-term economic growth in Nigeria. Sub-Saharan African countries, Kazakhstan, and Poland, in that order.

Table 5 indicated a negative influence of inflation rate (INFR) on economic growth that is significant at 5% level. Accordingly, a percentage increase in the inflation rate, while other explanatory variables remain constant, results in a 0.25% increase in economic growth. In order to maintain macroeconomic stability, inflation must be kept under control. High inflation, driven primarily by food and fuel prices, creates uncertainty for investors, reduces consumer welfare, and dampens growth. According to the findings, an unchecked sharp increase in the broad level of prices diminishes the worth of assets, disposable income, and pushes people into poverty. Consumers' ability to demand goods and services deteriorates as their incomes are decimated by rising prices, resulting in a decline in their standard of living and a decline in economic growth. The findings are consistent with those of Akinlo and Oyeleke [18] and Nguyen [51], who reported a significant negative relationship between inflation rate and economic growth in Nigeria and Vietnam.

From the results in **Table 5**, the long-run coefficient of effective interest rate (INTR) is positively related with economic growth and statistically significant at 1% level, acknowledging that an efficient and relatively stable financial system is vital for investment and inclusive growth. Explicitly, a percentage increase in interest rate other things remaining equal, triggered an increase of approximately 1.41% in economic growth. The availability of financial services, including a productive interest rate, is a critical component for encouraging healthy and equitable economic growth. According to McKinnon and Shaw [61], financial repression caused by low real interest rates frequently results in the withdrawal of funds from the banking sector as well as a disincentive to save. It decreases the availability of bank credit, which reduces investment and growth. According to the McKinnon-Shaw financial liberalization hypothesis, high real deposit interest rates boost financial savings, which induces a rise in the size and quality of domestic investment, thereby encouraging growth. The result is consistent with the findings of Nonvida and Amegnaglo [62], Miftahu [63], and Babu et al. [9] who found significant evidence of a positive effect of interest rate on economic growth in Benin, Nigeria, and Sub-Saharan Africa, respectively.

According to **Table 5**, the long-run coefficient of government capital expenditure (LOGCAPEX) displayed a negative effect on economic growth that is significant at 1% level. From the results, a percentage increase in government infrastructure spending activated a decrease in economic growth of about 19.57%. Nigeria's fiscal experience over the years explains the challenges of implementing effective fiscal policy responses in an environment with highly volatile revenue flows. In a dynamic situation, uncertain revenue flows tend to reduce the quality and efficiency of government expenditures in Nigeria, while private investments tend to be reduced. Revenue fluctuation leads to expenditure uncertainty, which frequently results in a large number of unfinished capital projects. Government spending in Nigeria has been largely unproductive due to spending volatility. The increase in capital spending may result in less thorough scrutiny of new projects, as many are premised on the belief that high revenue will continue unabated [64]. When revenue drops, many projects are unable to be sustained and must be abandoned, while those that do survive are either poorly executed or are only properly funded through borrowing. Ultimately, a procyclical spending pattern combined with poor oil earnings management caused low growth, persistent fiscal deficits, and debt accumulation. Sustainable growth and poverty reduction are unattainable without a significant reduction in volatility. The result agrees with the findings of Quashigah et al. [65] and Ogar et al. [66] who in their studies found evidence indicating a significant negative effect of capital expenditure on economic growth in Ghana and Nigeria, respectively, but in contrast with the views of Keynes [28], Easterly and Rebello [67] and Solow and Swan [68] who argued that government capital spending through its multiplier effects can stimulate investment and economic growth.

The long-run coefficient of domestic credit to private sector (LOGCPS) in line with a priori expectation is positively related to growth and statistically significant at 1% level. According to the results in **Table 5**, a percentage increase in credit to private sector is associated with an increase in economic growth of approximately 34.51%. Credit is the main channel through which savings are transformed into investments. Access to credit at low-interest rate enables an individual to build up finances that can support productive investment in various enterprises and private sector inventiveness that is important for growth and poverty reduction. The result is in accord with extant studies of Vincent et al. [69] who reported a significant positive impact of credit to private sector on economic growth in Nigeria.

The long-run coefficient of Foreign Portfolio Investment (LOGPINV) generated a positive impact on economic growth that is statistically significant at 5% level. Based on **Table 5**, a percentage increase in foreign portfolio investment, while holding other explanatory variables constant, elicited a rise in economic growth of around 3.96%. In light of the growing gap between their domestic capital stock and capital requirements, emerging nations are feeling the need for foreign capital to augment domestic resources. An important method for boosting the amount of funds available for domestic investment is through foreign capital inflow. To close the savings and foreign exchange shortfalls related to the quick wealth generation and growth required to end the pervasive poverty in developing nations, foreign capital inflow is necessary. In addition, foreign investors favor developing nations over developed nations due to the higher rates of return on investment in these countries. The result is in harmony with existing studies of Ezeanyanji and Ifeako [23] and Ozigbo [70] who reported a significant positive impact of foreign portfolio investment on economic growth in Nigeria.

4.5 Short-run impact of investment determinants on economic growth in Nigeria

Utilizing the most effective lag length, the researchers estimated an unrestricted Error Correction Model (ECM) linked to the long-run relationship from equation (1) to scrutinize the model's short-run dynamics. **Table 6** presents a summary of the short-run properties of the model's transition to equilibrium.

Table 6 lagged error term coefficient or adjustment speed (ECT(−1)) is, as predicted, negative, less than one and highly significant at the 1% level, further

Variables	Coefficients	Std. error	t-statistic	*P*-value
D(ELB)	0.0792	0.0293	2.7043	0.0145**
D(FDI)	−0.0152	0.0063	−2.4140	0.0266**
D(GFCF)	0.0032	0.0019	1.6771	0.1108^{NS}
D(GFCF(−1))	−0.0038	0.0018	−2.1839	0.0424**
D(INFR)	−0.0022	0.0005	−4.9315	0.0001***
D(INTR)	0.0022	0.0021	1.0663	0.3004^{NS}
D(INTR(−1))	0.0064	0.0029	−2.2306	0.0387***
D(LOGCAPEX)	−0.0179	0.0215	−0.8341	0.4151^{NS}
D(LOGCAPEX(−1))	0.1042	0.0282	3.6906	0.0017***
D(LOGCPS)	0.1072	0.0435	2.4628	0.0241**
D(LOGCPS(−1))	−0.1046	0.0458	−2.2862	0.0346**
D(LOGPINV)	0.0109	0.0065	1.6748	0.1113^{NS}
C	12.2399	1.5619	7.8363	0.0000***
ECT(−1)	−0.8786	0.1123	−7.8228	0.0000***

*Cointeq = LOGRGDP − (0.1529***ELB − 0.0195*FDI + 0.0073***GFCF − 0.0024**INFR +0.0141***INTR − 0.1957***LOGCAPEX +0.3451***LOGCPS +0.0396**LOGPINV.*

Table 6.
ARDL short-run estimated results.

supporting the existence of a unique long-term relationship between the indicators of investment and economic growth in Nigeria. In the current year, approximately 87.86% of the short-run disequilibrium caused by shocks in previous years converges back to long-run equilibrium. Because the pace of adjustment is relatively quick, any short-run outliers should take about 1.14 years to recover from and return the economy to its long-run optimum growth path.

From **Table 6**, the short-run coefficient of the present level of Economic Liberalization D(ELB) in Nigeria in agreement with the long-run results motivated a positive impact on the current level of economic growth that is significant at 1% level. Clearly, an increase in the present rate of deregulation of the Nigerian economy is expected to produce an escalation of about 7.92% in the current level of economic growth. This variable's positive sign indicates that increased deregulation of the Nigerian economy will open up more sectors of the economy to private sector participation and result in greater efficiency in resource allocation, thereby stimulating private investment and inclusive growth.

From **Table 6**, the current level of foreign direct investment inflow D(FDI) in covenant with the long-run result is inversely related to the current level of economic growth in Nigeria and statistically significant at 5% level. Clearly, a percentage increase in the present rate of foreign direct investment inflow is associated with about 1.52% decline in current level of economic growth. Foreign direct investment (FDI) is frequently asserted as a viable vehicle for economic growth because it is thought to be less vulnerable to crisis since investors typically have better investment arrangements and comprehend the host country's economic complexities. While it appears that FDI can provide greater technology transfer to host economies, the results indicate that Nigeria has not successfully attracted FDI commensurate with its vast resources or accomplish a high growth rate because it failed to develop the absorptive capacity to benefit from foreign investment. The amount of FDI inflow has decreased as Nigeria's level of insecurity has risen. The gradual exodus of foreign direct and portfolio investment from Nigeria to other West African nations, which has a negative impact on government revenue generation and economic growth, is caused by the government's apparent inability to provide a safe and secure environment for people, property, and the performance of business and economic activities.

Gross fixed capital formation in the current period D(GFCF) had a negligible positive impact on the current level of growth, whereas its one-year lag value D(GFCF (−1)) was negatively related to the current level of economic growth and significant at the 5% level. As a result, a percentage increase in the variable's one-year lag value reduces the current rate of economic growth by approximately 0.38%. Pervasive and structural security issues generate economic risks and uncertainties that change people's saving, investing, and consumption habits, skewing the equilibrium resource allocation within a nation. Infrastructure damage brought on by terrorist actions can disrupt commerce and increase a nation's cost of doing business. Reduced profits as a result of these higher costs translate into a lower return on investment. Because of its blatantly detrimental effects on inclusive growth, insecurity in Nigeria hinders and undermines domestic investment. All of these obstacles impede Nigeria's growth by suppressing domestic capital formation and private investment.

The short-run coefficient of present inflation rate in Nigeria D(INFR) in concord with the long-run result initiated a negative influence on the current level of economic growth that is significant at 1% level. Evidently, a percentage increase in the present inflation rate will stimulate a decline of approximately 0.22% in the current rate of economic growth. Monetary policy, in contrast to fiscal policy, can address the problem of economic shocks very quickly. Monetary policy goals include managing a variety of monetary targets, such as fostering economic growth, achieving full employment, stabilizing prices, preventing economic crises, and maintaining real exchange rates and interest rates. However, the importance of securing price stability is typically highlighted because rising prices erode disposable income and plunge people into poverty. A decline in standard of living results from consumers' declining purchasing power as a result of income erosion brought on by price increases.

The coefficient of present rate of effective Interest Rate D(INTR) initiated a marginal positive impact on the current level of economic growth, whereas the one period lag value of the variable D(INTR(−1)) initiated a significant negative impact on the current rate of economic growth, which is significant at the 1% probability level. According to **Table 6**, a percentage increase in the previous interest rate is associated with a 0.64% decrease in the current rate of economic growth. The interest rate has the potential to have an impact on the overall economy by determining the magnitude of macroeconomic indicators such as capital flows, investment, exchange rate, and credit demand. The McKinnon-Shaw hypothesis stipulates that a high deposit rate is a necessary policy tool for galvanizing financial savings for investment. It can, however, be self-defeating if executed during inflationary periods because the relatively high real lending rate impedes investment spending.

An effective and largely stable financial system is essential for investment and growth, as is widely acknowledged in the empirical literature. Low interest rates are thought to facilitate capital accumulation or encourage investment spending. Contrary to the McKinnon-Shaw hypothesis, the Neo-Keynesians hold that financial liberalization is bad for investment and growth. They stress that saving is determined by investment, not the other way around, and that a high interest rate may lower saving by suppressing investment. Besides, financing working capital with borrowed money at high interest rates may result in cost-push inflation. They place more value on the possibility of profit and a plentiful and flexible supply of credit for the private sector than on prior saving. According to the study's findings, high interest rates caused short-term financial hardship and economic stagnation even though they seem to have improved economic performance over the long term.

The current level of Government Capital Expenditure D(LOGCAPEX) in consonance with the long-run results, is inversely related to the current level of economic growth and statistically significant at 5% probability level. A percentage increase in current capital spending provoked a 1.79% increase in the current rate of economic growth. In contrast to the long-run result, the coefficient of the one-period lag of government infrastructure spending D(LOGCAPEX (−)) reinforced a positive and significant impact on the current level of growth at the 1% probability level. As a result, a percentage increase in previous levels of infrastructure spending resulted in a 10.42% increase in current economic growth. Increased government spending on infrastructure facilities lowers businesses' overhead and per unit cost of production, stimulating private investment growth and lowering poverty levels. Improved government spending is frequently designed to support growth and its use must be both economically and politically efficient and effective. As a result, effective management of social regulations is required so that government expenditure policies remain optimal, efficient, and effective in stimulating economic growth. However, the study result indicated that government infrastructural spending in Nigeria has been inefficient and retarding growth during the review period.

The current level of domestic Credit to Private Sector D(LOGCPS) has a significant positive influence on economic growth at the 5% probability level, in line with the long-run result. Specifically, a percentage point increase in current private sector credit stimulated a 10.72% increase in current economic growth. The coefficient of the one-year lag of private sector credit D(LOGCPS(−)) variance with the long-run result, on the other hand, is associated with a negative and significant impact on the current level of economic growth, which is significant at 5%. As a result, a percentage increase in previous levels of private sector lending motivated a drop in current economic growth of around 10.46%. The private sector may seek credit to improve labor productivity in both existing and new businesses. This is because lower labor productivity reduces the value of a company's assets. Credit supply influences labor productivity through investments in human capital, research and development for modern technology, and physical capital to improve the capital-labor ratio. Nigeria has insufficient domestic savings, which may make it difficult for financial institutions and markets to meet domestic credit demand solely through savings. These gaps imply that additional funding sources, such as foreign capital inflows, may be needed to supplement domestic savings in order to meet the private sector's credit demand. However, the risks associated with the financial system's information asymmetry could limit the amount of money available to the financial intermediaries and credit demanders. Due to this restriction, both funds from domestic and international sources are uncertain. Potential credit supply restrictions for investments in human and physical capital—the catalysts for higher labor productivity—are brought on by the uncertainty.

According to **Table 6**, the current rate of foreign portfolio investment D (LOGPINV), in tandem with the long-run results, caused a positive but statistically insignificant impact on the current rate of economic growth in Nigeria during the evaluation period. Foreign capital enhances domestic resources by advancing capital stock, technology, managerial aptitude, entrepreneurial prowess, brands, and market access. Consequently, increasing the inflow of foreign capital should improve the economic well-being of the country's economic agents.

4.6 Econometric diagnostics checks

The validity, stability, and fulfillment of the desirable statistical assumptions of an effective ARDL model were evaluated by a number of diagnostic tests such as normality, serial correlation, heteroscedasticity, and specification error. The regressors were tested for serial correlation to confirm they did not share a serial correlation, the residuals were tested for normality to guarantee they are normally distributed, and lastly, the model was tested for heteroscedasticity to certify there is no ARCH effect. Additionally, the stability of the ARDL model was assessed using CUSUM (Cumulative Sum of Recursive Residuals) and CUSUMsq (Cumulative Sum of Squares of Recursive Residuals). The results of the diagnostics tests are presented in **Table 7**.

Diagnostic tests statistics of **Table 7** indicate that the model's residuals are normally distributed and do not exhibit any problems with multi-collinearity, serial correlation, heteroscedasticity, or model misspecification error. The estimated model is regarded as being properly defined because the foregoing qualities are desired ones for OLS models. The CUSUM and CUSUM of squares tests, which are shown in **Figures 1** and **2**, also verified that the model's parameter estimates are relatively robust over a variety of structural modifications and that the estimated outcomes are reliable and adequate for economic forecasting and decision-making.

Problem	Test	Probability	Conclusion
Normality	Jarque Bera	0.3892	Normality exists
Serial correlation	Breusch-Godfrey LM Test	0.1146	No serial correlation
Heteroscedasticity	Breusch-Pagan-Godfrey	0.2385	No heteroscedasticity
Specification error	Ramsey RESET	0.7746	Correctly specified

Table 7.
ARDL diagnostics tests results.

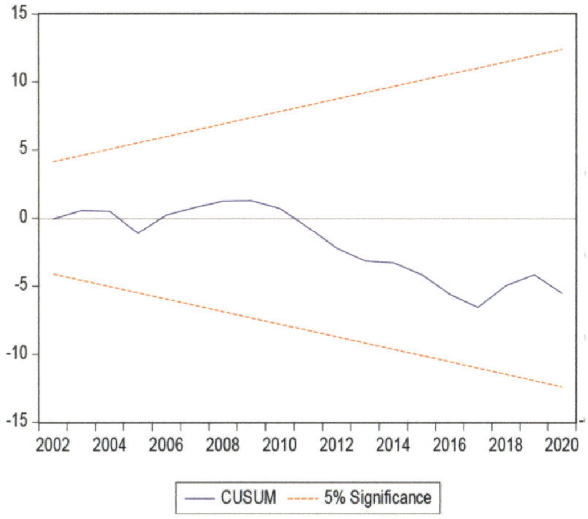

Figure 1.
CUSUM plot.

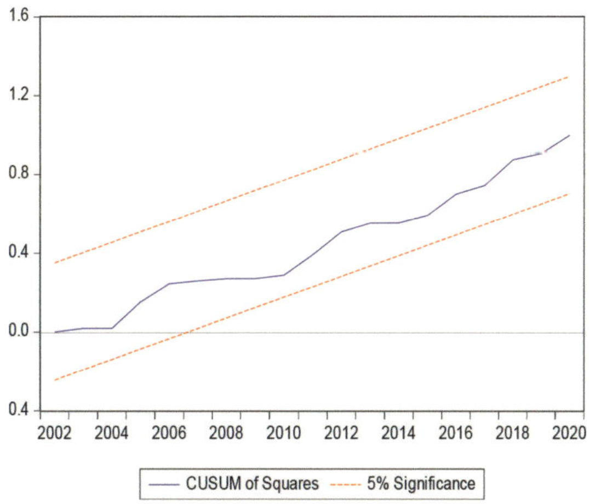

Figure 2.
CUSUM of squares plot.

5. Conclusion and recommendations

Due to low levels of income and domestic savings, Nigeria has a very large gap between investment and saving. In order to increase job creation, combat poverty, and foster growth, the nation has opened up several economic sectors to foreign investors and provided a number of investment incentives after realizing the ineptitude of domestic capital. The study therefore, conducted a disaggregated analysis of the impact of various investment indicators on economic growth of Nigeria over a 40-year period from 1981 to 2020. Domestic investment was disaggregated into private and public investment while foreign investment was disaggregated into foreign direct and portfolio investment. Credit to private sector, inflation, interest rates and economic liberalization were adopted as control variables and their relative effects on economic growth were tested using the ARDL methodology.

The empirical findings confirm co-integration among the study variables and demonstrate a significant positive impact of economic liberalization on growth both in the long and short-term while credit to private sector, domestic investment, foreign portfolio investment, and interest rate were efficient and associated with a significant improvement in economic growth only in the long-run. Furthermore, inflation rate significantly inhibited growth in the long and short-run, government infrastructure spending was ineffective and significantly suppressed growth in the long-run while foreign direct investment crowded-out growth but significant only in the short-run. The error correction mechanism revealed a high adjustment process of the selected macroeconomic indicators of investment in Nigeria, as the speed of adjustment to long-run equilibrium was 87.86% approximately while the diagnostics and stability tests showed that the model is appropriately specified and dynamically stable over time.

As a result, the study advocated for effective fiscal and monetary policy coordination to lower the cost of doing business, incentivize and create an enabling environment for domestic and foreign investors, and improved infrastructure spending to generate jobs, alleviate poverty, sustain growth and achieve overall macroeconomic stability. This study has important policy implications, including the need to liberalize the financial industry. According to McKinnon and Shaw, such liberalization entails getting rid of excessive reserve requirements, interest rate ceilings, and enforced credit distributions while also using the proper macroeconomic tools to secure price levels. Improved savings and investment are anticipated, along with a decrease in the profitability of investing in various economic sectors. The study therefore suggests limiting the growth of the money supply, lowering the cost of governance, and deficit financing in order to reduce the negative effects of inflation, particularly in the long run.

JEL classification codes:

A22, E62, F16, G18, H26

Author details

Abdulkarim Yusuf
Department of Economics, Nigeria Police Academy, Kano, Nigeria

*Address all correspondence to: abdulkarimyusuf01@gmail.com

References

[1] Bidemi JO, Olulu MR, Paul OS. Impact of private domestic investment on economic growth in Nigeria. Asian Journal of Economics, Business and Accounting. 2018;**9**(2):1-9

[2] Kinyanjui MW, Muturi W, Njeru A. Government expenditure on infrastructure and growth of private domestic investment in Kenya. African Journal of Emerging Issues (AJOEI). 2022;**11**(4):40-50

[3] Victor EO, Dickson OO. Modeling private investment behaviour in Nigeria: A cointegration approach. Accounting and Finance Research. 2013;**2**(3):14-23

[4] Hussain ME, Haque M. Fiscal deficit and its impact on economic growth: Evidence from Bangladesh. MDPI Economies. 2017;**5**(1):37-56

[5] Nyoni T, Bonga GW. An empirical analysis of the determinants of private investment in Zimbabwe. Dynamic Research Journals' Journal of Economics and Finance. 2017;**4**(2):38-54

[6] Eslon N, Andrew P. Do FDI and public investment crowd-in/out domestic private investment in the SADC region. Managing Global Transitions. 2021;**19**(1):3-25

[7] Marcus SS, Vale S. Is there a nonlinear relationship between public investment and private investment? Evidence from 21 Organization for Economic Cooperation and Development countries. International Journal of Finance and Economics. 2022;**7**(3):1-16

[8] Kumo WL. Macroeconomic uncertainty and aggregate private investment in South Africa. South African Journal of Economics. 2006;**74**(2):190-204

[9] Babu WA, Pantaleo IM, Ndanshau MO. Econometric analysis of the impact of taxes on private investment in Sub-Sahara Africa. African Journal of Economic Review. 2020;**8**(1):176-197

[10] European Commission. A stronger role of the private sector in achieving inclusive and sustainable growth in developing countries. Brussels. 2020;**13**(5):1-16

[11] International Finance Corporation. International Finance Corporation's engagement in fragile and conflict-affected situations: Results and Lesson. In: A Synthesis Report of IFC, August 26, 2021. Washington D. C.: The World Bank; 2021

[12] Herman S, Surjatno WS, Daniel FM. The role of domestic investment, foreign investment, and micro, small and medium-sized enterprises for poverty reduction in Indonesia. Journal of Eastern European and Central Asian Research. 2022;**9**(5):901-913. DOI: 10.15549/jeecar.v9i5.1072

[13] Abdulkarim Y, Mohd S. The impact of fiscal policy variables on private investment in Nigeria. African Finance Journal. 2021;**23**(1):41-55

[14] Gitahi NS, Ombuki C, Wawire N, Okeri S. Taxation and private investment: Evidence for Kenya. International Journal of Economics. 2013;**29**(11):78-93

[15] Bage C. The performance and future allocation of credit to selected sectors in Nigerian economy. CBN Economic and Financial Review. 2003;**34**:43-56

[16] Nigerian Investment Promotion Council. Compendium of investment

incentives in Nigeria. Abuja, Nigeria: NIPC; 2021

[17] World Bank. Debt in low-income countries: evolution, implications, and remedies. Policy Research Working Paper No. 8794. Washington, DC: World Bank Group; 2019

[18] Akinlo T, Oyeleke JO. Effects of government expenditure on private investment in Nigerian economy (1980–2016). Emerging Economy Studies. 2018;**4**(2):147-156

[19] Osuka BO, Ezedike GO, Mbanasor CO. Foreign portfolio investment and the growth of Nigeria's capital market. Fuoye Journal of Finance and Contemporary Issues. 2022;**3**(2):107-129

[20] Chinasa E, Urama CE, Ezema DC, Ndubuisi DO, Ukwueze ER, Eze AA, et al. The effect of foreign capital inflows on economic growth in Nigeria. Regional Economic Development Research. 2022; **3**(2):253-267. DOI: 10.37256/redr.3220221550

[21] Niels H, Robert L. Foreign direct investment, financial development and economic growth. The Journal of Development Studies. 2003;**40**(1):142-163. DOI: 10.1080/0022038041 2331293707

[22] Babatunde AG, Emmanuel OG, Henry O, Oluwasogo SA. Empirical analysis of the effects of foreign direct investment inflows on Nigerian real economic growth: Implications for sustainable development goal-17. Cogent Social Sciences. 2020;**6**(1):21-38. DOI: 10.1080/23311886.2020.1727621

[23] Ezeanyeji CI, Maureen I. Foreign portfolio investment and economic growth in Nigeria: An impact analysis. International Journal of Academic Management Science Research. 2019;**3** (3):24-36

[24] Idolor EJ, Omehe R. Effect of inflation and investment on economic growth in Nigeria. African Development Finance Journal. 2022;**4**(1):49-72

[25] National Population Commission. Census and national development in Nigeria: A historical review. Abuja, Nigeria; 2021. Retrieved from: www.nigerianstat.gov.ng

[26] United Nations Conference on Trade and Development (UNCTAD, 2010). Trade and Development Report 2010. From recovery to resilience: The development dimension. UNCTAD; 2010

[27] Clark JM. Business acceleration and the law of demand: A technical factor in economic cycles. Journal of Political Economy. 1917;**25**(1):217-235

[28] Keynes JM. The General Theory of Employment, Interest and Money. London: Palgrave Macmillan; 1936

[29] Samuelson D. A synthesis of the principle of acceleration and the multiplier. Journal of Political Economy. 1939;**47**(6):786-797

[30] Chenery HB. Overcapacity and the acceleration principle. Econometrica. 1952;**20**(1):1-28

[31] Koyck IM. Distributed lags and investment analysis. Econometrica: Journal of the Econometric. 1954;**65** (259):523-525

[32] Lucas RE. Optimal investment policy and the flexible accelerator. International Economic Review. 1967;**8**(1):78-85

[33] Treadway AB. The rational multivariate flexible accelerator. Econometrica. 1971;**39**:845-855

[34] Jorgensen WD. Capital theory and investment behaviours. The American Economic Review. 1963;**53**(2):247-257

[35] Jorgenson WD. Econometric studies of investment behaviour: A survey. Journal of Economic Literature. 1971;**9**(4):1111-1147

[36] Vartia L. How do taxes affect investment and productivity? An industry-level analysis of OECD countries. OECD Economics Department Working Papers, (No. 656). Paris: OECD Publishing; 2008

[37] Irving F. The Theory of Interest. New York, NY: Macmillan; 1936

[38] Duruechi AH, Ojiegbe JN. Determinants of investments in the Nigerian economy: An empirical approach (1990–2013). International Journal of Financial Research. 2015;**6**(4):217-227

[39] Tobin J. A general equilibrium approach to monetary theory. Journal of Money, Credit, and Banking. 1969;**1**(10): 15-29

[40] Nwokoye GA, Rolle RA. Tax reforms and investment in Nigeria: An empirical examination. International Journal of Development and Management Review. 2015;**10**(1):39-51

[41] Talpos I, Vancu I. Corporate income taxation effects on investment decisions in the European Union. Annales Universitatis Apulensis Series Deconomica. 2009;**11**(1):513-518

[42] Zouhaier H, Kefi MK. Interaction between political instability and investment. Journal of Economics and International Finance. 2012;**4**(2):49-54

[43] Babalola A, Onikosi-Alliyu OS. The crowding-out effect of fiscal policy on capital inflows in Nigeria. Economics and Organization. 2020;**17**(1):43-56

[44] Omojolaibi AJ, Tochi-Nze P, Ekundayo PM. Fiscal policy and private investment in selected West African Countries. CBN Journal of Applied Statistics. 2016;**79**(1):277-309

[45] Kengdo AAN, Ndeffo LN, Avom D. The effect of external debt on domestic investment in Sub-Saharan regions. The Economic Research Guardian. 2020;**10**(2):69-82

[46] Pesaran MH, Shin Y. Bounds testing approaches to the analysis of level relationships. Journal of Applied Econometrics. 2001;**16**:289-326

[47] Engle RF, Granger CWJ. Cointegration and error-correction representation, estimation and testing. Econometrica. 1987;**55**(2):251-276

[48] Johansen S, Juselius K. Maximum likelihood estimation and inference on cointegration with applications to the demand for money. Oxford Bulletin of Economics and Statistics. 1990;**52**(2): 169-211

[49] Ewetan OO, Osabohien R, Matthew OA, Babajide AA, Urhie E. Fiscal federalism and accountability in Nigeria: An ARDL approach. Journal of Financial Economic Policy. 2020;**5**(1):40-63

[50] Rahman M, Islam A. Some dynamic macroeconomic perspectives for India's economic growth: Applications of linear ARDL bounds testing for co-integration and VECM. Journal of Financial Economic Policy. 2020;**12**(4):641-658

[51] Nguyen HH. Impact of foreign direct investment and international trade on economic growth: Empirical study in Vietnam. The Journal of Asian Finance, Economics, and Business. 2020;**7**(3): 323-331

[52] Shin Y, Yu B, Greenwood-Nimmo M. Modelling asymmetric co-integration and dynamic multipliers in a non-linear

ARDL framework. Econometric Methods and Applications. 2014;**24**: 281-314

[53] Robert MO. A caution regarding rules of thumb for variance inflation factors. Quality & Quantity. 2007;**41**(5): 673-690. DOI: 10.1007/s11135-006-9018-6

[54] Abdulkarim Y, Mohd S. Growth and fiscal effects of insecurity on the Nigerian economy. European Journal of Development Research. 2022;**2022**:1-27. DOI: 10.1057/s41287-022-00531-3

[55] Glynn J, Perera N, Verma R. Unit root tests and structural breaks: A survey with applications. Journal of Quantitative Methods for Economics and Business Administration. 2007;**3**(1): 63-79

[56] Zivot E, Andrews DWK. Further evidence on the great crash, the oil-price shock, and the unit root hypothesis. Journal of Business & Economic Statistics. 1992;**106**:251-270

[57] Narayan PK. The saving and investment nexus for China: Evidence from Cointegration Tests. Applied Economics. 2005;**37**(17):1979-1990. DOI: 10.1080/00036840500278103

[58] Solow RM. A contribution to the theory of economic growth. Quarterly Journal of Economics. 1956;**70**(1):65-94

[59] Apanisile TO, Okunlola CO. Does military expenditure influence economic growth in Nigeria during 1989–2013? A bound testing approach. Romanian Journal of Fiscal Policy. 2014;**5**(2):56-71

[60] Daniel FM. The relationship between domestic investment, country risk, governance and economic development of Kazakhstan versus Poland. Journal of Eastern European and Central Asia Research. 2022;**9**(6):21-38. DOI: 10.15549/jeecar.v9i6.1196

[61] Shaw ES. Financial Deepening in Economic Development. New York, NY: Oxford University Press; 1973

[62] Nonvide GMA, Amegnaglo CJ. Effect of tax revenues on economic growth in Benin: The role of investment. Journal of Advanced Studies in Finance. 2017;**2**(16):139-145

[63] Miftahu I. Macroeconomic analysis of interest rate and economic growth in Nigeria: A time series approach. International Journal of Finance and Banking Research. 2019;**5**(4):91-104. DOI: 10.11648/j.ijfbr.20190504.14

[64] Blanchard O, Perotti R. An empirical investigation of the dynamic effects of shocks to government spending and taxes on output. Quarterly Journal of Economics. 2002;**117**:1329-1368

[65] Quashigah OP, Ofori-Abebrese G, Pickson BR. Empirical analysis of the potency of fiscal policy on economic growth in Ghana. International Research Journal of Finance and Economics. 2016; **154**(10):25-36

[66] Ogar A, Eyo IE, Arikpo OF. Public expenditure and economic growth in Nigeria: VAR approach. European Journal of Economic and Financial Research. 2019;**3**(3):36-60

[67] Easterly W, Rebelo S. Marginal income tax rates and economic growth in developing countries. European Economic Review. 1993;**379**(2):409-417

[68] Swan TW. Economic growth and capital accumulation. Economic Record. 1956;**32**(2):334-361

[69] Vincent AO, Marcus I, Oluchukwu A. Non-oil export and economic growth

in Nigeria: A time series econometric model. Economics and Business. 2018;**3** (2):115-134

[70] Ozigbo AS. Foreign direct investment, portfolio flows and economic growth in Nigeria. International Journal of Development and Economic Sustainability. 2021;**9**(1): 63-76

Chapter 6

Investing in Sustainable Development Goals: Opportunities for Private and Public Institutions to Solve Wicked Problems That Characterize a VUCA World

Olivier Sempiga and Luc Van Liedekerke

Abstract

We live in a world full of global challenges, such as global warming, the COVID-19 pandemic, and only recently the Russia-Ukraine crisis, all of which confirm that we live in a volatile, uncertain, complex, and ambiguous (VUCA) world. Most of these challenges are considered to be wicked problems. For many decades, wicked problems have been viewed as difficult, even impossible to solve. This chapter examines how institutions can navigate the VUCA world through investing in SDG so as to solve wicked problems. The chapter argues that adopting socially responsible investment as a strategy allows both private and public organizations to improve economic, social, and environmental performance; and is a fine way of investing in SDG, which could be a long-term solution to wicked problems. Using a multivariate analysis of variance (MANOVA), the chapter examines the relationship between SDG investment and climate change solutions at the local level. Results show a significant effect of investment in SDGs on a solution to wicked problems like climate change. The chapter concludes that the difficulty or impossibility of solving global challenges is likely to be caused by a lack of investment in the SDGs.

Keywords: sustainable development goals, socially responsible investment, wicked problems, VUCA world, MANOVA

1. Introduction

In the past few decades, the world has witnessed global challenges, such as global warming, economic crisis, the COVID-19 pandemic, and only recently the Russia-Ukraine crisis, all of which confirm that we live in a volatile, uncertain, complex, and ambiguous (VUCA) world. A great body of literature calls most of these problems wicked problems in the sense that it is difficult, even impossible, to find a lasting solution to them [1–3]. The least governments can do is to find a partial solution. In some instances, they have to just buy themselves some time while in the meantime the wicked problems become more serious. Prime examples of wicked problems that this chapter will refer to our global warming, whose consequences keep getting worse year after year and the COVID-19 pandemic, which has been challenging governments around the world. While global warming proves that the world is witnessing a climate crisis, the COVID-19 pandemic has plunged the world into a global health crisis. These and similar major crises are clear evidence that we live in a VUCA world.

There have been claims that the more we advance in achieving Sustainable Development Goals (SDGs), the better chance we stand to deal with crises, such as COVID-19 and global warming [4]. Despite considerable efforts and some progress during the years that followed the adoption of the SDGs (e.g., reduction of extreme poverty and child mortality rates, fighting against diseases such as hepatitis, and better electricity access in developing nations), the world is unlikely to achieve the SDGs by 2030 [5]. Recent studies show that the shift in development pathways and level of financing and investment is not taking place as it is supposed to. The lack of investment in the SDGs suggests that global challenges will be hard to solve. Consequently, there will be a continued increase in greenhouse gas emissions and hunger; a continued loss of biodiversity at unprecedented rates; and the extreme poverty rate could still be high in 2030 [5]. There is little empirical knowledge on how these challenges can be tackled and to what extent investing in SDGs leads to less wicked problems. We verify whether more investment in SDGs is a solution to the intractability of the wicked problems.

A great body of literature has studied wicked problems and their relationship with SDGs [6, 7]. However, this has never been done in the context of a VUCA world. Recent studies show that investment in the SDGs seems to be the best way to build resilience against shocks and avoid backslides into poverty and other global challenges [8]. Yet, there is still a lack of empirical research. A small body of literature has studied the types of investments that can be made around SDGs [9]. To better invest in the SDGs, governments as well as public and private institutions need to identify SDG investment areas and embrace socially responsible investment (SRI). While some organizations have started doing that many more will need to join the efforts. SRI entails that as well as making their financial interest, private as well as public institutions have to be oriented toward social and environmental issues to provide solutions to the problems we face as human beings [10]. To contribute to the alleviation of problems associated with climate change many different investors and actors are parting ways with a "traditional view" of economic theory, which considers investors as rational and wealth maximizing [11].

Using a multivariate analysis of variance (MANOVA), this chapter seeks to establish the relationship between investing in SDGs and solution to wicked problems like global climate. The chapter argues that adopting SRI is an investment strategy that will improve economic, social, and environmental performance; it is a fine way of investing in SDG, which could be a long-term solution to wicked problems. The main aim of this study is to establish the relationship between investing in SDGs and the solution of wicked problems. At the same time, we hope to contribute to the body of existing knowledge and to inform policymakers in making informed decisions. The study will allow us to understand why wicked problems have been difficult to solve and to propose better ways to navigate them and by so doing give a different image of wicked problems. Finally, the research will guide private and public institutions examining their behaviors in tackling or contributing to challenges the world faces in the VUCA world and possibly how to navigate these challenges.

The remainder of the chapter is organized as follows: Section I explores how we live in a VUCA world with wicked problems, the implications of that, and the theoretical and conceptual framework that surrounds that. This will allow us to understand the nature and gravity of the problems that humanity faces. Section II explains how investing in SDGs matters if we are to tackle the wicked problems that exist in the VUCA world and how three SDG logics can be used to guide SDG investment and their implications. Here, we will also discover how SRI is one of the most effective ways of investing in SDGs. Section III explains how data were collected and analyzes the results. The final section gives concluding remarks and avenues for future research.

2. Living in a VUCA world with wicked problems

2.1 Conceptualization of the "vucability" of the world

The world faces problems that are more and more intractable. The intractability of these challenges that humanity deals with on a daily basis makes the world look more complex, uncertain, ambiguous, and volatile. These are all characteristics of a VUCA situation. The VUCA concept was introduced after the end of the Cold War to refer to a world ever more difficult to predict and rely on [12]. Following the financial crisis in 2008–2009, which led many organizations and countries to be confronted by volatile, complex, and ambiguous conditions in their social and economic environments and models, the VUCA concept was adopted in other domains like business and management science [13, 14]. After the financial crisis, across many industries, a rising tide of volatility, uncertainty, and business complexity roiled markets and changed the nature of competition [13]. A more or less similar situation took place when organizations and governments were confronted with the COVID-19 pandemic and the challenges brought about by the Russia-Ukraine conflict. To meet the challenges of a VUCA world, policymakers and strategic planners in private and public organizations will have to comprehend the differences and the implications of the main conditions of a VUCA world—volatility, uncertainty, complexity, and ambiguity [15].

Volatility refers to the unpredictability of the nature, speed, volume, and magnitude of change [16]. Dynamic and frequent instability brought about by drastic, violent, and rapid shifts witnessed in the past years is the main characteristics of volatility [17]. Global warming is as much an example of volatility as it brings with it constant changes and poses a great threat to the planet. We have witnessed temperatures breaking records in Europe and elsewhere in recent years and this trend is set to continue. Millions of people from different parts of the world have been victims of tsunamis, hurricanes, floods, and landslides. In a volatile world, global warming effects may keep increasing. Although not every scientist agrees that there is a causal connection between these outcomes and climate change, there is ample evidence that natural disasters are linked to climate change [18]. Similarly, the manner in which the COVID-19 pandemic spread to every part of the world bringing with it disruptions and changes and how it was difficult to contain makes us not only vulnerable to COVID-19 itself but to other unpredictable pandemics that may arise as result of different shifts and changes.

Uncertainty describes a situation characterized by a lack of knowledge. Such a lack pertains to whether a certain event is significant enough to constitute a meaningful cause [14]. The lack of knowledge also entails that forecasting is very hard and decision-making becomes extremely challenging simply because issues and events are difficult to predict [19]. While science can make some predictions of how much temperatures could increase in the climate change process and what consequences may arise thereof, there are still many factors that are involved in the process that we may not be certain about. The fact that we are vulnerable to different sorts of natural disasters and pandemics and do not know which ones and when exactly they would strike and to what extent they will affect us and how much we can protect ourselves makes us live in an uncertain world. While science can predict a number of disasters, other challenges, such as pandemics, earthquakes, and wars, are hard to predict.

Complexity is due to the presence of numerous difficult-to-understand causes and mitigating factors involved in a problem. The difficulty in grasping causes and mitigating factors leads to ambiguity and confusion [14]. The COVID-19 pandemic has proved to be an extraordinarily complex issue as it resulted from interconnected and sometimes difficult-to-comprehend causes. Its solution has required strategies that consider and integrate multiple and competing parameters, including the health and well-being of individuals, communities, and societies versus the strength of the economy at local, regional, and international levels. The climate crisis is even more complex as it impacts almost every aspect of our life. It is unprecedented and there is no prior experience to draw on [1].

Finally, ambiguity is the absence of clarity about the meaning of an event. In this case, real issues of threats and opportunities are not properly understood and the causal relationships are hard to establish. Here, also the situation is unprecedented, and individuals as well as organizations deal with the unknown [15]. For instance, climate change has likely highlighted gaps in knowledge, diverse perspectives, and a wide range of interests among stakeholders. Differences in perspectives and interests probably lead to even higher levels of ambiguity and uncertainty, which shows that the characteristics of a VUCA world (i.e., ambiguity and uncertainty) are sometimes interconnected and affect each other. Unfortunately, this interconnection not only poses analytical, political and managerial challenges for understanding but more importantly makes responding to different challenges very complicated [20]. The "vucability" of the world and the issues that we face daily can be better explained by the wicked problem theory. The difficulty in finding the solution or their insolvability has led researchers to refer to these problems as wicked problems.

2.2 Wicked problem theory

The climate change and the COVID-19 pandemic mentioned above are arguably prime examples of wicked problems that we have recently been confronted with in the VUCA world. According to wicked problems theory, it is literally impossible to find a linear and lasting solution to wicked problems and as a consequence, it is futile to set up a planning approach geared to solve them. The wicked problems theory has its origin in Rittel and Webber [3] who challenged the efficacy of scientific social planning. These authors claimed that contested and complex social problems cannot be "tamed" using standard managerial approaches that rely on rational-analytic models of planning and decision-making [20]. There exists no single mind capable of encompassing the full array of information necessary to provide a solution to a wicked problem. Not only wicked problems do not have a straightforward solution that can be carried out confidently but they have a multitude number of contributing factors and are often root causes of other issues and are very difficult to describe [3].

A lack of consensus on problem definition, combined with a lack of consensus on solutions make the fundamental characteristics of wicked problems [21]. Such problems are seen as more enduring and intractable, and thus more likely to defy resolution. At an international level, sustainable development, climate change policy response, international business regulation, and illicit migration are some examples of enduring complex problems. At a national and local level, wicked problems examples include family violence, environmental pollution, poverty, and drug control. Over the years and in many societies, these systemic and complex problems have provoked divergent views about the appropriate policy responses and approaches to adopt while dealing with them. Politicians find it hard to agree on the very nature of these issues and their relative importance [20]. Disagreements arise because key stakeholders' viewpoints are anchored in different assumptions, values, interests, and capacities. People with different perspectives and experiences view wicked problems through a variety of lenses [1]. These differences in perspective have major consequences since the way in which a problem is defined or scoped is closely linked to preferred remedial actions to address the identified problem [20]. Faced with the intractable and contentious aspects of wicked problems public policy responses are often partial or even counterproductive [22]. Even the best available policy responses are highly provisional rather than enduring [20]. The intractability and quasi-insolvability of these wicked problems strengthens further the idea that we live in a VUCA world. Conventional techniques are not sufficient to solve wicked problems [1].

What the wicked problem theory implies in our context is that it will be difficult to find a last solution to the grand challenges that the world has been facing. There are two main implications: (1) wicked problem theory challenges strategy-making, and (2) performance measurement. First of all, the wicked problem theory challenges the establishment of full-scale strategy like the Agenda 2030, which set terms, conditions, means, and ways to solve global challenges. By the time we get to 2030 and as we try to implement these terms and solutions, problems will have evolved and taken up other meanings and definitions. It is futile to contemplate the end of poverty, for example, the reduction of CO_2 gas emissions. Policymakers and their theories are doomed to fail simply because wicked problems are not only impossible to solve but lead to other challenges. Secondly, wicked problem theory entails that it is difficult to measure performance because problems are ever evolving and their solution are challenged by identifying the real causal issue. Making reports of what has been achieved in terms of SDGs hardly makes sense since by the time reports are finished the problems may have worsened. Humanity seems to be caught in a vicious cycle of problems. The existence of wicked problems is a sheer confirmation that the world is volatile, ambiguous, uncertain, and complex. At the same time, the "vucability" of the world explains the wickedness of the problems that we face. Ironically, it is because people live in a VUCA world with wicked problems that they are compelled to seek solutions to this situation even if they are uncertain that they may find solutions to the problems. While early scholars thought it was practically impossible to solve wicked problems, recent scholarship has moved to suggest ways of finding solutions.

3. Toward solving wicked problems

It is worthwhile asking oneself why wicked problems are difficult or impossible to solve. Of course, there may be many reasons explaining the impossibility to solve wicked problems. One of the reasons would be the fact that wicked problems in themselves are so complex and sometimes ambiguous that they require different approaches and methods to be solved and yet those approaches and methods are unachievable. If for example, solving climate change requires collaboration and cooperation of everyone, at every level of government and necessitates intergovernmental negotiation like those usually seen during COP meetings (e.g., 26 and 27), it is hard to imagine that a consensus can be reached on key issues like reducing CO_2 gas emissions and when achieved it is hard to believe that everyone will fully cooperate or have the means to perform what it takes to reach a solution. This is due to the fact that besides the fact that people have different perspectives on issues and understand things differently countries are at different levels of development and economic growth, have different needs, and above all else have different and competitive interests. However, despite the fact that people have different interests and perspectives and that problems may be hard to solve, people naturally never give up on finding solutions to problems that they face. With time scholars have tried to move away from the pessimistic view of Rittel and Webber [3] and have argued that it is possible to "find" solutions to wicked problems.

3.1 Tackling wicked problems and turning them into opportunities

Noordergraaf et al. contend that there is a paradox embedded in wickedness theory [22]. To frame global challenges as wicked generates obstacles for addressing wicked issues. Framing problems as such is, in itself and of itself, to make them so grand and remove them from daily practice so much that actors become scared and get compelled to retreat in front of the problems instead of addressing them. Addressing wicked problems calls for fundamental change starting from the vocabulary used *vis-à-vis* problems. Recently, scholars have replaced claims of "solving" or "fixing" a wicked problem with the language of tackling, managing, coping, and addressing wicked problems [20, 23]. Moreover, since there is no one best solution, wicked problems could be addressed using a range of instruments and approached from different levels of analysis [23]. During the past years, different governance approaches, such as collaborative governance, adaptive governance, interactive governance, or network governance, have been adopted to tackle wicked problems [24]. Others propose to convert wicked problems into micro problems to be able to solve them. However, each approach would find detractors. Some scholars suggest that the political attempt to convert messy unstructured problems into "well-structured" micro problems begs the question of whether it is possible to resolve messy issues by converting them into "technically controllable" issues. They conclude that wicked problems cannot be properly "tamed" or "fixed" by dissolving them into multiple elements, which are then reassembled in a manner suited to a series of small projects [23, 25].

Despite the fact that we live in a VUCA world, some scholars believe that we can still turn challenges into opportunities. Human beings have naturally evolved from owning challenges and seeing them as opportunities and this natural attitude has allowed them to survive in harsh environments and conditions. Earlier research shows that the VUCA world itself is an opportunity in the sense that "volatility provides profit opportunity" [26]; "Uncertainty is opportunity" [27] and "Ambiguity equals opportunity" [28]. Nevertheless, the opportunity is only as such when it is ceased especially at a time when Antonio Guterres warned that "A window of opportunity remains open, but only a narrow shaft of light remains. The global climate fight will be won or lost in this crucial decade" [29]. He urges people to win this fight together for the 8 billion citizens and for future generation. But to win this battle, to solve the global wicked problems, more investment in SDGs is the key so as to increase trust, which in turn could lead to better performance and with its solution to these problems [30]. Wicked problems we face in this VUCA world can still be turned into opportunities. If COVID-19 did not teach us tough lessons it also presented us with the opportunity and taught us that it was possible to reduce gas emissions [31].

3.2 SDG investment as a better solution to wicked problems

The natural conviction that challenges are meant to be dealt with is what makes leaders and policymakers engage in strategy-making. World leaders who gathered in New York in 2015 unanimously agreed to adopt SDGs. These goals which are the building blocks of the 2030 Agenda are an attempt to find a lasting solution to the problems that the world has been facing. SDGs are a continuity to the Millennium Development Goals (MDGs) that were concluded in 2015. However, despite some success, MDGs had weaknesses in the sense that they were designed for the developing world. After many years of consultation and negotiation at different and between levels, SDGs were adopted to solve this weakness, knowing that development is not just sustainable but it concerns every human being and every nation. Just like problems do not affect selected individuals from one part of the planet solutions or efforts to solve the problems are more efficient when they come from all levels and different parts of the globe, especially for challenges that affect everyone and everywhere. Sustainable development should not leave anyone behind and can only be achieved if every nation and person cooperates. SDGs are comprised of 17 goals (**Figure 1**) and 169 targets and 232 indicators. Essentially, the SDGs constitute a universal call to end poverty, protect the planet, and improve the lives and livelihoods of everyone, everywhere [32]. The problems that SDGs are trying to address fall into the category of wicked problems in the sense that these types of problems transcend the borders of traditional policy domains, involve a wide variety of actors across different scale levels, and resist our attempts to solve them [33].

Leaders adopted SDGs mainly because they had become more aware that in a globalized world, most problems are interconnected, and are likely to affect every human being and an attempt at finding a lasting solution requires involving everyone

Figure 1.
Sustainable development goals.

and every nation. Breuer et al. [34] put it well when they say that the achievement of some goals is heavily dependent on the international order and patterns of global cooperation, and action on these goals will have repercussions beyond national borders. For instance, if a country reduces its emissions and meets its national emission goals, the same country will still suffer from the effects of climate change if other countries increase (or fail to decrease) their own emissions. As CO2 emissions keep accumulating in the atmosphere, the contribution toward reducing emissions (e.g., SDG 7, SDG 12, and SDG 13) in one country goes beyond the actions taken by that country simply because we globally share one atmosphere. Investing in SDGs by every government and from every level starting from the grassroots is the way forward for humanity to stand a chance to handle intractable wicked problems that hinder sustainable development.

Since their adoption in 2015 private organizations and public organizations alike have invested in SDGs. As a result, there has been some progress in realizing SDGs. Nevertheless, the COVID-19 pandemic has slowed down the little progress made on implementing and achieving SDGs [35]. It has exacerbated existing constraints for the SDGs. While the COVID-19 pandemic has affected people differently, it has widened existing inequalities across population groups and created a sense of vulnerability and uncertainty. People in low-paying occupations, the young, people on fixed-term contracts, and those with lower levels of education have been particularly hit hard [36]. Ironically, COVID-19 justifies further why private and public institutions should invest in SDGs more than before. The COVID-19 pandemic has brought to the fore how central the SDGs are. A few SDG practitioners argue that the world would have better dealt with the COVID-19 pandemic and ensuing economic challenge if the world was better advanced in meeting the SDGs with stronger health systems, a healthier natural environment, less gender inequality, fewer people living in extreme poverty, and more resilient societies [4].

Investment in and progress on the SDGs is the best way to build resilience against shocks and avoid backslides into poverty [8]. SDGs provide a realistic approach to navigate societies through and beyond the COVID-19 pandemic [6]. Just before COVID-19, the UN announced the current decade as a decade of action to accelerate investing in SDGs to be able to achieve Agenda 2030. Even though a decade of action that the UN had announced was put in jeopardy by COVID-19, there is still some hope if the robust investment is made on SDGs. To solve wicked problems, private, nonprofit, and public organizations have to invest money, time, and energy toward the achievement of the SDGs. Prior research maintains that the SDG framework has a transformative potential, which can be realized only through appropriate implementation [32, 37]. Across world regions, however, the extent to which SDGs are addressed, and the means used to do so and the efforts committed vary enormously. While some governments are putting a lot of effort into SDG implementation and are involving their citizens, others are still lagging behind. The concrete realization of SDGs will depend on how they are implemented by a diverse set of competent agents [32], including governmental and nongovernmental institutions, companies, and individual citizens.

To advance the SDGs, there is a need to create investment policies and measures. Investment is a necessary input to help achieve SDGs 1 to 15. In addition, investment explicitly appears as a target in SDGs 1, 2, 7, and 17 [38]. Investment in SDGs leads institutions to establish actions and attitudes that help in resolving major challenges. A small body of literature has studied what types of investment can be made around SDGs. Schmidt-Traub [9] proposes different SDG investment areas to help public and private institutions achieve SDG. For instance, reducing poverty (SDG 1) is achieved through the adoption of many policies and a broad range of investments. Such a range interconnects with other SDGs and include *inter alia* investment in social capital (health and education), business capital (smallholder farms, artisanal fishing, small enterprises, manufacturing), and physical capital (infrastructure). Furthermore, private institutions are encouraged to regularly report on their progress. Reporting allows a thorough investigation and likely lead to a better outcome in the future and robust investment. The more organizations invest the more successful SDGs will be and the more likely wicked problems are tamed [9].

Private and public institutions that invest in SDGs have to establish SDG investment needs to be addressed. In some organizations, the analysis currently focuses on mapping investors' corporate holdings to a selection of the SDG. Several investors (e.g., the Dutch APG and PGGM, or the Swedish AP2) are trying to work out investment possibilities associated with SDGs [39]. For instance, the bulk of investment needs for achieving gender equality must be included in gender-sensitive sector investments, including education, health, and access to basic infrastructure services. This has to be done at the local level, as well as national and other levels and sectors through a reduction of gender equality in employment, an increase in women's political participation, and combatting violence against women [9]. Establishing investment needs will determine whether organizations put massive or modest investments. For instance, achieving SDG 11 on cities and human settlements will require vast investments in urban infrastructure, social services, resilience and environmental protection, and economic development. These are a series of solutions that in one way or the other, separately or concurrently contribute to solving wicked problems. As we will see, investment in one area is connected and affects investment in other areas. Urban investment needs in social services and infrastructure are connected with investments in climate change adaptation or resilience as well as mitigation. A substantial share of urban environmental investment needs is also covered under water supply and sanitation as well as energy systems [9]. Most of these investments, however, face different challenges that may hinder their putting into practice or materializing.

3.3 Three logics to guide SDG investment in a VUCA world

It may be hard to resolve many problems in a VUCA world, but it is possible to navigate them as we invest in SDGs. According to van Zanten and van Tulder [6], this navigation can be done by finding a solution to the main three challenges we face [6]. The three challenges are governance challenge, systems challenge, and strategic challenge. To these three challenges correspond three logics (**Table 1**). Such logic can facilitate a sustainable transformation and respond to the three challenges [6].

First of all, there is a governance challenge that any SDG investment is faced with. Some of the problems we face (i.e., climate change) affect the whole world. In a such

Challenges	SDG logics
• a governance challenge	• governance logic
• a systems challenge	• systems (nexus) logic
• strategic challenge	• a strategic logic

Table 1.
Challenges and associated SDG logics.

situation, the challenge is how to respond to such a global threat and how to fill a multitude of global governance gaps brought about by climate change, all this in an increasingly volatile and uncertain (VUCA) world. Finding a solution to that global challenge is one way to increase the speed with which global problems (e.g., climate change, pandemics) can be addressed. SDGs provide a solution to the global challenge through the "hybrid" governance that they entail, since they involve different actors at different levels. Such a governance logic sets goals, adopts policies, and tracks progress to steer impacts. By involving multilevel actors and stakeholders, the hybrid governance specifies "pathways" to leverage innovation and partnering as ways to achieve the SDGs, rather than by generically prescribing "one-size-fits-all" measures into hard laws [6]. Hybrid governance is likely to present the best and most realistic approach to global ("wicked") sustainable development challenges, which feature complex governance problems. The COVID-19 pandemic and global warming are some of the challenges that need hybrid governance to be solved [6].

Secondly, SDG investment needs to consider a systems challenge in which global challenges are embedded. A systems logic is attached to this challenge. A systems logic manages SDG interactions. At first sight, it is easy to view SDGs as 17 distinct goals, with each of them trying to solve an individual sustainability problem, such as hunger, biodiversity, or poverty. However, nearly all sustainability challenges facing the world are deeply entwined, and therefore systemic in their nature [40]. Consequently, tackling sustainability challenges requires systemic solutions that manage interactions between different SDGs, rather than cherry-picking individual SDGs that align with an organization's interests [6]. The SDGs suffer from a lack of a systems approach to their successful implementation. Arguably the biggest challenge plaguing the SDG agenda is the priority given, in theory and practice, to SDGs that drive economic growth compared to SDGs that promote social development and ecological sustainability [41]. COVID-19 underscores how important a systems logic is to solving sustainability challenges especially in terms of social justice and equity. While COVID-19 is mainly about SDG 3 (good health and well-being), it is closely related to SDG 10 (reduced inequality). This is because the spread of the virus across populations has been regarded as being closely linked to inequality (i.e. people living in poverty and those having underlying health conditions — which are correlated— were the most vulnerable during COVID-19. The fact that SDGs are interconnected justifies further the idea that public and private organizations need to respond to SDGs in a systemic way rather than picking one that is at their advantage [42].

Finally, there is a strategic challenge that those who invest in SDGs have to deal with: how to align countries and companies' strategies to advance resilient and sustainable societies. Van Zanten and van Tulder [6] argue that in order to align countries and companies' strategies SDGs need to be revamped as a navigating platform that will help navigate a VUCA world endangered by wicked problems [6]. A strategic logic is key for it enables (micro-level) companies to develop strategies that impact (macro-level) policy goals. The strategic logic allows private organizations to promote and invest in SDGs as they complement the investment of public institutions. The advent of the SDGs in 2015 provided businesses with a clear logic for aligning their corporate sustainability strategies with the world's most pressing sustainable development challenges. SDG framework provides private organizations with massive business and investment opportunities. For instance, achieving the SDGs is argued to present an annual US$12 trillion investment opportunity [43]. Achieving the SDGs requires investments, as well as technological and managerial innovation, that can deliver on the goals. Businesses are well positioned to provide these inputs and consequently seize these opportunities and reap long-term rewards. In this sense, SDGs reflect business opportunities that are waiting to be seized [6]. Companies lack a thorough understanding of the business case that the SDGs represent. This is the main barrier to aligning core operations with the SDGs. Companies "are struggling to articulate the business case within their own operations" [44].

There are different implications associated with the three logics. Hybrid governance challenges and complement wicked problems theory. We saw that wicked problem theory, at least in its early formulation, seems to discourage strategy-making approaches like the one that brought up in the Agenda 2030. Hybrid governance shows that it is relevant to set goals and measure outcomes for a better solution to challenges. In other words, policymakers and leaders are right to set goals, measure performance to steer impacts, and find solutions to grand challenges. It is only when one is able to measure the progress that one can be able to know how much effort are needed and to what extent the challenges have reduced. Without measurement, there is no improvement and without strategy-making, there is no taming of problems. The second implication concerns the interaction between solutions. Whereas wicked problem theory tells us that one problem may be the root cause of another problem, the systems logic shows not just that but more importantly that solutions are interlinked. One solution to a wicked problem may lead to another wicked problem solution. For instance, by investing in education (SDG 4), there are chances that those who are educated will adopt attitudes and receive knowledge that will allow them to protect the environment and prevent more global warming (SDG 13). This systemic approach gives more power to solve challenges simply because one does not solve one problem at a time but more problems in a more or less synchronized way and from different angles. If problems are interconnected, their solution should interact and require coordination. Finally, the strategic logic implies not only that it is important to make strategy but it provides better ways to adopt those strategies, through for instance mutual collaboration between companies and government institutions. On their own, governments are unable to solve wicked problems without relying on the know-how of companies. But companies need to adopt strategies that allow them to invest in SDGs. To truly cease the investment opportunity that SDGs present and at the same time work toward achieving the Agenda 2030, companies will have to adopt Socially Responsible Investment.

3.4 Sustainable investment: adopting socially responsible investment

One of the most efficient ways to invest in SDGs that cut across different levels of government and institutions is adopting Socially Responsible Investment (SRI) as a way of being and acting (i.e., new *modus vivendi*). Adopting SRI is the best way to reduce a negative impact on society as a whole, thereby making change and contributing to solving the ills that have been affecting human lives for many years. Nonetheless, to have a truly lasting impact more institutions need to align their investment strategies with SRI. The challenges are so great and extensive that they cannot be left to the voluntary initiatives of some companies. The characteristics of a VUCA world seem to oblige us all to join the efforts of transforming the world for better. SRIs—also known as ethical or sustainable investments—are gaining momentum among scholars and practitioners. The extant literature defines them not only as "a result of increasing social awareness by institutions but primarily as a result of the increasing public (beneficiary) interest in social responsibility" [45]. SRI can be also defined as an investment process that integrates ethical values, environmental protection, improved social conditions and good governance into traditional investment decision-making [46]. SRI takes into consideration social, environmental, and governance factors in its management strategies and policies [6].

Over the past years, there has been an increase in sustainable investment. Reports show that toward the beginning of 2020, global sustainable investment increased by 15% for the 2018–2020 period totaling USD35.3 trillion in five major markets. The unprecedented growth in global sustainable investment is first of all due to the fact that the financial crisis of 2007–2008 increased the fear that weak corporate governance and risk management practices can have telling consequences on financial markets and world's economies. Second, the challenges entailed in the climate change process and depletion of natural resources and biodiversity loss have led to people calling public as well as private economic organizations to embrace more responsible behavior and coordination at the global level [47]. Many are becoming aware that if open societies are unable to transform from fragile into more sustainable and resilient economies, repeated systemic crises are inevitable [6]. To encourage more sustainable development, regulators, investors, media, and civil society have been called upon to reward sustainable behavior and condemn unsustainable behavior [38]. Some scholars have predicted that all assets, including fixed income, will increasingly be measured also by social and environmental outcomes and externalities [39]. Proponents of SRI are convinced that a well-developed and ethically oriented financial system can contribute to the achievement of the global goal of sustainable development and build a more sustainable society to live in [48].

To reflect the urgent need of SRI, financial institutions, among others, have parted ways with the exclusive focus on profit maximization and shareholders' wealth to a growing attentiveness about environmental issues like the green and low-carbon economy and the climate change adaptation and mitigation. Such a shift is becoming fundamental in the transition toward sustainable development [46]. To contribute to the alleviation of problems associated with global warming many different investors are moving from a "traditional view" of economic theory going back to expected utility theory, which argues that investors are there to maximize wealth [11]. In similar moves, companies are making investments that combine the traditional financial perspective with a perspective that is influenced by and oriented toward social and environmental issues [10]. For instance, many asset owners are looking to increase investments that make a positive social and environmental impact on top of their financial objectives. Others are reassessing their investment policies in the light of climate change risks and policies in line with Paris COP21 r and SDGs. We are entering an era where companies are adopting the integration of ethical values, environmental protection, improved social conditions, and good governance into traditional investment decision-making [49]. Such a combination represents one of the major drivers of the transition toward and the contribution to sustainable finance and, consequently, to sustainable development [46]. This shift needs to be accelerated and adopted on a great scale to have a meaningful impact on people's lives and on future generations.

Embracing SRI means that institutions have to be aware of interactions that may exist between SDGs. SDG investment will bring about synergies, that is, situations in which achievements on one goal contribute toward progress on other goals—as well as trade-offs—, that is, situations in which progress achieved on one goal will produce effects detrimental to other goals (or parts thereof) [34]. For example, investments and interventions in the field of childhood health are regarded as having large returns due to long-term gains. Moreover, childhood health is assumed to have important synergetic effects on education and poverty [34]. Similarly, infrastructure investment impacts not only SDG 9 on infrastructure, but also SDGs 7, 11, and 13, respectively, on energy, cities, and climate. Current energy, transport, building, and water infrastructure make up more than 70% of global greenhouse gas emissions. Therefore, as new investment replaces existing infrastructure, there is an opportunity for such investment to contribute to

Variable	Obs	Mean	Std. dev.	Min	Max
Solar panels	294	408.9712	208.7047	37.13	1164.06
Wind turbines	294	0.5774221	1.352458	0	8.35621
Sewerage	294	83.02432	14.74722	3.15	100
sdg4_index	300	56.74667	5.805299	29	74
sdg6_index	300	60.53333	8.707177	24	91
sdg7_index	300	38.67	4.85038	19	51
sdg9_index	300	50.05	7.438544	21	74
sdg11_index	300	52.18667	6.291032	26	69
sdg12_index	300	55.66667	6.760268	38	83
sdg13_index	300	71.15	6.531183	54	88

Table 2.
Descriptive statistics.

climate change solutions [38]. In a particular way, infrastructure investment has to abide by SRI principles simply because the decisions today have repercussions for the duration of the infrastructure's lifespan and have an especially large effect on climate change [38].

4. Methodology and data collection

The analysis above will be supplemented by an empirical quantitative analysis. To do that, we use datasets developed by Gemeente-en-stadsmonitor (GSM) and IDEA Consult for the year 2016, 1 year after the launch of SDGs. This data are gathered for all 300 municipalities and cities of the Flemish Region in Belgium. GSM carries a survey once in 3 years, while IDEA Consult gathers data every year to include in its SDG monitor. In order to come up with the final SDG indexes per municipality and city, GSM and IDEA Consult rely on many indicators that are related to SDGs. Cities and municipalities try to invest in SDGs using the means at hand so as to contribute to the achievement of the UN Agenda 2030.

To analyze these data sets, we use a Multivariate Analysis of Variance (MANOVA). This multivariate statistical method allows us to find out the multivariate effects of investing in SDGs in solving wicked problems, using the example of climate change. To solve the issue of collinearity between independent variables, the collinearity test allowed us to select variables that are not so much related among themselves. We were left with SDG 4, SDG 6, SDG 7, SDG 9, SDG 11, SDG 12, and SDG 13. For dependent variables, we have three variables that are used to protect the environment or reduce the effects of global warming in the Flemish municipalities and cities (i.e., solar panels, wind turbines, and sewerage). Before performing a MANOVA, we conduct descriptive statistics (**Table 2**).

5. Result analysis

Table 3 shows that four test statistics are reported for the group effect: Wilks' lambda (W), Pillai's trace (P), the Lawely-Hotelling trace (L), and Roy's largest root (R).

Source	Statistic	df	F(df1,	df2) =	F	Prob>F	
Model	W	0.0069	225	675.0	199.0	1.26	0.0264 a
	P	2.4060		675.0	204.0	1.22	0.0413 a
	L	13.4663		675.0	194.0	1.29	0.0164 a
	R	6.6187		225.0	68.0	2.00	0.0005 u
Residual			68				
sdg4_index	W	0.2315	31	93.0	198.4	1.35	0.0432 a
	P	1.1235		93.0	204.0	1.31	0.0566 a
	L	1.9718		93.0	194.0	1.37	0.0346 a
	R	0.9681		31.0	68.0	2.12	0.0050 u
sdg6_index	W	0.1741	40	120.0	198.6	1.31	0.0459 a
	P	1.3110		120.0	204.0	1.32	0.0415 a
	L	2.4198		120.0	194.0	1.30	0.0504 a
	R	1.1522		40.0	68.0	1.96	0.0072 u
sdg7_index	W	0.1559	26	78.0	198.2	2.19	0.0000 a
	P	1.3003		78.0	204.0	2.00	0.0001 a
	L	2.8734		78.0	194.0	2.38	0.0000 a
	R	1.7846		26.0	68.0	4.67	0.0000 u
sdg9_index	W	0.1447	40	120.0	198.6	1.50	0.0058 a
	P	1.3724		120.0	204.0	1.43	0.0121 a
	L	2.9296		120.0	194.0	1.58	0.0023 a
	R	1.7657		40.0	68.0	3.00	0.0000 u
sdg11_index	W	0.2995	30	90.0	198.4	1.09	0.3005 a
	P	0.9714		90.0	204.0	1.09	0.3146 a
	L	1.5301		90.0	194.0	1.10	0.2913 a
	R	0.7402		30.0	68.0	1.68	0.0401 u
sdg12_index	W	0.2598	28	84.0	198.3	1.34	0.0487 a
	P	1.0275		84.0	204.0	1.27	0.0925 a
	L	1.8593		84.0	194.0	1.43	0.0225 a
	R	1.2205		28.0	68.0	2.96	0.0001 u
sdg13_index	W	0.1900	30	90.0	198.4	1.64	0.0023 a
	P	1.2412		90.0	204.0	1.60	0.0033 a
	L	2.3311		90.0	194.0	1.67	0.0016 a
	R	1.3153		30.0	68.0	2.98	0.0001 u
Residual			68				
Total			293				

Number of observations = 294.
W = Wilks' lambda; L = Lawley-Hotelling trace; P = Pillai's trace; and R = Roy's largest root.
e = exact, a = approximate, and u = upper bound on F.

Table 3.
Multivariate tests.

All four are used to test the null hypothesis that the means of the dependent variables are equal across all levels of the independent variables. Roy's largest measures the largest eigenvalue of the between group covariance matrix. This refers to the amount of variability in our dependent variables, which are explained by the independent variables. Although Tabachnik and Fidell (2006) support reporting Wilks' lambda instead of the other values [50], we will use all four tests. Opposite of the other test statistics, Wilks' lambda's values close to 0 indicate large omnibus effects [51]. In our case, the Wilks' lambda is 0.0069. This means that our independent variables have a strong effect on the dependent variables. The value of Pillai's trace ranges from 0 to the number of dependent variables (3 in our case), with larger values, indicating a stronger effect of the independent variables on the dependent variables. The Pillai's value is 2.4060, which again shows a strong relationship between independent and dependent variables despite the variability among variables. As expected, SDG 11 (0.9714) has the weakest effect, while SDG 9 has the strongest effect (1.3724). The same conclusion applies to the Lawely-Hotelling trace test. In addition, the value of the Lawley-Hotelling trace is used to calculate the corresponding p-value, which is then used to assess the statistical significance of the independent variables. In our case, the Prob>F ranges between 0.0000 and 0.0504, which means that the p-value is less that 0.05 (i.e., the level of significance). Again, this proves that there is a significant effect of our independent values and the dependent variables.

We, therefore, reject the null hypothesis that investment in SDGs does not lead to a solution of wicked problems. The same conclusion applies to Roy's largest root, which shows a significant effect between independent values and dependent values since the p-value 0.005. Prior research shows that multivariate analysis helps in outcome variable selection [52]. This would entail that SDG 9 is the most important aspect to consider for organizations making an effect on climate change.

The advantages associated with using MANOVA include the fact that it allows us to test multiple independent variables at the same time, unlike methods such as ANOVA. In that case, we are able to assess patterns between dependent variables. While MANOVA has the advantage of providing a single, more powerful test of multiple dependent variables, it can be difficult to interpret the results [53].

6. Concluding remarks

The main aim of this chapter was to examine how investing in SDG relates to finding solutions to wicked problems in order to navigate the VUCA world. Practitioners and scholars of public administration and investment strategy have recently begun to recognize that a state capacity to manage a crisis such as global warming is dependent on the cumulative investments that a state has made in its ability to govern, do and manage. While crises and ensuing challenges are serious for all, it is especially a challenge for countries that have ignored those needed investments [54]. We conclude that there is a significant relationship between investing in SDGs if one has to solve wicked problems, such as global warming. All the SDGs we examined as our independent variables (i.e., SDG 4, SDG 6, SDG 7, SDG 9, SDG 11, SDG 12, and SDG 13) have a significant effect on solutions to climate change. These solutions include installing solar panels, wind turbines, and sewerage. It must be acknowledged that each element has an impact that is different from other elements. Secondly, the research was carried out at a local level. Future research needs to carry out the investigation at a macro level.

The chapter contributes to the existing body of knowledge by offering support to the many findings that point out the growing challenges of a VUCA world and the expectations that wicked problems that result thereof need to be solved. The chapter proposed that investing in SDGs by embracing SRIs as *modus vivendi* for both public and private institutions is a realistic way of tackling wicked problems. Our analysis showed and is in agreement with prior studies that demonstrated that achieving the SDGs *would* bring about a safer, more stable world with fewer natural and manmade hazards, thus lowering the likelihood of future crises occurring [6]. Backsliding on the progress already made on the SDGs imperils prospects for eradicating basic deprivations and reduces resilience to other shocks in the future [8]. This justifies the argument that there is a need for more investment in SDGs. Results will inform policymakers and politicians in their quest to solve wicked problems.

Theoretically, the chapter showed that wicked problems can be tackled and a VUCA world can still be navigated if more SRI investments are made. The theoretical and conceptual analysis adopted also allowed us to understand why wicked problems have been difficult to solve. We proposed better ways to navigate wicked problems. This gives a different image of wicked problems which were once thought to be insolvable. In line with the implication for practice, the chapter showed that collaboration between private and public sector in tackling wicked problems is paramount. Leaders across sectors now recognize that the challenges are too great and too systemic for any one of them to tackle alone and that mobilizing more resources for the SDGs will require a continued and close collaboration between the public and private sectors. The importance of collaboration and networking among actors is highlighted in SDG 17. Encouraging the joint engagement of a multiplicity of actors, such as governmental and nongovernmental institutions, businesses and individual citizens will be a critical condition for the achievement of Agenda 2030 [32]. Tackling grand challenges requires not just collaboration but revitalizing private and public investment [54]. These symbiotic public–private collaborations will bring more value and meaning to SRI and embracing SRI as an investment strategy will improve economic, social, and environmental performance, thereby providing a lasting solution to global challenges.

There are a number of limitations to the findings in this chapter. There is a need to provide more rigorous empirical research at the macro level to examine the extent to which SDG investments at different levels and in different sectors help tackle wicked problems. Future studies could adopt other quantitative methods of analysis to complement this MANOVA conceptual analysis.

Author details

Olivier Sempiga* and Luc Van Liedekerke
University of Antwerp, Antwerp, Belgium

*Address all correspondence to: o.sempiga@ags.edu

References

[1] Ross D, Leonard B, Inayatullah S. Leadership beyond the great pause: Climate change and other wicked problems. Journal of Futures Studies. 2022;**26**(4):15-22

[2] Termeer CJAM, Termeer A, Biesbroek R. A critical assessment of the wicked problem concept: Relevance and usefulness for policy science and practice. Policy and Society. 2019;**38**(12):167-179

[3] Rittel HWJ, Webber MM. Dilemmas in a general theory of planning. Policy Sciences. 1973;**4**(2):155-169

[4] UN. Progress towards the Sustainable Development Goals. Report of the Secretary-General. July 2020 session. High-level political forum on sustainable development. 2020

[5] Carpentier CL, Braun H. Agenda 2030 for sustainable development: A powerful global framework. Journal of the International Council for Small Business. 2020;**1**(1):14-23

[6] van Zanten JA, van Tulder R. Beyond COVID-19: Applying "SDG logics" for resilient transformations. Journal of International Business Policy. 2020;**3**:451-464

[7] Shulla K, Voigt B-F, Cibian S, Scandone G, Martinez E, Martinez F, et al. Effects of COVID-19 on the sustainable development goals (SDGs) discover. Sustainability. 2021;**2**(1):15

[8] U. DESA. Achieving the SDGs through the COVID-19 response and recovery. Policy Brief. 2020;**78**

[9] Schmidt-Traub G. Investment Needs to Achieve the Sustainable Development Goals: Understanding the Billions and Trillions. Sustainable Development Solutions Network. 2015

[10] Michelson G, Wailes N, Van Der Laan S, Frost G. Ethical investment processes and outcomes. Journal of Business Ethics. 2004;**52**:1-10

[11] Laurel-Fois D. Beyond appearances: The risk-reducing effects of responsible investment practices. Business & Society. 2018;**57**(5):826-862

[12] Shambach CSA. Strategic Leadership. Pennsylvania: Carlisle Barracks; 2004

[13] Doheny M, Nagali V, Weig F. Agile operations for volatile times. McKinsey Quarterly. 2012:1-7

[14] Bennett N, Lemoine GJ. What a difference a word makes: Understanding threats to performance in a VUCA world. Business Horizons. 2014;**57**:311-317

[15] Ramakrishnan R. Leading in a VUCA world. Ushus-Journal of Business Management. 2021;**20**(1):89-111

[16] Sullivan J. Talent Strategies for a Turbulent VUCA World—Shifting to an Adaptive Approach; 2015. Available from: https://www.ere.net/talent-strategies-for-a-turbulent-vuca-world-shifting-to-an-adaptive-approach/

[17] Reeves M, Love C, Mathur N. The Most Adaptive Companies 2012: Winning in an Age of Turbulence. Boston: BCG. 2012

[18] Banholzer S, Kossin J, Donner S. The impact of climate change on natural disasters. In: Reducing Disaster: Early Warning Systems For Climate Change. Dordrecht: Springer; 2014

[19] Kinsinger P, Walch K. Living and Leading in a VUCA World. Thunderbird University; 2012. pp. 1-4

[20] Head BW. Forty years of wicked problems literature: Forging closer links to policy studies. Policy and Society. 2019;**38**(12):180-197

[21] Roberts NC. Wicked problems and networks approaches to resolution. International Public Management Review. 2000;**1**(1):1-19

[22] Noordegraaf M, Douglas S, Geuijen K, Van Der Steen M. Weaknesses of wickedness: A critical perspective on wickedness theory. Policy and Society. 2019;**38**(2):278-297

[23] Head BW, Xiang WN. Why is an APT approach to wicked problems important? Landscape & Urban Planning. 2016;**154**:4-7

[24] Torfing J, Peters BG, Pierre J, Sørensen E. Interactive Governance: Advancing the Paradigm. Oxford: Oxford University Press; 2012

[25] Hoppe R. The Governance of Problems: Puzzling, Powering and Participation. Bristol: Policy Press; 2010

[26] Warwick-Ching L. Currency wars: Volatility provides profit opportunity. The Financial Times. 25 Mar 2013. Available from: http://www.ft.com/intl/cms/s/0/e17e1ab0-8714-11e2-9dd7-00144feabdc0.html#axzz2r3QHfbxW

[27] Hemingway A, Marquart J. Uncertainty Is Opportunity: Engage with Purpose. Edelman; 2013

[28] Amerasia Consulting Group. Ambiguity equalsopportunity: The story of the new HBS application. 3 Jun 2013. Retrieved from: http://www.amerasiaconsulting.com/blog/2013/6/3/ambiguity-equals-opportunity-the-story-of-the-new-hbs-Amerasia Consulting Group. (2013, June 3). Ambiguity equals opportunity: The story of the new HBS application. Available from: http://www.amerasiaconsulting.com/blog/2013/6/3/ambiguity-equals-opportunity-the-story-of-the-new-hbs-application

[29] Guterres A. Secretary-General's remarks to High-Level opening of COP27 [Retrieved 19 December 2022]

[30] Sempiga O, Wyen J, Van Liedekerke L, Mestdagh B.Does government performance cause trust? The case of SDG policies at local level. Forthcoming

[31] Sempiga O. Un Soir pas comme les autres. Paris: Edilivre; 2021

[32] Fiandrino S, Scarpa F, Torelli R. Fostering social impact through corporate implementation of the SDGs: Transformative mechanisms towards interconnectedness and inclusiveness. Journal of Business Ethics. 2022;**180**:959-973

[33] Termeer CJAM, Dewulf A, Biesbroek R. A critical assessment of the wicked problem concept: Relevance and usefulness for policy science and practice. Policy and Society. 2018;**38**(2):167-179

[34] Breuer A, Janetschek H, Malerba D. Translating sustainable development goal (SDG) interdependencies into policy advice. Sustainability. 2019;**11**(7):2092. DOI: 10.3390/su11072092

[35] Sempiga O, Mestdagh B. The impact of external shocks on sustainable development goals (SDGs). Forthcoming

[36] Brezzi M, González S, Nguyen D, Prats M. An updated OECD framework

on drivers of trust in public institutions to meet current and future challenges, OECD Working Papers on Public Governance 48, 2021

[37] Bowen KJ, Cradock-Henry NA, Koch F, Patterson J, Häyhä T, Vogt J, et al. Implementing the "sustainable development goals": Towards addressing three key governance challenges—Collective action, trade-offs, and accountability. Current Opinion in Environmental Sustainability. 2017;**26**(27):90-96

[38] Morton S, Pencheon D, Squires N. Sustainable Development Goals (SDGs), and their implementation: A national global framework for health, development and equity needs a systems approach at every level. British Medical Bulletin. 2017;**124**(1):81-90

[39] Inderst G, Stewart F. Incorporating Environmental, Social and Governance (ESG) Factors into Fixed Income Investment. Washington: World Bank Group Publication; 2018

[40] Leach M, Reyers B, Bai X, Brondizio ES, Cook C, Díaz S, et al. Equity and sustainability in the Anthropocene: A social–ecological systems perspective on their intertwined futures. Global Sustainability. 2018;**1**(13):1-13

[41] Gupta J, Vegelin C. Sustainable development goals and inclusive development. International Environmental Agreements: Politics, Law and Economics. 2016;**16**(3):433-448

[42] Ahmed F, Ahmed NE, Pissarides C, Stiglitz J. Why inequality could spread COVID-19. The Lancet Public Health. 2020;**5**(5):e240. DOI: 10.1016/S2468-2667(20)30085-2

[43] BSDC. Valuing the SDG Prize. London: Business & Sustainable Development Commission; 2017

[44] WBCSD. Business and the SDGs: A Survey of World Business Council for Sustainable Development (BCSD) Members and Global Network Partners. Geneva: World Business Council for Sustainable Development; 2018

[45] Cummings TG, Worley CG. Organization Development & Change, Nineth, Canada. South-Western: Cengage Learning; 2009

[46] Sciarelli M, Cosimato S, Landi G, Iandolo F. Socially responsible investment strategies for the transition towards sustainable development: The importance of integrating and communicating ESG. The TQM Journal. 2021;**33**(7):39-56

[47] Martini A. Socially responsible investing: From the ethical origins to the sustainable development framework of the European Union. Environment, Development and Sustainability. 2021;**23**:16874-16890

[48] Bouma JJ, Jeucken M, Klinkers L. Sustainable Banking: The Greening of Finance. London: Routledge; 2017

[49] Matallín-Sáez JC, Soler-Domínguez A, de Mingo-López DV, Tortosa-Ausina E. Does socially responsible mutual fund performance vary over the business cycle? New insights on the effect of idiosyncratic SR features. Business Ethics: A European Review. 2019;**28**(1):71-98

[50] Tabachnick BG. Using Multivariate Statistics. 5th ed. Boston, MA: Allyn and Bacon; 2006

[51] Grice JW, Iwasaki M. A truly multivariate approach to MANOVA. Applied Multivariate Research. 2007;**12**(3):199-226

[52] Huberty CJ, Morris JD. Multivariate analysis versus multiple univariate

analyses. Psychological Bulletin. 1989;**105**(2):302-308

[53] Stockburger DW. Multivariate Analysis of Variance. In: The SAGE Encyclopedia of Educational Research, Measurement, and Evaluation. Thousand Oaks: SAGE Publications; 2018. pp. 1120-1126

[54] Mazzucato M, Kattel R. COVID-19 and public-sector capacity. Oxford Review of Economic Policy. 2020;**36**:S256-S269